ROGUE STATE

ROGUE STATE

How a Nuclear
North Korea
Threatens America

WILLIAM C. TRIPLETT II

Since 1947
**REGNERY
PUBLISHING, INC.**
An Eagle Publishing Company • Washington, DC

Library of Congress Cataloging-in-Publication Data
    Triplett, William C.
    Rogue state: how a nuclear North Korea threatens America / William C. Triplett II.
    p. cm.
    Includes bibliographical references and index.
    ISBN 0-89526-068-9
    1. Nuclear weapons—Korea (North) 2. Korea (North)—Military policy. 3. United States—Foreign relations—Korea (North) 4. Korea (north)—Foreign relations—United States. I. Title.
    UA853.K7T75 2004
    355'.03305193—dc22

                             2004000450

Published in the United States by
Regnery Publishing, Inc.
An Eagle Publishing Company
One Massachusetts Avenue, NW
Washington, DC 20001

Visit us at www.regnery.com

Distributed to the trade by
National Book Network
4720-A Boston Way
Lanham, MD 20706

Printed on acid-free paper

Manufactured in the United States of America

10 9 8 7 6 5 4 3 2 1

Books are available in quantity for promotional or premium use. Write to Director of Special Sales, Regnery Publishing, Inc., One Massachusetts Avenue, NW, Washington, DC 20001, for information on discounts and terms, or call (202) 216-0600.

Every good faith effort has been made in this work to credit photo sources. If any copyrighted photo has been inadvertently used in this work without proper credit being given in one manner or another, please notify the publisher in writing so that future printings of this work may be corrected accordingly.

CONTENTS

1

ROGUE STATE

Not only YES, but HELL YES, and you tell that to your president!

— Kang Sok-ju, senior North Korean diplomat responding to accusations that North Korea was secretly building nuclear weapons

In early October 2002, President George W. Bush's assistant secretary of state James Kelly told the North Koreans that the game was up: The U.S. knew about North Korea's secret plan to build nuclear weapons despite its solemn pledge to the Clinton administration that it would do no such thing. Further, the U.S. had discovered that North Korea had traded long-range ballistic missile technology to Pakistan in exchange for nuclear weapons-making equipment and technology. Kelly had traveled to Pyongyang to confront senior North Korean diplomat Kang Sok-ju about the North's illegal uranium enrichment program. Kelly and his team were expecting that, as usual, the North Koreans would issue a denial. They were stunned when the North Koreans not only admitted to cheating on its agreement with the Clinton administration, but did so with insolent audacity. In response to Kelly's questions about the existence of Pyongyang's secret nuclear weapons program, Kang shot back, "Not only YES, but HELL YES, and you tell that to your president!"[1]

Here were all the elements of a nuclear nightmare:

- A belligerent, secretive, rogue regime that had previously threatened the Clinton administration with "preemptive strikes"[2]
- A rogue regime with a history of arms proliferation insisting that it had the right to sell nuclear weapons to anyone
- A rogue regime closing in on nuclear weapons capability (if it hadn't already achieved it)
- A rogue regime that had traded long-range ballistic missiles to Pakistan and to terrorist regimes in the Middle East
- A rogue regime that had massively cheated on a critical nuclear agreement it had signed with the Clinton administration

The North Koreans were unrepentant about being caught violating their agreements. If the North Koreans followed through with their threats, the lives of millions of people—Americans, South Koreans, Indians, Israelis, Japanese, and others—would be at risk.

The Bush administration tried to keep Pyongyang's threats out of the press, hoping for a diplomatic solution, but the story broke just as communist Chinese President Jiang Zemin was due to arrive for a visit with President George W. Bush at his ranch in Crawford, Texas.

COMPLETELY IN THE DARK

At the traditional joint news conference at the ranch, the press asked Jiang what he knew about the North Korean enriched uranium program. Jiang said that Chinese officials were "completely in the dark" about it. There were no follow-up questions, but there should have been because the long-standing political, military, economic, and even geographic ties between the two communist states make Jiang Zemin's denial hard to accept.

The North Korean and Chinese communist parties have been mutually supportive military and political allies for almost sixty years. Their military units fought shoulder-to-shoulder, first against the anti-communist Chinese Nationalists under Chiang Kai-shek during the Chinese Civil War, and later against South Korea, the United States, and the United Nations during the Korean War. Chinese and North Korean political and military leaders frequently describe relations between the two countries as close as "lips and teeth."

They are, of course, geographic neighbors. The Korean peninsula sticks out like a thumb from the northeast coast of China. North Korea's border with South Korea has been sealed off since the end of the Korean War by the heavily fortified Demilitarized Zone, which makes North Korea's long, porous northern borderwith China—marked by the Yalu and Tumen rivers—all the more important. Many ethnic Koreans live on the Chinese side of the border—a reminder that ancient Korean kingdoms once dominated a large portion of that part of China known as Manchuria. But there is no doubt who is the master in the relationship today. While North Korea's population is in the twenty millions, China's is well over one billion. North Korea's economy is virtually nonexistent, while China is a major manufacturing economic power. North Korea's land mass is but a puny one percent of China's, and even as North Korea remains isolated from the world, China is courted.

Because of North Korea's status as a rogue or pariah state, it has few international contacts and relies heavily on the support of its communist neighbor. Its only regularly scheduled civilian airline flights are the twice-weekly connections between the Chinese and North Korean capitals of Beijing and Pyongyang. Much of North Korea's limited trade flows to China. The North Korean economy is always in a state of imminent collapse, but communist China serves as its life support system. Beijing will not let the regime in North Korea die.

For Jiang Zemin not to know about North Korea's nuclear program, Chinese intelligence on its immediate neighbor and ally would have had to fail completely. Such failure would subsequently have led to swift punishment. In 2003, after a submarine accident claimed the lives of its crew, Beijing immediately relieved the commander of the entire Chinese Navy, the equivalent in American terms of our Chief of Naval Operations. Also canned were the chief political commissar for the Navy, the commander and chief political commissar of the East Sea Fleet, and several other high-ranking naval officers. By contrast, no top official associated with communist China's North Korea policy has been purged for keeping the top leadership, including President Jiang Zemin "in the dark." General Xiong Guangkai, the chief of communist Chinese military intelligence, is still on the job. General Xiong is so highly regarded by his bosses that he was chosen to lead a military delegation to Washington less than two months after the press conference at Crawford. Diplomats have not been fired and no communist Chinese publication has created a scapegoat for this supposed intelligence failure. It is surely of great interest to Beijing to be informed whether or not its impoverished neighbor is developing nuclear weapons.

The fact is: communist China is central to all North Korean issues, from human rights to weapons proliferation. North Korea is not an island. It is a subordinate part of a communist Chinese empire. Previous efforts to explain North Korea's vile and perverse behavior have given scant attention to this perspective. Few people have thus far realized that if North Korea is to be contained and made peaceful, communist China will first have to be persuaded to stop being part of the problem.

ROGUE REGIME

The big five tyrannical mass-murdering regimes of the twentieth century have been Adolf Hitler's national socialists in Germany, the communist regimes of Stalin's Russia, Mao Zedong's China,

Pol Pot's Cambodia, and the Kim Dynasty in North Korea. Established by Kim Il Sung, whom the North Korean propagandists named the "Great Leader," it is now run by his oldest son, Kim Jung Il, known as the "Dear Leader." The North Korea-watchers in South Korea, Japan, and elsewhere are waiting to see if the Dear Leader designates one of his sons as his heir and if so, which one?

During the almost sixty years they have ruled the country, the Great Leader and the Dear Leader have:

- Started a war against the United Nations that killed millions and devastated the entire Korean Peninsula
- Allowed perhaps three million people in the North to die of starvation
- Established an "Army First" priority system and diverted international food aid to the military
- Established a chain of political prisons where entire families, from babies to grandparents, are incarcerated
- Established a kind of "Terrorism and Crime University" and sent out agents to kidnap and murder innocent civilians in foreign countries
- Murdered a First Lady, known as the "National Mother," of South Korea
- Assassinated almost a complete South Korean cabinet
- Exploded a bomb aboard a civilian airliner killing everyone aboard simply to disrupt the Olympic Games in Seoul
- Become the major illegal drug smuggler to Japan and South Korea, including to American military personnel serving in these countries
- Kidnapped South Korea's leading film director and film actress and imprisoned them in the North Korean gulag until they agreed to make North Korean propaganda films

While the North Korean people starve, the Kim family enjoys marble palaces, hunting lodges, seaside villas, jet skis, racing cars and motorcycles, women, liquor, and gourmet food imported from around the world. Their medical care is looked after in a world-class facility with the latest equipment, which is reserved for their and their selected cronies' exclusive use. There is even a "Longevity Institute" to serve the Kim family.

While the Kim family and their supporters live like modern pharaohs, the North Korean people are in bondage, both physical and spiritual. The regime operates one of the most comprehensive efforts ever made to keep a people ignorant of the larger world. Party propaganda fills the newspapers. Televisions and radios are wired to receive only one state-controlled station. Torchlight parades channel the people's energies into a frenzy of fanaticism reminiscent of Nazi Party rallies in the 1930s. In the midst of a famine, the regime spent almost a billion dollars glorifying the Great Leader after his death in 1994.[3]

Foreigners who visit North Korea notice that the people won't make eye contact and any conversations are stilted and ritualistic. Those who have not been brainwashed into submission have been terrorized. A system of surveillance—by three separate sets of secret police and informers—places enormous pressures on everyday life. The entire country has been impoverished and some people driven to cannibalism in order to survive. Those children who do survive are stunted, malnourished, and without medical care. Many older people have starved to death, sacrificing their meager rations so that their children and grandchildren might live.

The Kim family dictatorship has elements of an organized crime family that has taken over a country. About one percent of the population is in the ruling elite, while the rest of the population suffers. Without the murderous terror of the regime's secret police, the rulers could not sustain their power and position. Crime comes naturally to this gang of thugs, which explains why the Kims turned to narcotics and arms trafficking to sustain themselves.

An organized criminal conspiracy such as that of North Korea will have allies and accessories among its own kind. In fact, from the beginning, North Korea owes it existence to a notorious thug in his own right, Joseph Stalin, whose Soviet troops occupied the northern half of Korea after the allied defeat of the Japanese in 1945.

PAYING THE PRICE

Since then, the Korean people and the non-communist world have paid a heavy price for Stalin's creation and communist China's support of North Korea:

- More than 50,000 American soldiers, sailors, airmen, and marines were killed in action, and many others grievously wounded, during the Korean War
- Other soldiers—South Korean, British, French, Greek, Thai, Columbian, Brazilian, and Filipino—died defending South Korea under the United Nations flag during the same war
- Perhaps a million South Korean civilians were killed, wounded, or made orphans and homeless by the North's aggression
- An American sailor was murdered by North Koreans aboard the USS *Pueblo*
- Thirty-one Americans died aboard a U.S. Navy plane shot down on the Great Leader's birthday in 1969
- U.S. Army Captain Arthur Bonifas and First Lieutenant Mark Barrett were murdered while carrying out their duties along the Demilitarized Zone (DMZ) between North and South Korea
- South Korean servicemen, police, and civilians have been murdered in gun battles with North Korean saboteurs and commandos
- A high school girl singing in a chorus was killed in the same shootout that killed the South Korean first lady
- Korean women have been captured and made sex slaves for the amusement of the Kims and their cronies. In addition,

young Japanese women have been kidnapped to serve the Dear Leader
- Thousands of religious believers have been executed or sent to death camps in North Korea

CLEAR AND PRESENT DANGERS

The situation has become even more dangerous today:

- North Korea's belligerence, its professed desire to conquer South Korea, and its massed artillery and rockets along the DMZ are a constant threat to South Koreans and the American troops that help defend them
- North Korean saboteurs have run amok in Japan for decades—allowing them to rehearse for future attacks on Japanese nuclear power plants and American military installations
- North Korean laboratories are turning out poison gas and germ weapons by the tons
- North Korean technicians are much closer to producing nuclear weapons than allied intelligence had previously suspected
- North Korea will soon be able to strike the American west coast with nuclear weapons
- North Korean missiles already threaten all of Japan and South Korea and the American troops stationed there
- North Korea is selling ballistic missiles to Pakistan, Iran, Libya, and Syria, and helping these countries develop their own missile systems
- There is reason to believe that North Korea, in cooperation with Pakistan, is helping the mullah regime in Iran to acquire nuclear weapons
- North Korea is training Islamic terrorists, worked with Osama bin Laden, and might have helped an international terrorist group acquire germ weapons

KILL WITH A BORROWED KNIFE

The history of North Korean aggression would not be complete without an account of its allies and accessories. The long-term alliance between North Korea and communist China can be accurately described as "killing with a borrowed knife," a phrase that comes from the *36 Stratagems*, a military classic focused on the ancient Chinese art of military deception. Probably compiled during the Ming Dynasty (1360–1644), it is as important and well known to the Chinese as Sun Tzu's *Art of War*, the latter of which is much more familiar to Americans.[4] An American specialist on the communist Chinese military explains, "It means to use covertly another country to annihilate your enemy."[5] Beijing and Moscow have over five decades created, nurtured, and sustained one of the most dangerous, volatile, and repressive communist states in the world—the Kim regime in North Korea. While they have made great efforts to disguise their involvement, they cannot hide the record:

- Joseph Stalin created the North Korean regime and installed the Great Leader as his puppet
- Aided by information provided by British spies, Stalin, Mao, Kim, and Ho Chi-Minh conspired in 1950 to launch a massive invasion of Asia (Tibet fell, Indochina fell, but Taiwan dodged the bullet)
- Moscow and Beijing helped Kim start the Korean War; Beijing intervened to block a United Nations victory in the war
- Moscow and Beijing have kept the North Korean regime afloat through economic subsidies over the last fifty years
- Moscow began Pyongyang's nuclear research program; Beijing converted it to a weapons program
- Moscow and Beijing launched Pyongyang's poison gas program
- Beijing's only formal military alliance is with Pyongyang
- Beijing has prepared its military forces to fight a new Korean War

- Beijing started Pyongyang's ballistic missile program, providing it with critical technology
- Beijing uses North Korea and Pakistan as its proxy distributors of weapons of mass destruction and ballistic missiles to terrorist countries such as Iran, Libya, and Syria
- Beijing serves as the diplomatic and military shield for Pyongyang

DENIAL AND DECEPTION

Killing with a borrowed knife only works if it can be disguised. The intention is two-fold: keep your opponent from learning vital information (denial) and mislead him about your true intentions (deception). For the last fifty-five years, Pyongyang and Beijing have operated one of the most successful denial and deception operations ever mounted. In spite of the ample evidence (which will be laid out in the pages of this book), North Korea and communist China have managed to deceive bureaucrats, diplomats, politicians, and academics in the democratic world. North Korea is often mistakenly seen as taking aggressive actions principally in order to protect itself. This is the victimization argument.[6] Communist China is likewise seen as a helpless giant who has no clue what the North Koreans are up to ("completely in the dark") and certainly has no power to stop it.

The two nations have been able to hide their joint participation in many projects involving weapons of mass destruction programs and missile proliferation. It is true that North Korea is the front man delivering the missiles to terrorist countries. But behind North Korea, the Chinese are enriching themselves by selling parts, service, production tools, training, and development of future models.

SELF DELUSION

The non-communist world—primarily the United States, Japan, and South Korea—has willfully ignored North Korea's close relations to Beijing. Time after time, our officials have been shocked, surprised, and forced to scramble to North Korean aggression and provocation. Being caught off guard has led to blunders and needless loss of life. Now that North Korea is acquiring nuclear weapons, the risk of such willful self-delusion as that exhibited by politicians in Washington, Seoul, and Tokyo is even higher.

There has been a tendency to ignore the inherently foul nature of the regime—such as when the Clinton administration signed agreements with Pyongyang without considering North Korea's record of flagrant noncompliance. It has always been easier to postpone the day of reckoning in the hopes that someone else will deal with it. The same willful blindness extends to the failure to acknowledge the true relationship between Beijing and Pyongyang. It is clear that Beijing serves as an "enabler," if not co-conspirator and participant, in all of North Korea's crimes.

The bottom line is this: As a rogue state, North Korea serves the larger purposes of the Chinese Communist Party. Beijing knows that a free and democratic Korea on its border would be a serious threat to the regime. It already has enough problems explaining to its own people why those living on Taiwan's tiny island of Quemoy can freely elect their leaders but those living a mile away on the Chinese mainland cannot. Beijing does not want millions of Koreans and Chinese living in Manchuria to have a full view of democracy across the Yalu River.

By using North Korea as its front man in weapons of mass destruction and missile sales, Beijing can participate in this lucrative business without openly getting its hands dirty. On the few occasions when such deals are discovered, China simply issues a denial, and many in the West have believed such denials. More ominously, one should consider whether Beijing's secret proliferation deals involve more than money; whether China's politburo thinks it gains by spreading nuclear weapons, chemical weapons, germ warfare weapons, and ballistic missile delivery systems to the least stable and most dangerous regimes in the world; whether, in fact, China is a threat to peace around the world and a promoter of terrorism.

IS THERE A SOLUTION?

There is no simple military solution to the North Korean problem—unless the North Koreans were openly prepared to launch a nuclear missile at the United States, in which case an obliterating American first strike would be justified. North Korea can fire between 300,000 and 500,000 artillery shells per hour on the Seoul metropolitan area. Even if allied air forces and counter-battery fire could knock out 90 percent of these incoming shells in the first hour (a rate of success never previously equaled on any battlefield) it would still leave tens of thousands of shells to fall on Seoul. Even if only 10 percent of those shells were equipped with poison gas warheads, thousands of them would blanket the area. In the fall of 2003, Republican Senator Pat Roberts of Kansas, the chairman of the Senate Intelligence Committee, told Tony Snow of FOX that a new Korean War would devastate 60 percent of the country. That is a conservative estimate. There are no warmongers in Seoul.

But the choice is not between Kim's way or war. Many countries have extensive influence with Beijing, if they choose to use it. Beijing can make or break the Kim regime. But so long as the issue is defined as "North Korea" and not "communist China and North Korea," there is unlikely to be any progress on issues involving human rights, the threat of regional aggression, and weapons proliferation. Only when the "borrowed knife" linkage between Beijing and Pyongyang is recognized will it be possible to consider feasible solutions to North Korea.

2

THE MOSCOW CONSPIRACY

If I had to choose between betraying my country
or betraying a friend, I hope that I would have
the courage to betray my country.

— E. M. Forster

he summer is a time of slow pace and uncharacteristic sunshine in England. At Oxford, home of the world's oldest
English-speaking university, bells atop medieval churches
ring through the air, the sound bouncing around narrow cobble-
stone streets and old yellow stone buildings. With Mao Zedong's
communist armies sweeping over China in the summer of 1949,
the British Foreign Office decided to hold a "summer school" for
diplomats and intelligence officers at Oxford. The chief lecturer on
"Red China," rising Foreign Office star Guy Burgess, made clear
that his sympathies lay with the communist revolutionaries.[1] Only
decades later would the Allied governments fully understand that
Burgess was a dedicated Soviet spy, part of a larger Soviet spy ring
of perhaps forty people recruited at England's Cambridge University in the 1930s.[2] At least three of them—Burgess, Donald
Maclean, and H.A.R. ("Kim") Philby—would exploit their positions to betray the Allied cause in Korea.

A bad drunk and a brawler, Burgess, along with some of the others, had been a member of a semisecret society at Cambridge dedicated to hedonism and Joseph Stalin. "We repudiated entirely existing morals,"[3] one member of the "Apostles" would later declare. The E. M. Forster concept of binding friends together against their country was the guiding spirit of the group. Very little that was of depraved nature escaped their attention, and committing treason for the Soviet dictatorship certainly fit their pattern.

Burgess began his career as a secret Soviet spy in World War II when he joined Britain's secret intelligence service, known as MI6, but by 1948 he had transferred to the Far Eastern division of the Foreign Office. His colleagues noted both the intensity and the ingenuity of his advocacy for Mao's cause.[4] Burgess was given access to a vast selection of materials from the Joint War Committee, the War Office (then Britain's Defense Ministry), and General Douglas MacArthur's headquarters in Tokyo, and immediately immersed himself in all Allied secrets regarding China and Korea.[5] In April 1950, he got his hands on a special document: a "TOP SECRET" Allied military intelligence analysis of what assistance Stalin was providing to Mao's forces. With this information, Moscow and Beijing would know where the Allied analysts were right, where they were wrong, and what gaps in intelligence to exploit.[6]

Maclean also had a history of drunkenness, disorder, and mental breakdown. On a drinking binge in Cairo, he once broke into an apartment shared by two secretaries of the American Embassy and totally trashed the place, breaking furniture and even an iron bathtub. Maclean kept his official career confined to the Foreign Office. Just after World War II, he worked in Washington with another of Stalin's spies, American State Department official Alger Hiss. The two Soviet agents participated in the establishment of the United Nations and exchanged information on the disposition of Allied military forces overseas, especially in Korea.[7]

Philby, yet another heavy drinker, spent his entire official career as a British intelligence officer for MI6, while working for the Soviets on the side. For his efforts, London awarded him the Order of the British Empire and Moscow gave him the Order of the Red Banner. At the KGB museum in Moscow, one cannot help but notice the admiration paid to the Cambridge spies, especially to Philby.[8] At his 1988 funeral in Moscow, Philby received the final respects usually reserved for a departed KGB general. When I visited his gravesite in 2003, however, it was overgrown and neglected.

His memoirs, written from Moscow in the late 1960s, do not offer much insight on the substance of his espionage activity, but they are revealing about the atmosphere of the time. Philby lived in an era when the British diplomatic and secret services made no serious effort to examine the background or even public views of those they recruited into His Majesty's services. If your family was rich enough, had the right friends, went to the right college, you were in the old boys' network. It did not matter if you had been widely known as a communist or emotionally unstable in college. Even when the FBI and its British counterpart, MI5, knew they had a Soviet mole in the system, they went looking for him among the "sweepers, cleaners, bottle-washers, and the rest." As Philby pointed out, "It has so far occurred neither to them [the FBI] nor to the British that a diplomat was involved, let alone a senior diplomat."[9] Philby further observed that, "The reluctance to initiate enquiries along these lines can only be attributed to a genuine mental block which stubbornly resisted the belief that respected members of the Establishment could do such things."[10]

Philby was a bit more discrete (though not always) than Burgess and Maclean, who made no effort to disguise their virulently anti-American outlook or their generally pro-Soviet leanings. A substantial percentage of the British political establishment held similar views in those days.[11] To them, President Truman was the real threat to peace in the Far East, not Stalin, Mao, or North

Korea's Kim Il Sung. The intensity of their views may well have had an impact beyond a spy's normal collection of secret information. They added their own anti-American alarms to the classified documents they passed to Moscow, which would have fed Stalin's paranoia about Allied intentions in Korea.[12] No one seems to have noticed the inherent contradiction—while the secret documents the spies sent to Moscow clearly showed that the Allies were on the defensive, the comments that accompanied these documents were skewed to make Stalin paranoid of Allied aggression.

In the time leading up to the Korean War and extending through the most severe fighting, all three of these British traitors were in ideal positions to provide vital information to their Soviet masters. Everything they saw, read, and heard went directly to Moscow. Every secret plan on the Korean War, every secret decision by the Allies was betrayed. From Moscow, these secrets went eastward to Beijing and Pyongyang.

During World War II, the Allies obtained a copy of the German encryption device, the "Enigma machine," and were able to decipher most of Hitler's orders and plans. Scores of German soldiers and U-boat sailors died without knowing of the Allied advantage. Together, the three Cambridge spies—Burgess, Maclean, and Philby—had a similar impact on the Korean War, but this time the Allies were on the losing end. Stalin had access to the entire range of Allied war plans, disposition of forces, and strategies. Maclean would later brag that he had given all of Truman's plans and "every significant secret decision on the war" to Stalin "on a plate."[13] For example, from Maclean, Moscow (and thus, Beijing) would know that President Truman had forbidden Allied forces to bomb the Yalu River bridges or even conduct armed reconnaissance over Manchuria.[14]

Maclean's former deputy at the Foreign Office declared that the documents Maclean passed to the Soviets would have been "of inestimable value in advising the Chinese and North Koreans on strategy and negotiating positions."[15] Ultimately, the soldiers, sailors, and marines who fought for the Allied cause in the Korean War would pay the horrific price for the treachery of the Cambridge spies.

A COMMUNIST SUMMIT

Stalin's seventieth birthday was celebrated in Moscow on December 21, 1949. His successor, Nikita Khrushchev, referred to this period in Soviet history as the time when "the sickness ... [first] began to envelop Stalin's mind in the last years of his life."[16] Just the previous year, Stalin had ordered the executions of all the leading communist party officials in and around Leningrad (present day St. Petersburg), as well as the prime minister of the Russian Federal Republic. By 1953, this mental illness would overwhelm him to the point that he would accuse the chief Kremlin physicians of treachery. The doctors, who were falsely accused, were nevertheless beaten into signing "confessions." (Since the doctors were mostly Jewish, a number of scholars believe that, had he lived, Stalin would have used the phony "doctor's plot" as an excuse for a wholesale assault on Soviet Jewry.[17])

In short, by the winter of 1949–1950, Stalin's naturally suspicious nature was beginning to exhibit signs of classic paranoia, which would ultimately lead to dementia. Outside forces, such as the America-hating Cambridge spies and the ambitious young communist leaders in Asia, only fed those fires.

Even with Stalin's deteriorating mental health, the communist world had a lot to celebrate at the end of 1949. Just five months earlier, the Soviets had shocked the Americans by exploding their first nuclear weapon, years before the West had expected it.[18] Communist regimes were consolidating their power all over Eastern Europe and communist parties in Western Europe seemed to be on the verge of taking power in a number of important countries.

In Asia, the international communist movement had made enormous gains, fueling ambitions for more. Mao Zedong's Chinese

Communist Party (CCP) had just come to power through military victory over the Chinese Nationalists. Formally established on October 1, 1949, the young People's Republic of China represented twenty-five years of struggle and sacrifice by Mao and his surviving comrades. The CCP's military arm, the People's Liberation Army (PLA), was then engaged in mopping up remnants of Chiang Kai-shek's Nationalist forces and looking for its next assignment: the invasion of Taiwan.

Stalin's man in Korea, Kim Il Sung, was busy consolidating his hold on power in North Korea and sending communist guerrillas into the South.[19] The Democratic People's Republic of Korea (DPRK) had been proclaimed in September 1948. Upon establishing its capital at Pyongyang, it immediately began a campaign of subversion and aggression aimed at Syngman Rhee's Republic of Korea (ROK) based in Seoul. By the end of 1949, Kim's communist guerrillas in the southern part of Korea were being rolled up by Rhee's police forces and Kim was looking for outside support to take his struggle to a new level.

When Japanese forces retreated home from Indochina at the end of World War II, they left behind a temporary political vacuum that was quickly filled by Ho Chi Minh's communist forces, then known as the "Viet-Minh." As the late French writer Bernard Fall would observe, Ho got his way with the local population through "well-applied terror."[20] Fall also noted, "Until the French returned to Hanoi in March 1946, it [the Viet-Minh] used its unhindered control to liquidate hundreds of Vietnamese anti-communist nationalists likely to get in the way."[21] High on the Viet-Minh target list were "the genuine Vietnamese nationalists who wanted a Vietnam independent from France but equally free of communist rule."[22]

The French quickly drove Ho's army back to the mountains along the Chinese border, but the arrival of the Chinese Army on the other side spelled the end of French rule in Indochina. As Fall notes, "It became strategically hopeless [for the French] when the

Chinese Reds arrived on Indochina's borders in late 1949 and China thus became a 'sanctuary' where Viet-Minh forces could be trained and refitted."[23] At the end of 1949, Ho didn't control much beyond a few jungle enclaves, but his prospects were excellent.

In other parts of Southeast Asia—Malaya, Singapore, the Philippines, Thailand, and Burma—communist guerrillas were making progress with the local people and they, too, had reason to be optimistic. The British colonial rulers of Malaya and Singapore had, in the summer of 1948, declared a state of emergency to deal with the mostly ethnic Chinese "communist terrorists" and the outcome of this conflict was in doubt.

In Japan, the communists had made a brief grab for power after the war through strikes and sabotage, but General MacArthur's occupation forces and the natural opposition of the Japanese people had stopped that cold. By the end of 1949, the Japan Communist Party was trying to transform itself into a traditional political party aiming for power, or at least a share of it, through the ballot box. With the Japanese economy still struggling after the war, that wasn't an altogether bad strategy.

What better than to celebrate this favorable turn of events with a summit in Moscow of the world's communist leaders? Mao's train pulled into Moscow on the stroke of twelve, on December 16, 1949. A senior Soviet delegation greeted him at the train station and he had dinner with Stalin that night. It was Mao's first known visit outside the boundaries of the People's Republic of China. His eldest son, Mao Anying, had accompanied his father as far as the Chinese border.

Ho arrived too late for the birthday celebrations but in time for the final deliberations. He began walking from the mountains of northern Vietnam in early January, passed through Beijing and finally reached Moscow the first week of February. His trip was apparently secret.[24]

Former Soviet leader Nikita Khrushchev reported in his memoirs that Kim Il Sung arrived in Moscow sometime in "late 1949."[25]

Unlike Kim's visit to Moscow earlier in the spring, this visit was not announced.[26] Keeping Kim's presence a secret would have served everyone's purpose. What Kim wanted to do in South Korea was nothing less than a communist blitzkrieg. If Kim had been visible in Moscow with Mao (soon joined by Ho), it would have been very difficult to maintain deniability, something high on Stalin's mind. As a longtime communist revolutionary and conspirator, Kim probably wasn't offended to be kept to the shadows for this trip, especially if the reward was Stalin's support for his attack on South Korea. Khrushchev writes that Stalin met Kim in his *dacha*, or country cottage.[27]

This was not the first nor would it be the last time the Kim regime's relations with its larger comrades were enveloped in a cloak of secrecy. When it came to North Korea, Stalin was so obsessed with secrecy and deniability that he told Khrushchev he wanted no "evidence" that Soviet military planners and advisors had participated in the preparations for Kim's attack on the South.[28] To this day, China refuses to admit its official participation in the war against the United Nations and continues to refer to PLA forces sent to Korea as "Chinese People's Volunteers."

The participants of this communist summit and their successors who are in power today are still reluctant to reveal what went on at the meeting. Some of the most critical files in Moscow appear to have been purged and others remain closed to outside scholarship.[29] Mao's interpreter for the Moscow Summit has an entry for "Kim Il Sung" in his memoirs but no discussion of what that might mean.[30] Even today, raising the issue of "Kim in Moscow" causes conversations in Moscow to fall silent.[31]

Since Kim's attack on the South ultimately turned out to be a failure, there has been a lot of finger pointing as to who gave Kim the "green light." Chinese sources have even tried to sell the idea of how "surprised" everyone was that Kim had launched his attack.[32] For that to be true, Mao's diplomats and secret agents covering North Korea would have had to have been totally asleep, an unlikely prospect. Considering the preparatory meetings before the Moscow Summit, the summit itself, and the post-summit meetings, it's safe to say that both Stalin and Mao were energetically behind Kim's enterprise.[33] With his characteristic directness, Khrushchev could say as late as 1970, "I would have made the same decision myself if I had been in his [Stalin's] place."[34]

The winter of 1949–1950 was the high water mark for the international communist monolith.[35] Major communist leaders had a unity of purpose in their desire for world communist domination that momentarily trumped their own individual agendas. In the decades to come, nationalist agendas and personal ambitions would supersede communist unity and lead to recriminations and even shooting between China and two of the other three. Even during this summit, when all sides were making an effort at unity, the seeds of future conflict were already being sewn. Both Mao and Stalin exhibited serious resentment with each other over matters large and small, and neither would forget.[36]

But their momentary unity produced a series of decisions that initiated a reign of terror over millions of people in the Far East and established the framework for East Asia today. They decided:

- To give Kim the green light to invade South Korea
- To give Mao the green light to conquer Tibet
- To give Mao the green light to invade Taiwan
- To recognize Ho's regime and give him the green light to conquer Indochina
- To attack the Japanese Communist Party for not taking up arms against U.S. forces stationed in Japan

Mao and Stalin ended the summit with a banquet and a mutual defense alliance between the Soviet Union and the People's Republic of China. In addition to the publicly announced treaty, there were a number of secret protocols, one of which is thought to have been an espionage-sharing agreement "on a global scale."[37] While the security clause of the treaty specifically named and was directed at Japan, it included the phrase "or any state allied with her" which widely meant the United States.

United States Secretary of State Dean Acheson immediately and forthrightly denounced the Stalin–Mao agreement as an "evil omen of imperialist domination."[38] Now Asia would become a major battleground of the Cold War—with the United States, Japan, and their allies on one side, the Soviets and China on the other. The communist leaders' grand design for conquest would result in millions of victims over the next fifty years and remains today as the source of potential conflict across a third of the globe.

PREPARING FOR WAR IN KOREA

For centuries, Koreans had had a cultural affinity for China and sometimes a military alliance. Korean troops, for example, joined the Chinese–Mongol attempts to invade Japan in the 1300s, attempts broken up by the "Divine Wind" (kamikaze) of typhoons.

However, in 1905 Korea became a colony of Japan and Korean partisans went looking for help in China. In the 1920s and 1930s, some of them joined Chiang Kai-shek's Nationalists and others joined Mao's Communists. Kim Il Sung initially went with Mao, learned to speak Chinese fluently, and joined the Chinese Communist Party. [39]

Perhaps because Mao wasn't in position to offer much material aid, by the late 1930s, Kim was in a Soviet Army uniform serving in an ethnic Korean unit the Soviets had established in their Far East.[40] When the Soviets took over Korea north of the 38th Parallel in 1945, they brought Kim with them, soon establishing him as their leader of what would become the DPRK or North Korea.

If Stalin chose Kim because he was more ruthless than the other contenders, his judgment has been vindicated. Kim and the

Soviets immediately began to militarize North Korean society on the Soviet model. As a result of the ensuing repression, even before the war broke out, nearly one million North Koreans fled in desperation to the South with nothing except what they could carry on their backs.[41] Korean Christians were a particular target for Kim's secret police dragnet.[42] Kim armed the new Korean People's Army (KPA) with captured Japanese weapons, supplemented with every sort of Soviet weapon his troops could absorb. In the spring of 1950, there was a great surge of Soviet weapon deliveries to North Korea. When the Soviets pulled out of Korea at the end of 1949, Col. Gen. Ivan Christiakov's 25th Army (120,000 men) turned over all of their weapons and equipment to the newly formed KPA. By the time of Kim's June 25, 1950, surprise attack on the South, Stalin had armed the KPA with 150 to 200 T-34 tanks, long-range artillery, and combat aircraft.

Considering the low level of the Chinese economy at the time, Beijing didn't have much in the way of war material to offer Pyongyang, but it did have soldiers with combat experience who spoke the Korean language. During the late 1940s, the Chinese civil war between the Nationalists and the Communists was raging in nearby Manchuria. Kim and the Soviets provided sanctuary for the Chinese Communist Northeast Army and gave Mao control of a large Japanese-built ammunition plant at Hungnam, North Korea.[43] By one Chinese scholar's estimate, "Without the assistance of the North Korean communists, CCP [Chinese Communist Party] forces in southern Manchuria could have been totally destroyed by the GMD [Nationalists]."[44] If he had lost Manchuria, it's not at all certain Mao would have ultimately prevailed in conquering the whole Chinese mainland.

Kim was generous even with his soldiers. As early as the spring of 1946 he sent North Korean troops to join Mao's forces fighting in China. They joined a larger group of ethnic Korean troops that the Chinese communists had already recruited from ethnic Korean people living in Manchuria. The Korean soldiers ultimately became the PLA's 156th, 164th, and 166th Divisions, part of Chinese General Lin Biao's Fourth Field Army.[45] These North Korean troops in PLA uniforms, ultimately numbering about 100,000, received valuable combat experience while fighting in China. With the end of the Chinese civil war, Kim wanted these troops for the KPA and Mao sent them to Pyongyang in two groups with all their military equipment. The first two ethnic Korean PLA divisions were stationed in Manchuria and were sent over the Yalu in 1949; the third division was still fighting Nationalist forces in southern China and did not arrive in North Korea until the spring of 1950.[46] The PLA's 166th Division became the 6th Division of the KPA; the PLA's 164th Division became the KPA's 5th Division; and the PLA's 156th Division crossed the Yalu River and became the KPA's 7th Division.

These troops, experienced in combat, would soon become the spearhead of Kim's attack on South Korea. In commenting on these "battle-hardened" Korean troops, a North Korean KGB general said, "They played a very important role in the attack on South Korea."[47] When the Chinese intervened in the Korean War later in 1950, it was their old comrades from the Fourth Field Army who came to their rescue under the name of the Chinese People's Volunteers (CPV).

With the Soviet war material onboard trains heading for North Korea and the ex-PLA troops crossing the Yalu, it was time to look at final plans and preparations. Even before the winter summit, communist leaders had been making preparations to assist Kim's military ambitions.

- July 1946: Chinese PLA opened an office in North Korea[48]
- January 1949: Chinese, North Korean, and Soviet military officers met in Manchuria;[49] and Soviet politburo member Anastas Mikoyan visited China[50]
- March 1949: Chinese and North Koreans signed a secret defense pact[51]
- April 1949: Kim signed secret military pact in Moscow[52]

- July–August 1949: Chinese leader Liu Shaoqi conferred with
  Stalin in Moscow on a communist "division of labor" for
  world conquest

While the senior communist political leaders met in Moscow,
Chinese and Soviet specialists were engaged in a military planning
mission in Beijing. After the summit, Kim visited Moscow and
Beijing to get final approvals and cover last-minute details.[53] That
spring, Stalin sent a team of advisors to help prepare a war plan for
the invasion of South Korea. Led by three generals with "combat
experience," they were the best the Soviet general staff had to offer.[54]

OTHER AGGRESSION

Stalin: "Any other questions?"

After thanking "Comrade Stalin" for having sent a Soviet air
transport regiment to China during the recent Chinese civil
war, Mao asks Stalin to let the regiment "stay a little longer, so
it could transport provisions to General Liu Bocheng's troops,
currently preparing for an attack on Tibet."

Stalin: "It's good that you are preparing to attack. The Tibetans
need to be subdued."[55]

With these few words, on January 22, 1950, the two dictators con-
signed an entire people to invasion, conquest, and fifty years of
horror. Mao's motivation for this "attack" is fairly easy to understand. Conquering the Tibetan homeland would almost double the
size of the PRC and puts his troops on the high ground to attack
India (which they did in 1962).[56] But what was Stalin's motivation?
Some scholars speculate that Stalin, along with Mao, had aggression against India in mind.[57] It may also be the case that Stalin

agreed with Mao that the conquest of Tibet would be an easy land grab because the Americans were not expected to intervene. The communist leaders guessed correctly: There was no American intervention in Tibet.

TAIWAN

If Tibet was on Mao's mind, so too was his planned invasion of Taiwan. He had already raised the issue during Mikoyan's visit to China a year earlier as did Liu on his trip to Moscow the previous summer. Like Kim, and as we shall see Ho, Mao was aiming for an invasion during the summer of 1950. If all had gone according to plan, communist armed forces would have launched attacks against South Korea, Taiwan, Indochina, and Tibet within weeks of each other. Chinese Premier Zhou En-lai called this "the concept of confronting the United States on three fronts."[58] A giant arc—from the Sea of Japan, down through the South China Sea, and ending on the border with Pakistan—would have been in flames. Eventually, other countries of Southeast Asia—Burma, Thailand, the Philippines, Indonesia, Malaya[59]—would have been engulfed. Japan and Australia would have been isolated and India threatened from two sides. This remains the goal of the Chinese Communist Party today; only the tactics have changed.

Taiwan then, as now, wasn't going to surrender. Mao and his supporters knew that the PLA as it then existed—a massive infantry on foot and sometimes horseback—could not conduct a D-Day style amphibious landing on Taiwan while Chiang's Nationalist forces controlled the sea and the air. He would need to restructure his forces, demobilizing many of the infantry divisions to free up resources for a new navy and air force, both of which would have to be created from scratch. Beginning in the spring of 1950, Beijing cut almost a million and a half soldiers from the ground forces of the PLA.[60] Quantity went down but quality, in the form of a modern, effective fighting force, was going up.

Above all, Mao needed Moscow's substantial help to create a modern air force and navy. During the civil war, the communists had captured a few transport aircraft and some small ships, but China had no aircraft industry, few pilots, no training schools, no naval shipyards, and no captains with ocean sailing experience. As the result of Liu's summer of 1949 visit to Moscow, PLA air force and navy delegations went to Moscow. The air force agreements with Moscow resulted in six aviation schools being established in China and 185 various types of Soviet aircraft being transferred to China by the end of the year. The navy talks produced agreement by Moscow to help found a naval infrastructure in China, "including shipyards, naval colleges, and extensive coastal fortifications."[61] Moscow sent hundreds of military advisors.[62]

The Mao–Stalin summit produced a Chinese order for an additional 1,000 Soviet bombers, fighters, trainers, and transports. Stalin also dispatched Soviet Air force units to defend Shanghai.[63] Mao had originally thought to divide the $300 million low-interest loan he received from Stalin evenly between the air force and the navy. However, pressing needs in Korea meant that most of it went to the air force.[64]

What neither Mao nor Stalin counted on was the bravery and determination of the soldiers, sailors, and airmen of the Republic of China, by then on Taiwan—that is, the Nationalists. After pushing Chiang's forces off the mainland in 1949, Mao thought the PLA would make short work of the Nationalist garrison on Quemoy Island (Jinmen in Chinese).

Today there are several tourist flights each day between Taipei, the capital of Taiwan, and Quemoy. A visitor to the island can look through binoculars and easily see people on the mainland going about their daily business.[65] A number of defectors have swam across the short body of water separating the island from mainland China.

But on the night of October 17, 1949, the PLA's 28th Corps and part of the 29th tried to make an amphibious landing on the island. The Nationalist defenders put up a fierce resistance and, after two weeks of heavy hand-to-hand fighting, staved off the invaders. The PLA lost 9,000 men (dead or captured), its worst defeat of the civil war,[66] The Quemoy defeat, coupled with another setback further north[67] shocked the Beijing leadership into postponing the Taiwan invasion from the summer of 1950 to the summer of 1951. No one knew it at the time, but the Nationalists' brave stand at Quemoy ultimately saved Taiwan and gave Chinese democracy a chance to flourish on the island of Formosa.

INDOCHINA (VIETNAM)

As with the Tibetans, the people of Indochina were not so fortunate as to escape a communist takeover. Ho Chi-Minh, like Kim, had had a long working relationship with the Chinese communists, having met such senior leaders as Zhou Enlai when they were all young communists in Paris in the 1920s. Also like Kim, Ho had lived in China, spoke Chinese fluently, and had been a member of the Chinese Communist Party, even a member of Mao's armed forces, in this case the Eighth Route Army. In 1946, Ho offered sanctuary to a Chinese communist regiment that had to slip over the border into Viet-Minh-held territory to escape the Nationalists during the civil war. These forces became the first communist Chinese military advisors and instructors to the Viet-Minh.[68]

It was probably Mao who summoned Ho to Moscow in January 1950. While Ho was en route, the Chinese formally recognized Ho's regime and persuaded a reluctant Stalin to do the same. The Soviet dictator's eye was on France where the French Communist Party was making important gains and he didn't want to stir up trouble in the French colony. But at that moment, communist solidarity prevailed.

At the precise time Mao and Stalin in Moscow were discussing diplomatic recognition for Ho, other officials in Beijing decided to send a representative from their Central Military Commission to Indochina to assess the Viet-Minh's military needs. Within two months, Chinese arms and ammunition began to flow south and the Chinese established military training camps near the border. There was even an artillery firing range for the Viet-Minh set up at Ching-hsi in southern China.[69] In April, the Viet-Minh formally asked for military advisors. In response, the PLA sent three senior generals to set up a full-fledged Chinese military advisory group. Also in the spring of 1950, Beijing began a massive transfer of war material to the Viet-Minh. This included rifles, pistols, machine guns, 105mm howitzers, bazookas, and recoilless rifles.[70] With the Chinese providing training and weapons, the Viet-Minh won an important series of victories over the French in the fall of 1950.[71]

BLUNDERS AND TREACHERY

The worst way to play a weak hand of poker is to let your opponent see your cards, proclaim in public how weak your hand is, and take actions demonstrating that you have a weak hand. The Americans did all of this in the period leading up to the Korean War.

Their hand was weak by choice, not the luck of the draw. General Douglas MacArthur in his memoirs noted, "General Marshall, then Army chief of staff, had reported to the secretary of war in 1945: 'Never was the strength of American democracy so evident nor has it ever been so clearly within our power to give definite guidance for our course into the future of the human race.'"[72]

Then the U.S. threw it away in mindless demobilization. The 12 million man military was only 1.5 million by 1949. The United States Eighth Army, which carried the bulk of army fighting in Korea, was "one-third below strength [in infantry]," according to their commander. "The regiments had only two instead of three battalions, light tanks instead of heavy, 105mm howitzers instead of 155mm cannon."[73]

Some military specialties, developed at great effort during World War II, were abandoned almost entirely. One of these was aerial photographic interpretation, known commonly as "PI." As General S. L. A. Marshall pointed out, "Beginning its war in Korea, the

Eighth Army did not possess even the shell of such a system. There were no interpreters, no air crews adequately trained for the mission, and no production apparatus working had the specialists been available."[74] When Mao's armies began to slip over the border into North Korea, this deficiency would cost the lives of UN soldiers. With adequate PI, the Americans might not have been taken by surprise.

With Europe-first thinking still pervading the American political establishment, what troops and military hardware the U.S. had were heavily committed there. General MacArthur commented that Secretary of State Dean Acheson made eleven trips to Europe while in office, but none to visit him in Tokyo.[75]

The State Department was in command when it came to Korea. In April of 1949, President Truman had announced that U.S. occupation troops would be withdrawn from South Korea and by June they were gone. The small military advisory team left behind was placed under the "operational control" of the State Department.[76]

State felt that it had to make certain South Korea did not provoke the North. First, it insisted that the South Korean military forces be set up as a lightly armed constabulary, i.e. police force, and not as a regular military. In a move that crippled the ROK even further, the United States State Department vetoed the kinds of defensive weapons that South Koreans needed to defend themselves.

State was not the only institution engaging in major blunders. On Capitol Hill, cutting the defense budget became a bipartisan sport. In the summer of 1947, Congress not only cut $45 million out of the South Korea economic aide package, it struck 70,000 officers and civilians from the Army payrolls.[77] Less than two months before the invasion, Democratic Senator Tom Connally from Texas, the chairman of the Senate Foreign Relations Committee, gave a published interview in which he declared that the U.S. would probably have to abandon South Korea.[78]

The first crucial moment when blunders and treachery came together so disastrously for the Korean people would have been in the first half of Mao's visit to Moscow. On December 30, 1949, the American National Security Council created a secret policy paper (NSC-48) that had the effect of excluding South Korea and Taiwan from the U.S. defense umbrella. NSC-48 called for checking the spread of communism in Asia "by means other than arms," a clear signal that the U.S. would not intervene.

There is no doubt that the Cambridge spies made certain that Moscow was immediately informed of the contents of NSC-48. As American historian William Stueck put it, "The NSC paper appears to have been available to Stalin courtesy of his spies in the United States, who included Kim Philby, the British liaison officer to the American Central Intelligence Agency."[79] Here was proof, if Stalin and Mao needed it, that the Allies had given up on South Korea and Taiwan.

Both President Truman and Secretary of State Acheson made public speeches confirming the idea that South Korea and Taiwan would be abandoned. President Truman said the United States would not defend Taiwan "at this time."[80] In his speech before Washington's National Press Club, Secretary Acheson even used a map of East Asia to show who was under the American defense umbrella (Japan) and who was not (South Korea, Taiwan, and Vietnam). Acheson would later claim that he was "eager and inexperienced" and that this led to "a very serious misunderstanding."[81] Perhaps in response to Acheson's signal, within a week, Congress killed the South Korea aid bill for that year.[82]

A "DIVISION OF LABOR"

Some scholars use the polite phrase "division of labor" to describe what the international communist leadership was doing in 1949–1950.[83] Others call it a "global division of spheres of responsibility."[84] It was the division of responsibilities in a massive conspiracy of world conquest. Mao would take Tibet and Taiwan. Kim would conquer South Korea with troops from Mao and arms from Stalin. Mao was the back up if things went bad in Korea. Ho would take Indochina backed by arms and training from Mao.

The troops were in place. Weapons were on hand. Planning was complete. The last element was intelligence. The communist leaders had to know if the Americans would intervene and how. We know the Cambridge spies had provided Stalin, Mao, Kim, and Ho with full details of Allied defense plans in the Far East, and allowed their fanatical anti-Americanism to feed Stalin's increasing paranoia. Until more archives are opened, however, we will not know if the spies, together with as yet unknown others, also helped to create the disastrously weak American policy towards Korea. Was the State Department's unilateral disarming of the South Korean forces just a function of weak minds at work, or was there a more sinister hand operating in the background? How could the American national security apparatus come to the conclusion that South Korea and Taiwan were irrelevant to our defense posture in Asia? Especially since they would conclude exactly the opposite in six months?

Stalin, Mao, Kim, and Ho, communist revolutionaries all, dreamed of first regional, then world, conquest. In what we know of their correspondence, they were constantly concerned about whether the Americans would try to block their ambitions. Stalin and Mao were as suspicious as they were cunning and ruthless. They would not have taken the Truman and Acheson public declarations at face value; they would have smelled a trap. The Cambridge spies put that worry to rest. Commenting on the new Truman administration policy to resist the spread of communism "by means other than arms," Russian scholar Vladislav Zubok dryly noted, "One may speculate that Stalin learned about the essence of this new policy before these official pronouncements, from various leaks and intelligence sources in Washington and London. It is even possible that . . . an intelligence coup might have been a pivotal factor in prompting Stalin to reassess his Far Eastern strategy."[85]

In the final analysis, the Allied war effort in Korea was betrayed even before it started. Speaking about Maclean, one British author remarked, "there is little doubt he leaked the results of the [British and American] [secret] talks, helping the Chinese inflict more British, American, and Commonwealth casualties."[86] Recovering from his disillusionment, one of Burgess' former friends would later write, "Even more, he had become in my eyes one who had voluntarily engaged in the cruel and murderous operations of an organization which was directly responsible for the destruction of millions of people by death, torture, starvation, and any other means which its ingenuity could devise to achieve that purpose. He was, no doubt, my friend; he was also a man with blood on his hands."

All of them—Stalin, Mao, Kim, Ho, Burgess, Maclean, Philby, and the others—had blood on their hands. The reign of terror they helped unleash is directly responsible for the death and continuing misery of millions of Tibetans, Koreans, Vietnamese, Cambodians, and others. The dangers we face in Asia today derive from what they put in motion over fifty years ago, and nowhere more so than on the Korean Peninsula.

3

BEIJING'S WAR

[There] was the complete, almost unspoken acceptance on the part of everyone that whatever had to be done to meet this aggression had to be done. There was no suggestion from anyone that either the United Nations or the United States could back away from it.[1]

— President Harry S. Truman

Saturday, June 24, 1950, was another monsoon day along the 38th Parallel. Heavy clouds loaded with moisture dropped sheets of rain during the morning. Good for farmers looking to the fall rice crop.

First Lieutenant William Hamilton, a U.S. Army advisor to the Republic of Korea forces (ROKs), decided nothing was going on along the border with North Korea, at least not that weekend. G–2 intelligence headquarters in Tokyo had told Washington "there will be no civil war in Korea this spring or summer."[2] There was a big falloff that spring in border incidents and guerrilla activity,[3] and it looked like the Stalinist North Korea had decided to concentrate on its own affairs for a while. They needed supplies, and Saturday night in Seoul was more promising than just looking out the window watching the rainfall. Hamilton got in his jeep and headed for the lights of town.[4]

Captain Joseph R. Darrigo, a senior advisor to South Korea, shared a billet with Hamilton and he stayed. The decline of North Korean border activity that spring, which should have brought him comfort, instead plagued him with suspicion. He even went so far as to share his concerns up the chain of command, but they garnered little interest and no response. He was just an Army captain out in the boondocks, what did he know?

A lot, as it turned out. That night Darrigo was the only American on duty at the border. Weekend passes meant that everyone else was in town or elsewhere. Somewhere around four o'clock in the morning he awoke to loud noises in the distance. Thunder? Not unlikely, given the stormy weather. But a different storm was brewing. Almost immediately he heard the unmistakable sound of small arms fire ricocheting off the side of his house. This was artillery. Time to get up and get moving.

This was it. A North Korean version of the German Blitzkrieg.[5] Soviet-made 122mm long-range artillery had opened up all along the border. Russian T-34 tanks led columns of battle-hardened North Korean infantry. Kim had thrown his best troops, 95,000 veterans of the Chinese Civil War, at the unsuspecting South Koreans. It was a total sneak attack—just as precisely calculated and much like the Japanese attack on Pearl Harbor nine years before, which also had occurred on a Sunday morning.

By striking in June, Kim knew the U.S. Far East Air Force (FEAF), stationed in Japan, would be severely hampered by the monsoon weather.[6] On most days during the monsoons, the rain-laden clouds reduced the ceiling to 200 feet and fog frequently closed down the runways. Not good flying weather.

As an advisor to the South Koreans, Darrigo had no troops to command; his job was to raise the alarm. He jumped in his jeep and headed for the center of Kaesong, the ancient capital of Korea and, at that time, a medium-sized town between Seoul and the border. He was looking for the South Korean 12th Infantry Regiment and its parent, the ROK 1st Division. But when he reached

Kaesong, he found he was too late: A full regiment of North Korean soldiers had already infiltrated the town and had turned their attention to him. Under fire, Darrigo managed to make it to the South Korean 1st Division Command Post.[7]

Although both the First Division commander and his own boss, U.S. military advisor Lt. Col. Lloyd Rockwell, were in Seoul for the weekend, an alert young South Korean watch officer managed to find them. Before dawn, the 1st Division was already moving out. The South Korean 1st Division could claim three infantry regiments, but they had no tanks and no effective antitank weapons. They were about to feel the force of two full-strength North Korean divisions led by a formidable battalion of T-34 tanks. The outcome was painfully clear: The South Korean troops would die valiantly, but they would die.[8]

All of the North Korean Army's heavy weapons came from Moscow. Even the preparation order was originally written in Russian,[9] but after that point Moscow handed the baton to Beijing.[10] The core of the North Korean fighting force was made up of ethnic Koreans who had fought with Mao's People's Liberation Army. At least one unit fought down the length of the Chinese mainland, clear to Hainan Island. Almost the entire high command of the North Korean Army, known as the "Korean People's Army" [KPA] or Inmun Gun, was composed of veterans who had fought in China.[11] With these prophetic opening shots, Beijing assumed influence and responsibility for North Korea, an unholy alliance the People's Republic of China affirms to this day.

MILITARY COMPARISON—JUNE 25, 1950

	KPA	ROK
Force Levels	135,000	100,000
Combat Experience	Yes	No
Adequate Training	Yes	No

	KPA	ROK
Leadership	Good	Mixed
Intelligence	Effective	Marginal
War Plans	Detailed	Poor
Tanks	150-200	None
Long Range Howitzers	122mm Soviet	None
Motorized Artillery	76mm Soviet	None
Heavy Mortars	120mm	None
Anti-Tank Weapons	Yes	Minimal
Anti-Tank Mines	Yes	None
Basic Infantry Weapon	Full-Auto	Semi-Auto
Ammunition	Sufficient	Low
Combat Aircraft	200	None

Such was the composition of forces when the Korean War began. The South Koreans did have some divisional artillery—obsolete American "snub-nose" 105 mm howitzers—but it had no armor shield and was out-ranged by the Soviet-supplied divisional guns (14,000 yards to 8,000 yards).[12] The Americans had not supplied South Korea with antitank shells and the 105s High Explosive rounds just bounced off the T-34s.[13] Likewise, South Korea's World War II vintage 2.36-inch bazookas and American 37mm antitank guns had no effect on the tanks. The American 75mm recoilless rifle, later introduced into the war, was the appropriate weapon for an infantry company facing an armored attack. In the words of the United States Army historians, "The South Korean armed forces had no tanks, no medium artillery, no 4.2-inch mortars, no recoilless rifles, and no fighter aircraft or bombers."[14]

It is difficult to explain adequately the sheer terror that a tank formation has on infantry soldiers in the open. Even observing a friendly armored force performing exercises can be unsettling.[15] This particular tank type, the T-34, is a 35-ton main battle tank, developed by the Soviets in the middle of World War II. In factories behind the Ural Mountains, the Soviets produced thousands of these and it was the machine that ultimately broke the back of the German Army. It was designed to be low slung, making it a relatively squat target, with an 85mm gun and two 7.62mm machine guns. Furthermore, it was heavily armored and largely invincible to the weapons South Korean defenders had on hand in 1950. As if to amplify the feeling of terror these beasts inspired, the North Korean Army mounted sirens on the front of their tanks. To the South Korean soldiers and later, the Americans, the T-34s were metal monsters. Nearly all the battlefield historians of the Korean War have focused on the critical role played by the KPA's Soviet armor in achieving the North's initial success. One historian explained, "It was the communist tanks, the ever present, ever leading T-34s which could not be stopped, and could not be destroyed, that wrecked every plan and every hope of the ROK commanders."[16]

Although some troops did panic, by and large the South Korean forces stood their ground and fought against overwhelming odds. Many individuals did great service and should be commended for their heroism and resourcefulness in fighting the enemy. In one case, an enterprising South Korean engineering officer stopped some tanks with satchel charges on long poles.[17] Even the South Korean police were able to pitch in and stop a tank on at least one occasion.[18] But these were the exceptions; in most cases, the T-34s rolled over the defenders, easily brushing them aside as they headed south.

War is about sacrifice and the Korean War saw its share. The Han River runs east and west, just below Seoul, and it was here that a major portion of the South Korean Army was lost. 44,000 soldiers trapped between Kim's invading forces and the river were killed when the South Korean government blew bridges over the Han River in the early morning hours of June 28.[19] Blowing the bridges was the pivotal action that kept Kim's armored forces from crossing the Han River until July 3.[20] Later, Kim Il Sung would

ascribe this high-priced delay as instrumental in North Korea's ultimate failure to drive the UN forces off the peninsula.[21]

Yet the destruction of the Han River bridges remains a con-
troversial issue in South Korea—not just because of the heavy
military casualties, but because a number of civilians were killed
in the explosion. After the 1953 armistice, the South Korean government tried and executed the South Korean chief of military
engineers.[22]

BLUNDERS, AGAIN

The United States has been well served by outstanding and dedicated Foreign Service Officers.[23] However, John J. Muccio, U.S.
ambassador to South Korea in June 1950, was not one of them.
Vain, with an affinity toward bow ties, he was essentially clueless
about what was going on around him. Even with full knowledge
of the coming storm, he contented himself with public statements
and private cables declaring the South Korean forces to be "supe-
rior" to the North Koreans in every way.[24] KMAG, the U.S. Military
assistance group in Korea, reported to him, not to General
MacArthur in Tokyo. It was Muccio and his team who should have
been reading and acting on Captain Darrigo's warnings.

But the major offense to be laid at Muccio's door was not his
disinterest in the warnings of Darrigo and others like him, but his
ignorance and panic when it came time to face the crisis. On the
first day of the war, he cabled Washington to say that the South
Korean forces "had made a gallant comeback by midnight and
seem to have stabilized the situation."[25] In reality, North Korean
armor was overrunning South Korea north of Seoul and the entire
South Korean army was in full retreat in the western part of the
country. Muccio's misleading reports caused the Pentagon to mis-
judge the situation in the critical first days.

When the Pentagon finally grasped the situation, Muccio and
his team were forced to evacuate American dependents and burn

all the embassy records relating to Americans. However, according to one report, what he and his team did not do is burn the records relating to South Korean citizens, many of whom had been in the employment or had other contact with the embassy. The North Korean secret police arrived in Seoul to find these remaining records, pointing to over 5,000 persons, waiting for them. Except for those who had already escaped south of the Han River, none of the South Koreans named in the U.S. embassy files survived the North Korean firing squads.[26]

In the months leading up to June 1950, the South Korean government had repeatedly begged the Americans for weapons to defend themselves. In August 1949, South Korean President Syngman Rhee wrote to U.S. President Harry S. Truman, "We Koreans believe that the Communists, under Soviet direction, intend to attack in force, that they will do so, and if they do, it is we Koreans, civilians and military who will pay the price, not the good-willed American advisors." President Truman advised President Rhee to take up his problems with Muccio.[27]

Based on Ambassador Muccio's reporting from Seoul, it was the U.S. State Department's policy to keep certain defensive weapons out of the hands of the South Koreans. The State Department was petrified that a well-armed Republic of Korea would attempt to liberate the people of North Korea, thereby dragging the United States into a major war with China and the Soviet Union. Further, the Soviet Union shares a border with North Korea and would not have allowed its protégé to be defeated by the South. Given the public mood in the United States, there was no chance that the United States would give South Korea the armor and combat aircraft really necessary for a march northward.

Despite these concerns, there was no excuse for the American State Department to deny South Korea the defensive weapons required to deter a North Korean attack on Seoul. American 75mm recoilless rifles and antitank mines alone would have made an enormous difference in defending the South, but would not have been enough to make them a threat to North Korea. In hindsight, the war that State Department so feared turned out to be unavoidable, costing hundreds of thousands of South Korean and American lives before it was over.

Washington had an even larger share of blunders, beginning at the top. Harry Truman first rose to prominence as President Franklin D. Roosevelt's first choice for vice president, mostly due to his reputation as a cost-cutter in the defense area. This philosophy that had served him so well in the past, was not forgotten after he became president in 1945. As a result, the United States underwent a staggering demobilization after World War II. The Joint Chiefs of Staff felt they needed at least $15 billion for the military; President Truman wanted to cut that to $6 billion.[28] A comparison of U.S. forces at the end of World War II in 1945 and in 1950 looks like this:

	1945	1950
Total Forces	12 million	1.5 million
Army	8 million	592,000
Air Force	218 air groups	38 air groups
Marines	480,000	75,000
Aircraft Carriers	40	11

At a time when downsizing was the rule, the military brass didn't help matters either. Post-World War II force reductions resulted in Army units that were short of subordinate units, meaning that regiments had fewer battalions, for example. The Army could have done either of two things: Retire more divisions and consolidate the remaining ones into "heavy" divisions, or develop new battlefield strategies for the "light" divisions. It did neither.[29] As a consequence, early in the war, the American army went into battle with plans and strategies it did not have the resources to carry out.

THE UNITED NATIONS ENTERS THE KOREAN WAR

Kim's surprise attack on Seoul came as a complete shock to Washington. The U.S. Army historians candidly reported that, "Agencies of the United States government failed to forecast adequately the North Korean attack."[30]

But not everyone in the army was oblivious to the North Korea threat. In the late 1940s, Major General John Singlaub, who was then a U.S. Army major running special operations for the CIA in Manchuria, established an intelligence network to monitor both the Chinese Communists and the North Koreans. According to General Singlaub, his agents were told to search for any indication that the North Koreans had intentions to attack the south.[31] The agents in the Singlaub network went to work at great personal risk to themselves, but that hard work paid off. By the late 1940s, it was clear from their intelligence that the North Koreans were building a tank-heavy force. The road bridges heading south were being reinforced to take the extra weight a tank would generate and railroads were also being repaired.

In midst of the finger pointing between Congress and the administration immediately after the North Korean attack, CIA Director Roscoe Hillenkoetter revealed that five days before the invasion, his agency had sent a detailed warning to the highest levels of the government. The CIA's warning, based on the work done by field agents from the Singlaub network, had been hand delivered to President Truman.[32] Although CIA has the signed receipts to show it was delivered, the intelligence report itself has disappeared.[33]

Despite these squabbles, the challenge that must now be confronted was immediately clear. Calling his senior aides together, President Truman himself described the drama of the moment: "[There] was the complete, almost unspoken acceptance on the part of everyone that whatever had to be done to meet this aggression had to be done. There was no suggestion from anyone that either the United Nations or the United States could back away from it."[34]

Secretary of State Acheson, who less than six months before had placed South Korea outside of the American defense perimeter, was now raising the alarm that Kim's attack "was the spear point of a drive made by the whole communist control group on the entire power position of the West—principally in the east, but also affecting the whole world."[35] George Kennan, a senior State Department official at the time, concluded that, for the communists, the underlying aim was not just Korea but rather the big prize, Japan.[36] Within twenty-four hours of the attack, President Truman had ordered the American Air Force and Navy into the Korean War and announced that the U.S. 7th Fleet would prevent communist China from invading Taiwan.[37]

The State Department requested and got UN support for the U.S. actions. By early July 1950, North Korea was at war with the United Nations and five-star General Douglas MacArthur was the commander of the UN forces. In time, sixteen nations would contribute military forces to the UN's war effort in Korea.

On June 29, General MacArthur led a personal inspection tour of the situation in Korea. From a hill overlooking the Han River, he could see the South Koreans in full retreat and hear the sound of artillery and mortars in the distance. Based on General MacArthur's report, the next day President Truman expanded American participation by including ground troops for Korea. Recognizing the wider challenge, President Truman also approved a military aid package for the French effort against the Viet-Minh.

The burden of rescuing Korea fell on the U.S. 8th Army, at that time scattered all over Japan on occupation duty. General MacArthur's chief of staff rated the 8th Army at "about 40 percent effective."[38] The troops didn't even have a physical training program adequate enough to keep them alive fighting in Korea's mountainous terrain.[39] They lacked every kind of military equipment, including working radios. They had a few light tanks, no match for T-34s, no antitank mines and their stocks of antitank rounds were small. Within the 8th Army, there were four under-strength divisions: the 7th, the 24th, the 25, and the 1st Cavalry. Of these, the 24th led by General William Dean, was the least prepared for battle. While General Dean was capable, some on his senior staff was not. His chief of staff was known as a "drunk" and a "weak spot."[40] In turn, the 24th Division had three infantry regiments: the 19th, the 21st, and the 34th. Of these, the 34th was the least effective. In training the year before, the 34th had performed so badly that General Dean had sacked the regimental commander.

A battalion of the 19th Infantry ("Task Force Smith") went to Korea in early July, one day ahead of the 34th. Facing thirty-three tanks, with no antitank mines, and armed with only six rounds of antitank munitions, Task Force Smith was summarily defeated by one o'clock in the afternoon.[41] With the South Koreans having lost the heart of their army when the Han River bridges were blown, it was now up to the under-strength and under-equipped U.S. 24th Army Division and the surviving South Korean units to stop a dozen divisions of Kim's army. Their goal: the southern port of Pusan, where the conquest of the entire country of Korea could be had. Over the next three weeks, the 24th Division and the South Korean forces would fight dozens of individual battles. General Dean would spend most of the war as a prisoner of war. The 24th would take 30 percent casualties and many of its senior officers would be killed fighting from the front lines.[42] During July, the South Korean forces took 70,000 casualties (killed in action, wounded, or missing) but the Americans and South Korean forces inflicted 60,000 casualties on the North Korean war machine.[43] The 24th and the South Korean forces would retreat a hundred miles, but they had bought time with blood.

By the first of August, the 8th Army had brought in enough fresh troops, bullets, and beans to form a defendable perimeter around Pusan in the southeast corner of the country. For the next six weeks the Americans and the South Koreans would do battle with the North Korean Army. Knowing that time was running out, Kim threw everything he had, most of thirteen divisions including a hundred new T-34 tanks, at the Pusan Perimenter.[44] General John Walker, commander of the 8th Army, told his troops, in essence, "Stand or die."[45] They took note. Though the line bent in some places, it never broke. In a taste of the battles to come, one mountain ridge at Pusan changed hands no fewer than thirteen times.[46] All the while, UN troops continued to arrive at the port of Pusan. By the middle of September, the UN forces outnumbered Kim's, and had enough heavy tanks ready to at last take on the KPA's T-34s on an even footing. The North Koreans fighting forces were not finished, but the American landing at Incheon would break it open.

Despite this preparation, as the Cambridge spies continued to read and pass on every Allied war document to Moscow, the secrecy of the Allied amphibious landing at Incheon was more than probably compromised. Memoirs of Chinese leaders reveal that the international communist leadership had at this point deduced that the landing at Incheon was coming, but that Kim would not listen.[47] In reality, Kim had no choice but to focus on Pusan. He didn't have enough manpower to both defeat the UN at Pusan and adequately defend Incheon. He gambled everything on a knockout blow aimed at Pusan, and lost.

So it was, on September 15, 1950, that seventy thousand UN forces landed at Incheon, twenty miles west of Seoul on the Yellow Sea.[48] Extremely high tides and the good chance of inclement weather meant that General MacArthur would have to make his own gamble, over the objections of most of the Joint Chiefs of Staff.[49] It was an enormous, successful, and most of all, lucky gamble. The North Koreans had a garrison of about 2,000 at Incheon and could move up elements of one infantry regiment[50] with about a dozen T-34 tanks from Seoul. Compared with that, the U.S. forces had the full might of Air Force and Navy air support, Pershing tanks, and antitank weapons. UN forces also had the secret assistance of a number of Japanese ex-military officers and civilians with intimate knowledge of the port.[51] By the time the battle at Incheon was to take place, there was hardly a serious contest to be had—due in large part to General MacArthur's gamble. As it turned out, the most difficult fight was for Seoul. It took almost two weeks of vicious house-to-house, street-by-street fighting for the UN forces to throw the North Koreans completely out of Seoul.

The idea behind the Incheon landing, 150 miles from Pusan, was to catch the North Koreans between a hammer and an anvil. The UN forces landing at Incheon, the anvil, would take Seoul and drive eastwards across the Peninsula. The 8th Army would then break out from the Pusan Perimeter. Driving north, they would become the hammer. By the end of September, the North Korean Army was shattered and the UN was debating whether to liberate North Korea or halt at the old 38th Parallel.

As the UN forces liberated areas previously held by the North Koreans, a pattern of atrocities began to be unmasked. Tens of thousands of South Korean civilians, including women and children, were discovered in mass graves. As was common with other communist regimes, the victims were forced to dig their own graves.[52] South Korean, American, and other UN soldiers captured by the North Koreans also went to their deaths—hands tied behind their backs and a single bullet hole to the head. In one mass grave alone, American troops found seven thousand South Koreans and forty GIs, all murdered.[53] Again, when the UN forces liberated the North Korean capital of Pyongyang, they found thousands of people in mass graves outside the main prison—South Korean civilians driven north by Kim's retreating army.

In those days corruption was endemic, but most South Korean officials were patriots, thousands of them dying rather than join the communists. It is difficult to believe that any South Koreans could have collaborated with a regime as odious as North Korea, but as is the case throughout history, some chose to follow this route. Many of these communist collaborators were students. After Seoul had been liberated, both the CIA and British intelligence found that more than half of South Korean university and high school students had actively collaborated with the North Korean occupation. As one American historian put it, "No one who lived through the occupation of Seoul could deny that students were among the most ardent supporters of the [North Korean occupation] regime."[54] Even today, people who escape from North Korea are often astounded to discover a pro-Pyongyang bias among many South Korean students.[55] A July 2003 poll conducted by a South Korean presidential advisory panel found that South Korean young people substantially prefer North Korea to the United States.[56]

BEIJING'S WAR—THE MYTH AND THE REALITY

Beginning about 1960, the American academic community has accepted a myth regarding China's entry into the Korean War. According to this myth, if the UN had not crossed the 38th Parallel, there would have been no intervention from the Chinese. In this standard interpretation of the events, which is widely taught in American universities, Beijing was merely responding to a direct threat to its national security upon seeing the UN forces crossing the 38th Parallel.[57] In fact, nearly all Western scholars accepted this theory.[58] If true, such a theory would easily position the U.S. as the aggressors and punt all the blame for the death and the destruction that followed in the same direction.

As is often the case, the reality is both different and more complicated. It took two mainland Chinese scholars, Chen Jian and Shu Guang Zhang, now teaching in the United States, to point the way.[59] By accessing Chinese records, it became clear to them that the standard interpretation is patently false. As Chen put it, "Mao and his associates aimed to win a glorious victory by driving the Americans off the Korean peninsula."[60] Likewise, Zhang notes, "There is reason to argue that, rather than merely responding to what was perceived as a compelling threat to their security, Beijing authorities chose to act aggressively, regardless of the calculated high risk and cost."[61]

Were Mao and at least some of his comrades spoiling for a fight with the Americans? Yes. Let's look at the record.

From the communists' standpoint, the first reports from the Korean front were positive. Indeed, on June 26, 1950, Stalin's ambassador in Pyongyang sent in a glowing report, "The attack of the troops of the People's Army took the enemy completely by surprise."[62] However, within a week, the ambassador had the difficult task of keeping his own head while preparing the Soviet dictator for bad news. His message to Stalin on July 2 begins to hedge. The "general situation," he says, "continues to remain favorable." But he now writes that there is a "complicated military-political situation in Korea," and among the Korean population "individual attitudes of a lack of belief in the final victory have appeared."[63] By July 4, Stalin's man reported that Kim was already complaining of the "seriousness of the situation at the front and in the liberated territories."[64] Kim had three problems:

- The ROKs and the American 24th Division were fighting a tough rear-guard action
- The South Korean populace was not embracing the communist North Koreans
- American air power, even with the bad weather, was tearing up his rail yards and generally raising havoc with his supply system

The international communist leadership swung into action. The Chinese proposed to Stalin that nine Chinese divisions be moved to the North Korean border. Stalin agreed with this idea and stated, "We will try to provide air cover for these units."[65] As we will see, the issue of Soviet air cover for Chinese units in Korea would poison the well of PRC–Soviet relations for decades to come.

Beginning July 7, the Beijing leadership held a series of high-level political and military meetings to discuss preparing for war with the Americans. Beijing turned on the anti-American political propaganda to whip up popular support for war. Chinese armies also began to move to the North Korean border—by the end of July, there were over a quarter of a million Chinese soldiers on the Yalu border. For the next two months the PLA soldiers on the North Korean border trained intensively to prepare for fighting against U.S. troops. Under duress, former Nationalist officers with experience fighting along side American soldiers were forced to give lectures and briefings to PLA officers on American battlefield tactics.

In late August Chinese generals held a conference at which they came to the conclusion that they could beat the Americans. Wires between Moscow, Beijing, and Pyongyang hummed with accelerated discussions of Soviet war material headed for the Korean front.[66] By the end of September, the Chinese war machine was ready to strike the Americans with or without provocation. As Shu writes, "the Chinese military was geared for war. Like an arrow on a drawn bowstring, nothing could easily prevent its release."[67]

At the last moment, it almost didn't happen, not because of anything the UN did or did not do, but because Stalin got cold feet. He told Mao that there would be no Soviet air cover for Chinese troops fighting in Korea, at least not for awhile. At first, Mao countermanded his own marching order, but after twenty-four hours of intense discussion, Beijing decided to go ahead without Soviet air cover. General Peng Dehui would lead the "Chinese People's Volunteers" (CPVs) and Mao oldest son, Mao Anying, served on the general's senior staff.

Why did Mao decide to attack the Americans? Some members of the politburo were unenthusiastic about the project because they wanted to devote the government's energies to political consolidation and economic development.[68] Two of the PLA's best generals checked themselves into medical facilities rather than lead Chinese troops into Korea.[69] A key to Mao's thinking lies in his October 2, 1950, telegram to Stalin justifying the intervention in Korea:

> We have decided to send some of our troops to Korea under the name of [Chinese People's] Volunteers to fight the United States and its lackey Syngman Rhee and to aid our Korean comrades. From the following considerations, we think it necessary to do so: the Korean revolutionary force will meet with a fundamental defeat, and the American aggressors will rampage unchecked once they occupy the whole of Korea. This will be unfavorable to the entire East.[70]

The telegram goes on to state Beijing's intention "to fight American troops" (three times) and "annihilate American troops" (four times). At no point does Mao claim that China faces any sort of national security threat itself if they do not attack the Americans. Mao tells Stalin he fears the Americans will attack Chinese cities only if the Beijing does enter the war. It was naked aggression by the Chinese Communists, not actions by the UN, which led to two more years of war on the Korean Peninsula.

What motivated Mao was his concern that a UN (and American) victory in Korea would "be unfavorable to the entire East." Later in the telegram, Mao declares that only after they "annihilate the American troops in Korea" will the situation become "favorable to the revolutionary camp." To a veteran communist leader like Stalin, these are code words for the decisions Stalin, Mao, Ho, and Kim made in Moscow in the winter of 1949–1950. Mao is telling Stalin that unless the Americans are stopped, their entire plan to conquer Asia from Tokyo to New Delhi might be at risk.

The first elements of the Chinese forces crossed the Yalu River into North Korea on the night of October 18, 1950. By early November, they had committed thirty-six divisions to the fighting.[71]

BLUNDERS, SPIES, AND VALOR

After having missed the indicators pointing toward a North Korean attack, one might have expected that the American civilian and military leadership would have its guard up for the obvious next act in the drama, intervention by Soviet and/or Chinese forces. They did not. Again, a world of illusion based on how they wanted things to be, not how they were, obscured events.

The American civilian and military leadership wanted, and expected, the Korean War to end in the fall of 1950. President Truman and General MacArthur met at Wake Island in October to discuss the end of the war. Records of their discussions indicate that the only real arguments were over what to do after the North Koreans were chased into Manchuria. The Joint Chiefs wanted to transfer entire American divisions to Europe immediately and General MacArthur told them that the 2nd Division would be ready to move out in early January. He anticipated turning over all defense matters to the South Koreans and ending the U.S. presence in Korea within a very short period of time. Free and democratic elections would be held throughout the Korean Peninsula by the first of the year. The 8th Army would be back in Japan by Christmas.[72] "The Mirage of Victory" had completely taken hold.[73]

The same was true on the ground as well. UN troops were driving north in two columns, the 8th Army-led force in the west and 10th Corps in the east. Between them was the Taebaek Range, which forms a spine of mountains down the length of Korea. Restricted to the roads along the two coasts and separated by mountains, the two columns were not in physical contact with each other—leaving a vast empty space in the middle, perfect for an enemy's envelopment tactics.

In the 8th Army, many of the soldiers thought the war was essentially over. They went into battle with less than one hand grenade per man. Less than half of them had entrenching tools. Most of them had thrown away their steel helmets in favor of a pile cap to keep out the cold. Some soldiers carried as few as sixteen rounds of ammunition.[74]

By this time, the three major Cambridge spies—Burgess, Maclean, and Philby—were in position to do the most damage yet. Burgess stayed at the Foreign Office until he transferred to the British Embassy in Washington in the late summer of 1950. Philby was already in Washington as MI-6's formal liaison to the FBI, CIA, and Canadian intelligence. Maclean would soon head the American Desk at the Foreign Office in London. The three spies could have passed the word to Moscow that there was no risk to China or the Soviet Union from a massive attack by the Americans. The spies knew the mindset of the Allied commanders and the Rules of Engagement the Allies operated under. The Americans were going home; they weren't going to attack China. Mao's divisions could fall on the Americans, South Koreans, and other allies with impunity.

A year later, Burgess and Maclean fled to Moscow at the end of May. Soon thereafter, Philby was withdrawn from Washington at the demand of CIA Director Bedell Smith and FBI Director J. Edgar Hoover. Although many in London believed that Philby was also guilty of espionage, the old boy's network protected him until the early 1960s, when he, too, took off for Moscow.

But they had already done their damage. They had provided Stalin, Mao, Kim, and Ho with a unique look inside allied assumptions, strategies, and plans for the Cold War period, thereby helping to set in motion a reign of terror that continues today.

Over the next six months, UN forces would reel under the blows of five major Chinese assaults. Taken in by Chinese deception (as well as a measure of self-delusion), the UN commanders would be forced to retreat to the 37th Parallel and fight their way back to where the Demilitarized Zone is today. Seoul would change hands two more times in house-to-house fighting. For two years, the Korean War would return to the kind of trench warfare made famous by World War I.

The Chinese 38th and 39th Armies were among the first to cross into North Korea and go into combat against UN forces.[75] They had been part of the PLA's Fourth Field Army and had fought alongside ethnic Korean troops during the Chinese Civil War. Over the course of the Korean War, these two group armies would see long and serious combat. Commenting on one of the very first engagements, the U.S. Army historian's report noted, "The Chinese force that brought disaster to the [American] 8th Cavalry Regiment at Unsan was the [Chinese] 116th Division of the 39th Army."[76] Today 116th is on station in Manchuria, it is fully mechanized, and it has first call to fight the Americans again, should it come to that.

In the midst of the horror of war, there were numerous examples of valor:[77]

- The South Korean units, who always seemed to be singled out by the Chinese to be victimized first
- The eight hundred–man British Gloucester Battalion, which held a hill in front of Seoul until they were down to only fifty men
- The Dutch Battalion, badly shot up with their commander and principal officers dead, still standing
- The French Battalion that took on the Chinese, bayonet to bayonet, and drove them off
- The remarkable stand the Canadians and Australians made in front of Kapyong
- The U.S. Marines "advancing in a new direction" at frozen Chosen
- Mike Michaelis' 24th Infantry (The Wolfhounds), which fought from Pusan through the Chinese intervention

On the day the war ended, the Korean Peninsula was a smoking ruin. Mao himself lost a son in the war—Mao Anying, his son by his first wife. After his mother's death, Mao Anying had been sent to the Soviet Union to be educated. One Chinese general referred to him as "supremely gifted, smart, and capable."[78] He later became the Russian interpreter for General Peng, commander of the Chinese forces in Korea.

On the afternoon of November 24, an American F-51 fighter plane on reconnaissance found some activity around a small house in the very northern part of North Korea. The next day, the Americans came back in force and with napalm, hitting the little house repeatedly. The house had been General Peng's command post and Mao Anying was burned to death by the napalm.[79] Peng buried Mao Anying in North Korea but waited several weeks before he informed the chairman of his son's death in combat.

Senior Chinese officials split the blame for Anying's death between the Americans, who caused it, and Stalin, who had failed to provide air cover to the Chinese forces fighting in Korea. During a private discussion in Beijing in the mid-1980s, a senior Chinese diplomat remarked that of all of Mao's children, only one of them, Mao Anying, the eldest son, had any capability. "And you know, Mao always blamed Stalin for Anying's death," the diplomat said.[80] Mao himself probably never forgave the Americans or Stalin for the death of his only promising heir.

Much had been lost on all sides. The six-hundred-year-old capital city of Seoul had changed hands four times in the Korean War, leaving little standing to indicate its former glory. Five million Koreans were refugees. Millions of Koreans, North and South, were dead. Hundreds of thousands of children were orphaned. It could all have been prevented.

4

THE NEW
KOREAN WAR

The PRC [China] and DPRK [North Korea] are . . .
in the relations of lips and teeth, and the peoples
and armies of the two countries have a blood-
tied traditional relationship.[1]

— General Xiong Guangkai, deputy chief of staff
for intelligence in the People's Liberation Army

"**A**h, The Korean War Has Not Ended." So announced a special exhibit at Seoul's War Museum in the summer of 2003. Beijing and Pyongyang's war against the United Nations did not end with a peace treaty but rather with an armistice—one that was never signed by South Korea. Neither China nor North Korea has ever acknowledged their aggression that led to widespread death and destruction on the Korean Peninsula. Today, Kim Jung Il's regime is preparing to wage modern warfare against the South while carrying on a constant campaign of murder, provocation, and threats. Beijing has been secretly engaged in a military buildup in Manchuria, designed to support North Korea in the event of war. The Demilitarized Zone (DMZ) separating North and South Korea is the most highly fortified frontier in the world today. The return of war on the Korean Peninsula is a very real possibility.

THE DMZ TODAY

The Yongsan complex in the heart of Seoul is the center of Allied military activity for all of Korea. It is the command center for the UN, the combined U.S.–South Korea Forces, and the American Eighth Army. Yongsan was once located on the edge of Seoul, but the city has since grown all around it. VIP helicopter tours of the Korean DMZ usually take off from Yongsan's golf course. On a typically overcast day in 1990, with threatening rain, I took a ride on a UH-1H "Huey" helicopter.[2]

As the Huey headed north, flying low and fast, General William Carpenter—a famous West Point football player, war hero in Vietnam, and a senior general of U.S. forces in Korea—explained over the intercom that the unusual height restrictions were a defense against MANPADs—Man-Portable Air Defense—Soviet or Chinese equivalents of the American shoulder-fired "Stinger" type missiles. These are the same types of weapons that have been used against American helicopters in Iraq. A military visit to the DMZ is serious business.

A North Korean infiltrator probably wouldn't waste a shot on me, a visiting staff member of the United States Senate Foreign Relations Committee, but taking down a helicopter carrying a senior general of the U.S. forces in Korea would have earned the shooter big medals in Pyongyang. General Carpenter's helicopter landed behind a hill. The passengers walked up the back of the hill and around to the American observation post. From this sandbagged bunker North Korean observations posts are in plain sight. The general pointed out Chorwon Valley, the historic invasion route from north to south, and noted that the distant hills ahead were honeycombed with caves and tunnels. There, tens of thousands of North Korean long-range artillery, rockets, and missiles awaited the signal to fire.

In the summer of 2003, I took a drive laterally along the DMZ with a South Korean military escort. Dressed in civilian clothes and riding in an unmarked car gave me a sense of the daily routine around the DMZ.[3] The region surrounding the southern edge of the Korean DMZ is the most heavily fortified and dangerous frontier in the world. Every sort of conventional weapon can be found here in abundance. Allied soldiers are numerous, well armed and dug in. South Korean and American fighter-bombers are just minutes away.

Hundreds of thousands of civilians also live around edge of the DMZ, making the area a close mix of normal everyday living and imminent preparations for war. Farmers tend rice paddy fields and orchards. Kids walk to school. Grannies go to the market. A little tire store does business along the narrow road leading into town. A Korean barbecue place in Pajoo even has a menu in English. On the way out of town, a little park can be found on the right. The grass is moving ever so slightly, but there is no wind blowing—it's two South Korean soldiers in a foxhole with a light machine gun. They are completely camouflaged, right down to the war paint on their faces. Children playing on the slide just ten feet away ignore them.

The DMZ is a strip of land roughly a mile and a half wide and 155 miles long with a strictly limited military presence inside the zone. South of the DMZ, it's almost an unlimited military presence.[4] The southern edge of the DMZ has three fences eight feet apart, each about ten to twelve feet high, topped with razor wire. The fences have metal noisemakers attached, making it difficult for an intruder to cut the wire without alerting the guards.[5] Guard towers and flood lights run the length of the DMZ. Unseen devices such as motion detectors, sound detectors, and infrared heat sensors are at work. The South Koreans have created massive, multi-ton concrete barriers suspended fifteen feet above the major highway that leads into the South. In case of a North Korean invasion, explosives can be set off to drop these barriers and block the highway.

The DMZ is also heavily mined. Driving on the small roads along the southern edge of the DMZ, I was tempted to step out of the car for a photo. But after opening the car door, I found signs with the "skull and cross-bones" or "Mine" written on them.

Getting one's leg blown off is not the only hazard around the DMZ. With little human presence over fifty years, nature has taken over. *National Geographic* magazine has photographed wild cranes that thrive in the natural sanctuary of the demilitarized zone. So too have the poisonous snakes.[6] Some of them are related to the cobra family and give no warning before they strike. The North Koreans capture them to bottle a local brew, a health tonic called "Adder Liquor."

Crossing the initial three lines of fences would still not put a North Korean infiltrator in the clear. There are more fences, barriers, and guard posts. South Korean and American military policemen guard posts along the area south of the DMZ. They appear alert, professional, well trained, and unlikely to be taken by surprise.

I spotted the American Second Division infantry troops leaving a field exercise. It was late August in Korea, and the weather was hot and muggy. Carrying full field packs, the American troops had been making their way through the thick underbrush and up and down hills. Like the military police, they looked physically fit and on top of the situation.

The United States Army calls artillery the "King of Battle." By the end of the Korean War, the Allies had massed a lot of big guns along the front lines. These guns are still here. After passing the camouflaged machine gunners in the little park, the road bends to the left around a medium-sized hill. The hill has been hollowed out and turned into a firebase for South Korean Army 155mm howitzers. Only the barrels of the big guns protrude from the hill, pointed to the North. Between them are low bunkers covered with grass, probably for ready ammo. The main magazines would be located further inside the hill. Elsewhere along one of the four-lane expressways, a South Korean artillery convoy, towing 105mm howitzers, was on its way to a field exercise. The entire unit—at least twenty guns, supply trucks, and the medical van—was on the march.

TUNNELS

Faced with such heavy fortification by South Korean and American forces along the DMZ, the North Koreans have resorted to tunneling. Mining has a long tradition in North Korea, a country rich in minerals, including gold. The South Koreans have discovered four North Korean tunnels under the DMZ—the earliest in 1974 and the latest in 1989. No one knows exactly how many tunnels the North Koreans have built, but estimates say that there are at least twenty undiscovered tunnels.[7]

In 1974, a North Korean defector was able to point out the general location for a tunnel. The South Koreans bore test holes every two meters but still missed it. They filled the test holes with water. An underground explosion in 1978 caused the water in one of the test holes to rise and splash up onto the ground. Further excavations turned up a North Korean tunnel about a mile long and buried over two hundred feet under the ground. The tunnel has a gentle downward slope towards North Korea so any water dripping through the tunnel would flow out the back. Walking along the tunnel, neither the six-foot tall South Korean soldier nor his American guest could stand upright. The sides of the tunnel had been painted with charcoal—an effort by the North Koreans to disguise the operation as coal mining.

For the past fifty years, the border between North and South Korea has been one of the most dangerous on the globe. Although the Korean War ended in 1953, the North Koreans have continued to commit acts of aggression by land, sea, and air.

MURDERS ALONG THE DMZ

With the DMZ returning to nature, from time to time trees and brush grow up to obscure the view of soldiers manning the UN observation posts (OP) and check points (CP). North Korean infiltrators can take advantage of such blind spots to cross over into the South undetected. Over the summer of 1976, a large poplar tree grew up to obscure the view from UN CP No. 3 to UN OP No. 5. Since it was on the UN side of the demarcation line, the UN command sent local Korean workmen to cut down the tree. A group of North Korean soldiers arrived to chase off the workers.

The UN Command wanted to be firm about protecting its rights to operate but didn't want to cause an incident. So they sent the workmen back with two American officers and a small group of enlisted men. The Americans were armed with pistols which are permitted under the armistice agreement in the Joint Security Area (manned by the U.S., South Korea, and North Korea), but were given firm orders not to draw their weapons unless absolutely necessary.

Tension was high in the summer of 1976, with the North Korea guards throwing many threats and bullying. The North Koreans sent three times as many soldiers as the Americans, jumping the Americans when their backs were turned to supervise the tree trimming. Within minutes, U.S. Army Captain Arthur G. Bonifas and First Lieutenant Mark T. Barrett were murdered and the American enlisted men severely beaten with axe handles, crow bars, and iron pipes that the North Koreans had hidden in their clothing.[8] This was clearly a carefully planned and approved operation. The *Far Eastern Economic Review* reported that Kim Jung Il instigated the murders.[9]

The rest of the world couldn't turn their eyes from the situation in Korea, either. Back in the U.S., the election year had made Korea a sensitive issue. Governor James Carter of Georgia, the Democratic candidate for president, had pledged to withdraw American forces from Korea if he were elected.[10]

UN commander-in-chief General Richard Stilwell and his chief of staff, Major General John Singlaub, devised a plan to assert the authority of the UN without unduly escalating the situation. As a warning to the North Koreans, UN forces were moved from Def Con 4 to Def Con 3, a higher state of readiness.[11] Next a joint team of eight hundred American and South Korean soldiers moved in quickly to take down the overgrown tree before the North Koreans could react. This swift and well-executed reaction ended the incident with an apology from Pyongyang.[12]

THE USS *PUEBLO*

The USS *Pueblo* was a small American Navy intelligence ship sent in January 1968 to international waters off North Korea to listen in on North Korean communications. It soon came under attack by four North Korean warships. The *Pueblo* was armed with a machine gun on the bow, but the gun was under an ice-covered tarp that would have taken at least thirty minutes to remove. To get to the gun, the crew would have had to make a suicidal walk across open deck in full sight of the North Korean gunners. The North Koreans proceeded to seize the *Pueblo* in international waters. One U.S. sailor was gunned down and the rest of the crew were taken hostage for almost a year during which time they were savagely beaten.

Commander Lloyd Bucher, the captain of the *Pueblo*, writes that during the months of his captivity in North Korea he was expecting "some form of retaliation in the form of a punitive raid."[13] But the U.S. never took such retaliatory action. Bucher wrote, "At the time it was inconceivable to me that our country would take no forceful direct action to avenge the seizure on the high seas of one its ships by a third-rate communist power acting in defiance of international law."[14]

The *Pueblo* was on its maiden voyage when it was attacked, yet a sister ship had previously operated in the same area without incident.[15] Why the *Pueblo* was hit has never been satisfactorily explained. It is possible Kim was trying to regain some lost prestige after his commandoes had failed to assassinate South Korean President Park just a few days earlier. The commandoes got within a short distance of the "Blue House," home of the South Korean president, but failed to penetrate the grounds. Kim may have been looking for something spectacular and audacious to compensate for this failure.

There is another explanation. The *Pueblo* was attacked on January 23. North Vietnamese and Vietcong attack known as "Tet Offensive" occurred on January 30. If the communist leaders had been exchanging information, the Blue House, *Pueblo*, and Tet attacks could have been a coordinated attempt to destabilize U.S. President Lyndon Johnson's administration and affect the 1968 election. President Johnson's press secretary was bombarded by questions asking if the two events were related.[16] American and foreign press had been running daily front-page stories on the *Pueblo*. Combined with news of the Tet Offensive, the two stories helped to enhance the impression of military and political incompetence in the Johnson White House. Although Johnson won the New Hampshire primary, he withdrew from running for reelection. At the time, many members of the American intelligence community believed that the attacks were linked; but until the files are opened in Pyongyang and Hanoi, we will not be able to confirm that the three attacks were coordinated.

HAPPY BIRTHDAY TO THE GREAT LEADER

To celebrate the fifty-seventh birthday of Kim Il Sung, the Great Leader of North Korea, in April 1969 the North Koreans murdered thirty-one American servicemen.

Thirty-four year old Navy Lieutenant Commander James Overstreet had left his air base in Japan with twenty-nine American Navy officers and men plus one American Marine. The trip should have been routine. For many years the United States has been flying reconnaissance aircrafts similar to Overstreet's EC-121M over the Sea of Japan without problems. The airplane, a converted Lockheed Super Constellation, was never within fifty miles of the North Korean coast. Before U.S. Air Force and Navy radar operators could warn Overstreet, two North Korean MIG-21 fighters slipped in and shot down his plane. Only two bodies were recovered.

North Korea had scored a propaganda coup. The Great Leader's birthday was already being celebrated with "unprecedented fervour,"[17] and the thirty-one murders only added to the festive atmosphere. Americans had made over 190 similar flights in the previous six months, so the North Korean Air Force had been able to plan exactly when and where to strike.[18] The MIGs had laid in wait for the Great Leader's birthday present to come lumbering by. The EC-121 was old, slow, unarmed, and never had a chance. Radio Pyongyang had a field day and communist hearts were uplifted all over Asia.

The Nixon administration did nothing beyond a bit of brief posturing. As *Time* magazine wrote at the time, "For three days after the U.S. aircraft was officially declared missing, the president went ahead with business as usual at the White House. The matter did not even come up at a Cabinet meeting the morning of the announcement."[19]

Lieutenant Commander Overstreet and his crew were victimized three times: by the failure of American military authorities to provide fighter escort (inexcusable so soon after the Pueblo); by the North Korean Air Force; and by the Nixon administration for its callous failure to recognize their sacrifice.

U.S. AND SOUTH KOREAN DEFENSES

Through a Mutual Defense Treaty signed in 1953, the United States is the ultimate guarantor of the defense of South Korea. In the late fall of 2003, U.S. Secretary of Defense Donald Rumsfeld declared that the United States would use its nuclear forces to defend South Korea from attack if necessary.[20]

At the top of the U.S.–South Korea defense pyramid is the Combined Forces Command at Yongsan. Unique among American defense arrangements with foreign countries, the commander of

Combined Forces in Korea is always an American Army four-star general.[21] (His deputy is always a South Korean general.[22]) Heads of major sections within the Combined Forces alternate between Americans commanders with South Korean deputies and South Korean commanders with American deputies.

The United States and South Korea have another unique institution, the annual security consultation meeting. Alternating between Washington and Seoul, this two to three day meeting is led by the U.S. secretary of defense, the South Korean defense minister, and the respective Joint Chiefs of Staff—officials from the State Department, the Defense Intelligence Agency, and the Commander-in-Chief Pacific are also present. In addition, there are separate military-to-military meetings. The last security consultation meeting was held in Seoul in November 2003.

Until 1993, the United States and South Korea regularly held large military exercises, called "Team Spirit," designed to test our ability to respond to a North Korean attack. A large force would deploy from American bases in the United States and overseas to be integrated with units already in Korea. Tens of thousands of U.S. and South Korean troops engaged in these field exercises. In an effort to placate the North Korea, whose propaganda had been loudly protesting these exercises for years, President Clinton canceled all further exercises after 1993.

To compensate for the cancellation of Team Spirit, the U.S. and South Korea now hold a command post exercise each year during which political and military leaders practice mobilizing people and resources. This is a computer and tabletop exercise. There is another exercise called "RSOI"—Reception, Staging, Outward Movement, and Integration—a drill designed to practice dealing with an expected wartime influx of U.S. troops and equipment.

Having worked together for over fifty years, American and South Korean commanders have come to respect each other. Some keep in contact even after they retire. The social contacts that these commanders develop while on active duty eventually mature into a deeper understanding of each other's thinking. These social and personal relations between American and South Korean commanders translate to the ability to reach close coordination in case of an emergency.

MATCHING FORCES

The basic outline of South Korea's Table of Organization and Equipment include:

- Army—560,000 soldiers organized into twenty-two divisions and other units as well as twenty-three divisions in reserve
- Navy—63,000 strong including two Marine divisions of 28,000
- Air Force—63,000 strong in approximately eleven Wings and other units

The South Korean Army has over 2,000 modern tanks, including 80 Russian T-80Us, and massive amounts of artillery up to 203mm. The Army also has over 100 attack helicopters. The Navy has twenty submarines, six destroyers, and nine frigates. (The Navy's strength lies in its small craft, particularly important to South Korea's long coastline and many islands.) The Air Force flies American F-16C Falcons. In 2005, it will begin to use the most modern and capable version of the American F-15E Strike Eagle.

On the whole, the South Korean military—missiles, airlift, engineering, communications, and intelligence—is a modern and well-prepared one. It continues to improve. In the summer of 2003, the South Korean government announced a dramatic increase in a broad range of defense items and projects including missile defense and information warfare.[23]

The U.S. has 37,000 troops in Korea. Most of them are Army forces assigned to the Eighth Army. Of the Eighth Army, the bulk of the troops are in the Second Division (Mechanized) with almost 120 main battle tanks and over 200 other armored vehicles. The U.S. Air Force approximates eighty-five combat aircraft based in South Korea, including F-16 Falcon fighters and attack aircraft as well as the A-10 Thunderbolt, the world's most effective tank-killing attack aircraft.

Since the 1953 Armistice, the U.S. Second Infantry Division has occupied a two-kilometer stretch of the DMZ just north of Seoul. In early 2003 the U.S. Department of Defense signaled its intention to take the Second Infantry Division off the DMZ, depart the Yongsan base in Seoul, and possibly move to the southwest coastal area near the current Kunsan Airbase.

The Second Infantry Division's main mission has been to repel a North Korean–Chinese invasion for as long as possible. Its more understated purpose is to assure that any North Korean–Chinese attack on the South will automatically be an attack on U.S. forces. By serving as a trip-wire that will trigger the full and swift military retaliation of the United States, the Second Infantry Division's presence in South Korea acts as a deterrent against a North Korean–Chinese attack.

ALLIED WAR PLAN 5027

The principal Allied planning document is War Plan 5027, designed to counterattack in case of an all-out attack by North Korea, supported by communist China. A senior defense source in Seoul revealed that the war plan assumes communist China would intervene as a military ally and participant on the side of North Korea in case of a major war on the Korean Peninsula.[24]

5027 calls for South Korean and American forces now in South Korea to hold the line until help arrives.[25] The anticipated help would be:

- 50,000 to 100,000 additional U.S. troops
- Two U.S. Army Corps

- Two U.S. Marine Divisions
- Five U.S. Navy Carrier Battle Groups
- 30 U.S. Air Force Fighter Wings

Many of these additional forces would come from U.S. forces now stationed in Japan—Marines from Okinawa, a Navy carrier battle group from Yokota, USAF F-15 Eagles from Kadena Air Force Base also on Okinawa, and F-16 Falcons from their base at Misawa. The United States could also pull additional forces from Hawaii. The most potent U.S. Air Force units would be from the Eleventh Air Force, headquartered in Elmendorf Air Base in Alaska.[26] Most of these forces are hours away at best and would have to operate from bases in South Korea, Japan, and Guam under uncertain conditions.

It is not public information as to whether Japanese military forces would be directly involved. Japan must have some contingency plans for such a scenario. A secret 1994 Japanese Cabinet Security Office document leaked to the press covers the possibility of North Korean attacks on Japan itself, but did not include the deployment of Japanese forces on, over, or near the Korean Peninsula.[27]

Japanese participation is restricted by a host of legal and political issues at home.[28] If the Japanese Self-Defense Forces could become directly involved in a Korean emergency, they could add some serious muscle to the equation. Japan has about 240,000 well-equipped and well-trained servicemen and women—148,000 ground forces, 44,000 maritime, and 45,000 in the air force. It would most likely be the Japanese Air Self-Defense Force's F-15 and F-2 fighter aircraft that would get the first call for any crisis in Korea. Quickly following them would be the Japanese Naval Self-Defense Force's very competent minesweeping ships. U.S. and South Korean forces could also make use of Japanese medical resources. Japan could be the center for any massive civilian evacuation efforts, including thousands of Americans and Japanese working in South Korea and their dependents.

KIM'S ARMY

For many years the Kim family has been preparing to launch another attack on South Korea. Despite harsh suffering by the North Korean people, the regime has continued to squeeze the population to build up its assault forces. Kim's army is poised to strike without notice and with overwhelming force. In terms of numbers of troops, the North Korean armed forces are massive:

- Totaling over 1 million armed men on active duty and almost 5 million reserves—making it the fourth largest armed force in the world[29]
- Most are army troops armed with older Soviet-era tanks but they have huge amounts of artillery, including multiple-rocket launchers
- Kim's navy has twenty-six older submarines, most of which were acquired from communist China
- Kim's air force[30] has thirty to forty modern MIG-29s, but pilot flying hours are so low as to render it poor match in any conflict with the South Korean or American Air Forces (except during an initial surprise attack)[31]
- Kim's army is supplied by an extensive and expensive network of underground arms factories and depots[32]

In 1999 the North Koreans began moving the vast majority of their forces to areas very near the DMZ. Of particular concern is the fact that the North Koreans have continued to build fortified underground sites along the DMZ for missile and artillery positions.[33] A European diplomat, formerly stationed in North Korea, says he observed a number of "Kamikaze MIG" positions hidden near the north side of the DMZ.[34] These are suicide squadrons of older MIG fighters—they are based inside mountain bunkers with short concrete take-off strips leading out of the cave but no landing area. Pilots of these aircraft would be on a one-way flight south.

No one outside of North Korea or communist China really knows how many ballistic missiles the North Koreans have produced, how many have been sold abroad, or how many have been retained. Estimates by U.S. military leaders run as high as one thousand, a large increase in the last decade.[35] Many of these missiles are in hardened underground bunkers and silos connected to the North Korean command and control centers by buried fiber-optic cable. Even with a high explosive warhead, a ballistic missile falling on a civilian city can cause much death and destruction. With a chemical, biological, or nuclear warhead the cost in lives is even more frightening.

Modern warfare is dependent on electronics. Incredibly, the North Korean military was given an electronics industry, funded in part by the American taxpayer. For many years the North Koreans struggled to establish this industry without particular success. In a move of extreme bad judgment, in the spring of 1987 the United Nations Development Program funded an Integrated Circuit Test Facility in North Korea—"integrated circuits," or "chips," are the building blocks for any electronic product.[36] Under the "Military First" program established by the Dear Leader,[37] chips manufactured in North Korea go into nuclear weapons, ballistic missiles, cyber-terrorism, military communications, and other instruments of aggression. Almost none of the chips will end up in products that enhance the lives of the average North Korean.

American (and Japanese) taxpayer funds should never have gone into such a war supply facility. It is appalling and absurd that while western economic aid helps to prop up Kim's regime, he continues to commit aggression against North Korea's neighbors. Just four years before the UN gave Kim the chip factory, North Koreans had massacred almost the entire South Korean cabinet in Burma. Within six months of the UN gift, Kim's agents blew up a South Korean airliner, killing all passengers on board. Kim's regime has continued to gobble up international aid. Instead of promoting peace, such a UN gift gives an already aggressive rogue state the means to carry out its schemes of war.

The North Korean unconventional forces give Allied war planners the most pause. The Kim family regime has spent a lot of money and effort to build perhaps as many as one hundred thousand special operations forces. These commando units can be expected to target South Korea's civilian and military leadership as well as high-ranking U.S. military personnel for assassination. North Korean commando units are expected to undertake missions against U.S. and Allied targets in other countries. U.S. forces in Japan are especially lucrative targets, as are Japanese civil and military leaders. North Korean commando forces may also target U.S. forces based in Hawaii and Alaska.

To support these commando forces, North Korea has purchased or constructed a number of small submarines or semi-submergibles useful for navigating South Korea's long coastline and numerous small harbors and bays. One such submarine, supporting an infiltration exercise, ran aground off the South Korean coast in 1996. In the event of a conflict, Allied planners anticipate that many of these special-ops troops would infiltrate into South Korea to join other agents already inside. Some would come in by sea; others through yet undiscovered tunnels under the DMZ and still others might come by air using radar-evading wooden aircraft and gliders. Once inside, they would work to attack civilian infrastructure and sabotage South Korean military operations.

THE "INUNDATION WEAPON"

In 1950 most of Seoul was located on the north side of the Han River. In the past ten years, Seoul has grown so much that the city is almost the same size on either side of the river. Several million of South Korea's almost fifty million people live in this river valley. Upstream North Korea has recently constructed the Mount Kumgang Dam.

Construction of the dam began in 1986 but efforts were quickly abandoned. In 1995, amidst the North Korean famine, the new leader of North Korea ordered the completion of the dam on a rush. One of the largest known North Korean construction projects,[38] the Mount Kumgang Dam was built with forced labor in record time—a process that was called "storming" in Stalin's Soviet Union. Projects built in this manner were often poorly constructed and even dangerous. One North Korean defector claims that only half as much concrete as required was used in building the Mount Kumgang Dam.[39]

It may not be a matter of mere negligence; Kim's rush project may be less a civilian construction project than a weapon. Numerous defector reports claim that the Mount Kumgang Dam project is openly discussed in North Korea as an "inundation weapon." Kim Jung Il cannot be interested in this project or be willing to expend the resources to build it if the dam does not have some significant military potential. One North Korean hydraulic power professor predicted that if the water were released when the dam was at full capacity, it would send a wall of water down the Han River valley twelve feet or higher.[40] Such an event could cause as many as one million casualties in the area in and around Seoul.

BEIJING'S SECRET WAR PLAN

As we have seen, Beijing (and Moscow before it) has gone to great efforts to disguise and camouflage its military arrangements with North Korea. But let's consider the record:

- Communist China helped Pyongyang to start the Korean War
- Communist China bailed the North Koreans out after their losses at Incheon
- Beijing and Pyongyang have a formal defense alliance
- There are numerous pictures of Kim Jung Il meeting with Chinese military officers in China

- Beijing and Pyongyang have extensive Weapons of Mass Destruction connections
- Communist China keeps the North Korean regime on economic life-support

Just as the United States stands behind Seoul, Beijing stands behind Pyongyang. Beijing has only one formal, publicly known mutual defense alliance—its 1961 defense treaty with North Korea.[41] In recent years, China has been promoting the myth that this treaty is "ancient history" and "formality without substance."

But events have revealed that the true nature of Pyongyang–Beijing alliance is far from obsolete. For example, in late 1987 there was a thunderous explosion in North Korea. A munitions train from China blew up, killing 120 people and injuring over 5,000.[42] A more recent slip up by the Chinese Foreign Ministry in 1997 also confirms an alliance: The ministry published a book on China's treaty relations with foreign countries and failed to remove a reference table in the back that listed a 1996 agreement to provide "military assistance" to North Korea.[43] No details of this "military assistance" appear in the text of book, only a single reference in the back.

TRACKING THE "BEAR"

General Xiong Guangkai is deputy chief of staff for intelligence in the People's Liberation Army. Xiong, whose name means "Bear" in Chinese, is thought by some to be the PLA's chief conduit to the North Korean military. His movements shed some light on the extent to which Beijing is a backer of North Korea.

Xiong has been at many joint North Korea–China military functions and is famous for saying in 1999, "The PRC [China] and DPRK [North Korea] are . . . in the relations of lips and teeth, and the peoples and armies of the two countries have a blood-tied traditional relationship."[44] Xiong has also a habit of bragging to

American diplomats in private that he makes more trips to Pyongyang than are publicly revealed.[45] One of his public trips to North Korea occurred in early August 1998. At the end of that month, the North Koreans tested their long-range multistage missile for the first time, firing it across the Japanese islands and landing in the Pacific waters near Hawaii. This suspicious coincidence suggests that Xiong may have given the North Koreans the green light for the launch.

The general is also a frequent visitor to Japan where he tries to soften Japanese attitudes towards Chinese military modernization and North Korea. For example, in late 1997 he seemed to have convinced senior Liberal Democratic Party leaders that North Korea was on the "road to peace and stability."[46] But in fact, North Korea was then in the midst of a famine but still engaged in a massive conventional arms buildup, preparing new attacks and provocations on South Korea, and secretly trying to build nuclear weapons and long-range ballistic missiles. Xiong, as communist China's chief military spy, would have been well aware of these activities while he lied to Japanese politicians and academics.

In the U.S., Xiong is infamous for his late 1995 offhand comment to a Clinton defense official that the United States cares more about Los Angeles than it does about Taipei. Americans should take this to be a threat of nuclear war.[47]

FOLLOW THE MONEY

A key to determining Beijing's true intentions in Korea is to follow the money. For the last decade, the Pentagon has been looking, correctly, at the overall communist Chinese military buildup as "Taiwan-driven." That is, most of China's defense money has gone into applications that would have value if Beijing should invade Taiwan. However, an examination of Chinese forces in Manchuria reveals that Beijing is also preparing for the possibility of another Korean War. Although the U.S. and South Korea have always

assumed that communist China might intervene in any confrontation with Kim, the news that Beijing has poured a lot of
money into its military units in Manchuria has been a surprise.[48]

Any Chinese war planner considering a sustained military
engagement in Korea would expect heavy ground forces—armor,
mechanized infantry and artillery—to be employed. The People's
Liberation Army divisions are "regular" (mostly walking),
"motorized" (in trucks), or "mechanized" (tracked vehicles). It
costs money to upgrade a regular unit to a motorized unit, and
substantially more money to mechanize. A "heavy" Group Army
is one that has an armored division instead of an armored brigade,
effectively doubling its armor. Likewise, a "heavy" GA would double its firepower if it had an artillery division instead of a brigade.
To make a unit both mechanized and "heavy" (doubling its
armor) would require double budget demands and a high priority in Beijing.[49]

China's People's Liberation Army (PLA) has only two such
mechanized and "heavy" Group Armies—the 38th and 39th—
both stationed near North Korea.[50] Together, they cover
Manchuria and the border with North Korea.[51] Both the 39th and
the 38th are "almost heavy" in that they have attached armored
divisions but only artillery brigades. They are also attached with
helicopter regiments, a feature unique to these two armies in the
PLA. These two Group Armies were the same armies have a long
tradition of fighting alongside North Korean troops. During the
Korean War, they were the first across the Yalu River in October
1950. All of this suggests that the 39th and 38th Group Armies
have first call in the event of a confrontation on the Korean
Peninsula.

The decision to upgrade these mechanized Group Armies and
invest in defenses for a renewed Korean War seems to be related to
a rise in tensions between the U.S. and North Korea over nuclear
matters. Pyongyang and the Clinton administration conflicted over
the Kim's nuclear weapons program in 1994. The Chinese 39th

Group Army became fully mechanized in 1997, but the decision to do so was probably made in late 1994 or early 1995.

In recent years, the PLA's modernization has expanded from an intense focus on air and naval forces to include a greater focus on the army. The PLA is expected to produce 1,500 new T-96 tanks armed with 125mm guns, which may be able to fire very long-range laser-guided missiles. Save for a few Russian T-80 tanks in the South Korean Army, South Korean and American tanks do not fire these deadly missiles. The only conceivable purpose for these large and expensive war machines would be to prepare for a second Korean War. Many of these new T-96 tanks are now equipping Korea-designated armor units in the Shenyang, Beijing, and Jinan military regions.

Allied intelligence has identified six major PLA missile ballistic bases, one of which, "Base 51," is headquartered at Shenyang. At least three subordinate mobile missile launch brigades are scattered around Manchuria as well. These brigades, armed with the DF-3 and DF-21 intermediate range missiles, are believed to be targeted on Japanese Self-Defense Forces and American bases in Japan. They are to intimidate Japan from directly participating in the event of a new Korean conflict and to pressure the Japanese government to deny the U.S. the use of its bases.

China's Navy has three fleets. One of them, the Northern Fleet, has major bases along the Yellow Sea adjacent to North Korea. This force has the PLA's only nuclear powered ballistic missile submarine and all six of its nuclear attack submarines. The PLA Air Force's First Air Army is also headquartered in the Shenyang military region near the North Korean border and has airfields scattered through out the area.

Chinese Communist Party politicians have already made the financial commitment necessary to support Kim's regime. If Beijing chooses to fight alongside Kim in another ground war in Korea, the PLA will produce a much more effective force than the swarms of foot soldiers who crossed the Yalu River fifty years ago.

BOLDLY BACKING THE DEAR LEADER

Occasionally the communist Chinese military will directly signal to the Americans that it is standing behind North Korea. In the spring of 1994, during the first U.S.–North Korean crisis over Pyongyang's nuclear weapons programs, some American political leaders, including Republican Senator John McCain of Arizona, raised the "military option"—i.e. possibly bombing North Korea. In response, Beijing immediately swung into a shielding mode for its client state: First, in early June, China let the world know of its extensive military-to-military consultations between the PLA and a then visiting delegation headed by the North Korean Army chief of the general staff. Next, Beijing leaked to a newspaper the idea that it has pledged 85,000 troops to defend North Korea. Finally, in August the PLA held the biggest military exercises the Shenyang military region had seen in decades. These were conveniently staged on the Liaodong peninsula immediately adjacent to North Korea.

In the fall of 2002, China again threw its protective cloak over North Korea, this time after Kim revealed his second secret nuclear weapons program. The PLA's newspapers rushed out a series of feature articles on military exercises in the Shenyang military region. One article (with full color photos) featured the PLA's capability in river crossings, a point not lost on those who live in South Korea's Han River valley.[52] Allied defense specialists exchanged copies of these stories by e-mail with wry comments. The defense community in Washington and the senior members of the Bush administration took note that, once again, Beijing was backing North Korea, no matter what dangerous activity Pyongyang was engaged in.

In 2003, as the North Korean WMD issue heated up further, Beijing held more public military exercises, military-to-military visits, and consultations. In January, PLA publications featured "Red" force versus "Blue" force exercises in Manchuria. The "Red" forces were shown to have successfully defeated the "Blue" forces' "stealth aircraft," "cruise missiles," "helicopter gunships," and "precision strikes"—well-known parts of the American military arsenal and operation.[53]

Just before major talks were to take place between the U.S. and North Korea on nuclear matters, North Korean vice marshal Cho Myong Rok took a delegation to visit Beijing. He met with top Chinese leaders, including Chairman Jiang Zemin. Just before the August six-party talks in Beijing to discuss North Korea's nuclear weapons program, a large Chinese military delegation visited North Korea.[54] Communist China and North Korea were making it clear to the United States, Japan, and South Korea that Pyongyang and Beijing stood in communist solidarity as well as a united military front.

The American military has a saying, "How you train is how you fight." South Korean defense analysts in Seoul report there is no public evidence that the Chinese and North Korean armies are conducting joint field exercises similar to the now-cancelled U.S.–South Korean "Team Spirit."[55] North Korean fighters and PLA Air Force fighters do not join up over the Yellow Sea to practice together as Americans and South Korean air forces do on a regular basis. But it is possible to conduct fairly realistic computer exercises in secret. If the politicians in Beijing believe it is more important to keep the true extent of its military relationship with Pyongyang secret, it would do just that.

OLD TIES THAT BIND

Among American officers on duty in Korea, there are none who have any Korean War experience. But until the spring of 2003, Chinese Peoples' Volunteers veterans (those who fought alongside North Koreans in the Korean war) dominated the upper ranks of the Chinese Army. Politburo member and Chinese Defense Minister Chi Haotian, who retired in 2003, is reputed to have led a whole battalion into the fighting during the Korean War, returning with only twenty men. Another senior PLA leader who also retired in 2003, Central Military Commission vice chairman Zhang Wannian, was reportedly wounded while fighting the Americans in Korea. These two old generals had a great deal of influence on the promotion of the current generation of Chinese military leaders—the new PLA chief of staff was previously the commander of the Shenyang military region and oversaw the major arms buildup there in the late 1990s.[56]

THE NEXT KOREAN WAR

In the summer of 2003, former CIA director James Woolsey and retired USAF Lieutenant General Thomas McInerney wrote a much read and much discussed article for the *Wall Street Journal*.[57] They proposed that the United States and its allies eliminate the North Korean nuclear threat through "the use of force," mostly through airpower but also ground forces. That is, they suggested that next Korean War should be started by the United States and its allies.

While Woolsey and McInerney are outstanding officials and patriots, they are wrong on this issue.[58] Short of an imminent and confirmed threat to the United States or its allies, America should not initiate hostilities in Korea. One strong reason is that North Korea has enough forces in place, particularly missiles and long-range artillery with chemical warheads, to devastate Seoul and cause enormous damage to large parts South Korea. In addition, the likelihood is very high that China would stand behind North Korea. Beijing has done so in the past and has already made preparations to do it again with clear signals to Washington.

A confrontation with North Korea backed by China would mean putting a large portion of the American forces now serving in Korea as well as their dependent wives and children in the direct line of fire. South Korean forces and civilians would also die in the millions. War could also spread to American forces in Japan to risk

Japanese military personnel and civilians. It might take South Korea fifty to a hundred years to recover. Japan would be repairing the damage for decades. North Korea would cease to exist.

Allied soldiers, airmen, sailors, and Marines train every day, but this may not be enough of a deterrent. Not only must Pyongyang be convinced it cannot succeed in a surprise offensive, Beijing must be convinced as well. The temptation to use North Korea as a "borrowed knife" to distract the United States while it moves against Taiwan or some other target might become too enticing. Making certain that Beijing does not bless a North Korean attack should be a priority on Washington's agenda.

5

TERRORISM AND CRIMES

This day a year ago was the longest of my life, the most painful and sad. My mind went blank with grief and despair. I felt as though I had lost everything in the world. All things became a burden, and I lost my courage and will. A year has passed since then. And during that year I have cried alone in secret too many times to count.[1]

— South Korean president Park Chung Hee, writing in his diary, a year after the assassination of his wife by a North Korean agent

To Westerners, the symbol at the center of the South Korean flag looks like two interlocking commas. This symbol actually represents the ancient Taoist principles of the yin and yang, the origin of all things in the universe:

The yin is female, "motionless grandeur" contrasting with the male and "fiery vigor" of the yang. The moon is yin; the sun is yang. Other contrasts in the yin versus yang duality include night

and day, earth and sky, winter and summer. Together they create harmony and balance. If either is missing, there is only chaos.

The president of the Republic of Korea in 1974, Park Chung Hee, was definitely yang. Park was a tough, intensely patriotic, no nonsense ex-South Korean Army general who inspired loyalty and respect in some, and undying opposition in others. He is generally credited with having been the father of the economic miracle in postwar South Korea. He made peace with the Japanese, a move that was not popular with many of his constituents considering the lingering memories from the 1905–1945 Japanese occupation.

The South Korean first lady, Yook Young-soo, was clearly the yin.[2] The *New York Times*' Richard Halloran, no admirer of her husband, noted, "She was widely considered to have been a gracious and cultured woman whose image was warm and gentle."[3] She was even admired and popular among those who did not support her husband.

On August 15, 1974, she was murdered by a twenty-two-year-old good-for-nothing the North Koreans scraped up off the floor in Japan. The assassin, Mun Se Kwang, was an ethnic Korean whose family had been in Japan for at least a generation. After dropping out of high school, he drifted from job to job—janitor, window washer, and general laborer—on the fringes of society. He was ideal cannon fodder for a suicide mission. He first came to the attention of two Japanese communists, a husband and wife team, who steered him to the North Korean–based association of Korean residents in Japan. They nurtured him for two years, filled his pockets with cash, gave him orders on board a North Korean ship, and then sent him on his way with a forged Japanese passport and a stolen Japanese police revolver.[4]

The first lady's killer arrived a few days early, checked into a five-star hotel in Seoul, and proceeded to enjoy a level of luxury he had never experienced. When the time came to act, he hired a limousine and set off. Passing himself off as a Japanese VIP, he wormed his way into the back of the National Theater where

President Park was giving an Independence Day speech. About half way through the speech, the gunman leaped out of his chair, rushed down the aisle, and began firing wildly. One of his bullets bounced harmlessly off a clear bulletproof shield in front of the president's podium but another bullet stuck the first lady sitting behind him. Surgeons at the Seoul University Hospital desperately tried to save her, but she did not survive the evening. Pictures, sent around the world, showed her in her bloodstained Korean national dress, the chogori jacket and the chima skirt.[5]

Over a million people, many weeping openly, lined the streets from Seoul to the national cemetery where she was buried after a combined Christian and Buddhist funeral. Cardinal Kim said of her, "You gave us hope when we were in despair. You gave us light when we were in darkness."[6] Koreans today speak of their lost first lady with the deepest sadness and reverence, commonly using the term "national mother" to describe her.[7]

Although North Korea did not reach their intended target, President Park, the assassination of the South Korean first lady has to be considered a significant success for Pyongyang. First, she was only forty-eight when she died and if she had lived there is no doubt she would have been able to accomplish much more. Second, she was the restraining influence on her husband's authoritarian tendencies. After she died, he went into a downward spiral of anguish, ultimately leading to his death at the hands of his most trusted subordinates. Without the yin, the yang was nothing.

It is not known if the murder of the South Korean first lady was ordered by North Korea's "Great Leader," Kim Il Sung, or the "Dear Leader," Kim Jung Il, who was just then taking over more and more of the state's terrorist activities. Probably both of them had a hand in it. This event best illustrates the vile and corrupt nature of the Kim regime, demonstrating that it is beyond redemption.

In the fall of 1975, the North Korean leadership held an intense ten-day meeting to review the previous two and a half decades of failed efforts to conquer the South. The final judgment was harsh.

A number of high-level officials were purged and sent to a reform through labor camp. Kim Jung Il, at the age of thirty-three, took "complete control of North Korea's covert operations organizations into his own hands."[8] Kim told the North Korean leadership, "[B]asically, the only way is the violent method and peaceful means is nothing but an illusion. Fundamentally, there has to be violence."[9]

To fulfill his ambitions of conquest, Kim sent out waves of North Korean agents, many of them on suicide missions, to commit acts of terror and commit heinous crimes against innocent people around the world. He has set up the most extensive and sophisticated training facilities for his terrorists, criminals, and spies in the world.

TERRORISM AND CRIME UNIVERSITY

North Korea's prime terrorist and spy school is the Kim Jung Il University of Political and Military Education, although there are other spy training centers including the KPA language academy.[10] Reportedly, competition for entrance into Kim's university is quite high. The one-year and three-year courses are mostly for spies, called "operatives," although some spies are later used for terrorist operations.[11]

The four-year course is called the "combat section" and is almost exclusively for training terrorists. As might be expected, this course has heavy emphasis on physical and military training, including the use of explosives.[12] The students learn marine navigation, how to maintain marine engines, and the use of wireless radios. Graduates of this section man the spy ships as well as become the assassins and saboteurs sent overseas. As we will see, they are also the kidnappers.

Graduates of Kim U. describe the training as rigorous with a heavy emphasis on physical training and endurance. At the same time, it's a privileged existence with a substantially higher food ration than even submariners and pilots receive in North Korea. The facilities are excellent, including a large swimming pool and other luxuries outside the reach and even the imagination of average North Koreans.

There is, however, a price to be paid for entering Kim U. Once students enter the school, they are stripped of all personal effects and identification, such as family pictures, in order to impress upon them that they have cut off all ties with the past. Each student has to undergo intense ideological training with suicide as a central theme. Among the slogans students have to memorize is the following: "Let us become complete revolutionaries determined to blow ourselves up and commit suicide for the sake of our great leader and our fatherland!"[13]

SPY CITY

During the time of the Soviet Union, the "organs of state security" (mostly the KGB) maintained a large mockup of an average American town. It had a school, a range of stores, and so on. Agents preparing for an overseas assignment would train there in order to learn how to operate in a capitalist environment without giving themselves away.

According to defector reports, North Korea has far exceeded Moscow's efforts, building its own underground spy city. By one account, the North Korean espionage and terrorist training facility is about six miles long and 130 feet wide.[14] It is divided into sections, one of which recreates Seoul, another Tokyo, and others perhaps the United States, Europe, and the Middle East.[15] The facility has everything from slums to jewelry stores, even a pharmacy.[16] According to one defector report, the various sections are staffed with kidnapped victims from around the world, including Americans, British, Australians, Taiwanese, Turks, Lebanese, as well as Japanese and South Koreans.[17] Known as the "Environment Hall," it is so realistic that once when a defector was stuck in traffic in

Seoul, he was able to guide his police escort through a side street that allowed them to avoid the congestion. The students become very familiar with the areas around the homes of prominent politicians and other potential targets of assassination in foreign countries. Terrorists and spies in training spend about six months immersed in this facility, learning how to get on and off a subway or bus, cash a check at a bank, send a letter at the post office, buy food at a supermarket, handle themselves at a five-star hotel, and even how to sing the latest popular songs of the target country.[18]

TRAINING "ARAB" TERRORISTS

North Korean officials go to great lengths to compartmentalize the students and training areas so that a spy or terrorist preparing for an operation in one area, say South Korea, will not be able to identify students targeting Japan or other areas.[19] Only by accident—a door opening as they pass by, for example—can the students catch a glimpse of other students and other training areas. This way, if they are caught while on a mission and do not successfully commit suicide, they can only tell their interrogators what they know about their own training or assignment. Even in their own target area, North Korean terrorists and spies rarely know the full picture.

But sometimes the most severe discipline breaks down and people learn things they should not. According to one eyewitness report by a defector, not all the students being trained in terrorism are North Korean. "I saw a group of Arabs who received training for terrorism, kidnapping, and explosives while I was a student at Kim Jung Il Political and Military University," he said.[20] Further, he reported that one of the secret offices directly reporting to Kim "is involved in every Arab criminal syndicate."[21] The "Arab" students receiving a free education were apparently from "Syria, Libya, Iran, Iraq, and Palestine." The defector's adds, "It can be said that North Korea is the boss of the terrorist world."[22]

THE RANGOON ASSASSINATIONS

The father of Burmese democracy, Aung San, and six of his cabinet officers were assassinated in 1947 by a rival politician. It is his daughter, 1991 Nobel Peace Prize winner Aung San Suu Kyi, who carries the torch for democracy in her country today. On a hill overlooking the capital, Rangoon, the people of Burma erected a mausoleum in honor of Aung San and his cabinet officers. The building is open on the sides but has a solid roof. Important foreign visitors are often asked to place a wreath out of respect. In July 1983, a North Korean delegation went through such a ceremony. Later, investigators would determine that it was a "dress rehearsal" for a later attack on a visiting South Korean delegation—giving the North Korean agents a clear picture of the sequence of events, timing, where foreign dignitaries would be gathered, and the crucial fact that few high-ranking Burmese officials would be on hand.[23]

Three assassins from the North Korean People's Army chose a "Claymore" type landmine. This kind of mine contains around 700 steel ball bearings embedded in a convex shape. Mounted in the ceiling, the powerful bomb blew the roof off the building and rained death on the South Korean officials paying their respects below. In the confined space of the mausoleum, bodies were thrown into the air; at least one of the visiting dignitaries' bodies was blown to bits and never recovered.[24]

Even for North Korea's Dear Leader this was an audacious attack. He was after no less than the president of the Republic of Korea, the South Korean ambassador to Burma, the entire South Korean cabinet, and about fifty top South Korean business leaders, including the chairman of the Hyundai Group. Had the plot been successful, the North Korean bomb would have completely decapitated the South Korean political and economic leadership. This would have led to the chaos the North was looking for as an opening to conquer the South.

An errant bugle call partially saved the day. A Burmese military bugler thought the limousine coming up the road with flags flying was the visiting South Korean president. Actually, it was the South Korean ambassador arriving a bit ahead of his president. The North Korean terrorists took the bugle call as their signal and set off the remote-controlled bomb.

Still, the carnage was tremendous. South Korea lost one fifth of its cabinet, among them the brightest and the best—the deputy prime minister, chief presidential secretary of economic affairs, foreign minister, minister for commerce and industry, and energy and resources minister—all slain in a moment. Seventeen South Koreans and three Burmese were murdered and about fifty more were horribly wounded.[25] The businessmen and the ambassador survived because they were standing outside preparing to greet the South Korean president.

Within a few hours, Burmese police were in a firefight with the perpetrators. One was killed and the other two were captured, but not before they had killed three policemen. It was later determined the three terrorists had slipped ashore from a North Korean freighter that had docked in Rangoon two weeks earlier. When Burmese investigators tried to draw them out by telling them (falsely) that the South Korean president had been gravely wounded, one of the terrorists gave a clenched fist salute and shouted "Mission Accomplished!" from his hospital bed.

One of the two surviving terrorists refused to cooperate and he was executed. The other one gave a full confession. He seems to have been motivated by the discovery that his weapons had been booby-trapped by his own superiors. When he pulled the pin on his hand grenade, instead of going off in six or seven seconds as is normal, it detonated instantly injuring him severely. He apparently concluded that Pyongyang wanted to make certain there were no witnesses.[26] Reportedly, he remains in prison in Rangoon.

The Rangoon bombing took place on October 9, 1983. The day before, North Koreans had initiated a new peace move, using

Chinese officials to carry their message to Seoul.[27] This has been a very common North Korean negotiating tactic—to lull the enemy to sleep with peace offerings, just before striking. They did the same thing in the late spring of 1950, before the all-out assault on the South.

The motivation and details of this attack are not so mysterious. The North Koreans were presented with an opportunity—the political and economic elite of the South all in one place and away from their usual security at home—and took it. They had scouted other places that the South Korean president was going to visit on his five-nation stop and concluded Rangoon was their best shot.

However, two facts have never been explained. First, the two surviving assassins were fluent in Chinese. Burmese investigators had to find Chinese-speaking interrogators to talk to them in hospital.[28] Second, who hid them for the two weeks they were in the country preparing to strike? Did the assassins have a safe house in Rangoon's Chinatown—Burma has a large ethnic Chinese community—that they expected to return to after the attack?

Certainly, the Chinese government told Western diplomats that they were "aghast and appalled" at North Korea's actions.[29] Beijing even suggested to the Japanese that it was considering taking action together with the Americans against North Korea.[30] Nothing ever came of it. In those days, Pyongyang and Beijing were so close that the PRC would not even allow South Korean officials to attend UN meetings on economic and social subjects held in China.[31] Did Beijing know about the attack beforehand? Was it acting as an accomplice?

KAL 858 BOMBING

The Korean Air Line pilots had the big Boeing 707 at cruising altitude and on autopilot as it crossed the Andaman Sea, approaching the coast of Burma. It was early afternoon and in a few more minutes they would have begun their pre-landing checks for Bangkok. But on this particular day, terrorists had left behind a small, but effective, bomb in an overhead locker. One hundred and fifteen people lost their lives in an instant. The pilots never even had a chance to issue a distress call. Very little debris was ever found on the ocean below.

There the tragedy would have remained an unsolved mystery but for a slipup. North Korea's counterfeiters have the deserved reputation for high quality work, but an alert immigration agent at the international airport in Bahrain detected the phony Japanese passport carried by one of the two terrorists. When confronted, they both immediately bit down on their cyanide pills. The young woman survived but the older terrorist did not.

South Korea's National Intelligence Service was particularly clever. Rather than subjecting the woman terrorist to the usual intense grilling, they took her on a tour of Seoul and let her see how the people actually lived. Within two weeks, she had signed a confession revealing that she was a trained North Korean assassin.

Her name is Kim Hyon-hui. A child of privilege from Pyongyang, at the time of the attack she was in her mid-twenties. She had been recruited to Kim Jung Il University eight years before and prepared for this assignment by taking intense courses in Japanese language and culture, taught to her by one of the Japanese women kidnapped by North Korean agents.

Kim and the older agent traveled as father and daughter although they were not related. They began in Pyongyang, passed through Moscow and then on to Budapest. They drove across the border to Vienna where North Korean agents gave them the fake Japanese passports. In Belgrade, they picked up the bombs—350 grams of C-4 type plastic explosive disguised as a Panasonic portable radio and a liquid explosive disguised as a liquor bottle. From Baghdad, they joined KAL 858 en route to Seoul with stops in Abu Dhabi and Bangkok. The two North Korean terrorists got off in Abu Dhabi but left the bomb in an overnight bag aboard the South Korean jetliner. It was November 29, 1987.[32]

Kim told the investigators that Kim Jung Il had personally directed the murder of innocent people aboard KAL 858 and his motive was to disrupt the preparations for the 1988 Seoul Olympics. The South Korean government concluded her contrition was genuine and pardoned her. These days, she tries to live a quiet life in South Korea with her husband and son.[33] The memory of the victims lives with their families.

The Reagan administration responded to this outrage by putting North Korea on the list of countries that engage in state-sponsored terrorism. Pyongyang has never admitted its guilt in this case and still insists on being taken off of the list whenever it engages in negotiations with the United States. Communist China responded by demanding that both North and South Korea exercise restraint.

Over the past fifty years, North Korea has been suspected of more acts of terrorism than there is space to report. For example, just prior the holding of the Asian Games in South Korea in 1986, a bomb went off in Seoul's Kimpo airport, killing five and injuring over thirty people. In another instance, investigators looking into the Rangoon bombing discovered that the battery used on that bomb had the same date as the battery used in the bomb that blew up the U.S. Cultural Center in Taegu, South Korea, killing one person and wounding five, just the month before.[34]

NARCOTICS TRAFFICKING

North Korean narcotics trafficking came to international attention in Europe in the 1970s, when there was a sudden rash of cases involving North Korean diplomats. For example, the North Korean ambassador to Switzerland was declared persona non grata and forced to leave the country in 1976. Around the same time, North Korean diplomats were expelled from Sweden for the same reason and for a while some Scandinavian countries ordered North Korea to close its embassies.

The drug smuggling through the diplomatic pouch system seems to have stemmed from Pyongyang's requirement that its overseas missions become more than self-supporting. There was, and remains, a requirement of positive cash flows from embassies and consulates to the home country. North Korean diplomats turned to crime (not just narcotics trafficking) because it was an easy way to make money. With diplomatic immunity, even if they were caught, the most that could happen was to be sent home. These activities began about the same time that Kim Jung Il took personal control of North Korean covert activities.

Most of the early North Korean busts were for trafficking in opiates—opium, heroin, and morphine—although there was at least one hashish bust in Egypt. The general theory in the law enforcement community is that in the 1970s and 1980s some of the drugs came from North Korean fields but most of it came from purchases by North Korean agents from the international drug market, principally the "Golden Triangle" where Burma, Thailand, and Laos come together in Southeast Asia. The North Korean government became purchasers and suppliers like any other criminal syndicate.

In the early 1990s several factors sent North Korean drug trafficking skyrocketing. First, with the demise of the Soviet Union, their economic subsidies came to an end and there was a sudden need for money. Second, the Japanese economy went into recession and there was less illicit money flowing from Korean residents of Japan to Pyongyang. Third, North Korea was ramping up its weapons of mass destruction programs and the advance payments from Iran, Libya, Pakistan, and other customers probably couldn't cover everything. Finally, it seems that Kim Jung Il's appetite for foreign toys—cars, electronics, liquor, and women—was becoming insatiable.

The land and climate of North Korea is not particularly suited to opium poppy growing. But, for over one hundred years, in the northeastern part of the country the local people have produced poppy in limited amounts. The opium was and still is mostly used for medicinal purposes, given the unavailability of regular medicines.

According to a defector from North Korea's KGB,[35] Kim Il Sung ordered farmers in North Hamgyong Province to step up poppy growing in about 1992.[36] North Hamgyong Province is the traditional poppy-growing area along the Tumen River separating North Korea from China and Russia. North Korea's KGB supervised the poppy growing on the ground and the North Korean Academy of Agricultural Sciences provided technical assistance to the farmers.[37] North Korean farmers were forced to convert land normally set aside for food production and to growing poppies. As a result, food production in poppy-growing areas declined. One extensive opium poppy farm on a North Korean hillside can be easily seen from the Chinese side of the Tumen River.[38] There have been a number of reports that political prisoners have been dragooned into this dirty business as well.[39]

Around 1996, North Korea's current leader, Kim Jung Il, ordered an even greater expansion of poppy growing into a number of other provinces of North Korea, even some areas near the DMZ.[40] In order to bring in this bumper crop, middle school boys and girls were mobilized in the late summer and early fall for fieldwork. South Korean authorities are increasingly concerned over reports that agricultural fertilizer they have donated to North Korea for food production may have been diverted to increase the yield of poppy fields.[41] Interpol, the international police network, estimated that by the end of the 1990s, North Korea was producing about 45 tons of opium per year. Seoul's National Intelligence Service gave a higher estimate of 50 tons per year.[42]

There are two press reports, both very speculative and unconfirmed, that North Korea may have arrangements to grow or refine narcotics abroad. One report accuses North Korea of refining narcotics in pharmaceutical plants it has built as joint ventures in Africa.[43] The output of these plants, it is said, is shipped to North and South America. The other report points to Cuba. The

South Korean Agricultural Economic Research Institute claims that the North Korean military is "operating a 15 hectare [37.5 acres] opium farm in the mountainous area of Cuba together with the Cuban authority." The institute also claims that 150 North Korean soldiers are growing opium along a river north of Hanoi, Vietnam.[44]

North Korea sells some of its opium in the raw form for others to refine. There are also two known North Korean refining facilities controlled by the North Korean People's Army used to turn raw opium into heroin and morphine. Both are at chemical plants built by Japan before World War II.[45] The North Koreans apparently recruited specialists from Thailand[46] for the refining operation and the production equipment used is Chinese.[47] A special hospital, No. 915, has been identified as the location of further refining operations.

Also in the mid–1990s, Kim Jung Il and the North Koreans expanded the variety of drugs being smuggled. For example, in 1998, a North Korean diplomat stationed in Mexico was caught at the Moscow airport trying to smuggle cocaine into Russia. This so outraged the Mexican government that they sent the North Korean ambassador home and closed the embassy for a time.[48] Another North Korean diplomat stationed in Syria was discovered trying to bring the "date-rape" drug "Rohypnol," a kind of hallucinogenic similar to LSD, into Egypt.[49]

It was on methamphetamines, known as "crystal meth" or "speed," that the North Koreans found their biggest profits. Meth is created in a laboratory and thus not affected by climate or soil conditions. In 1997, suspicious Japanese Customs officers found 70 kilos (150 pounds) of meth inside some jars of honey being imported from North Korea. The street value of the shipment would have been about 10.9 billion yen or around $90 million dollars. These were found aboard a North Korean ship that docked at a small port in western Japan. At the time, there was some speculation that the North Koreans chose this port because it had no drug-sniffing dogs, but good police work made the difference.

In league with criminal syndicates based in Hong Kong, South Korea, China, and Japan, the North Koreans went into meth in a big way. They set up meth processing laboratories in North Korea and across the border in China.[50] The meth made in North Korea even developed its own trade name, "Philopon." Customs officials and police all over Asia have since had their hands full. Japanese officials believe that the North Koreans supply at least 30 percent of the meth market in Japan. By one estimate, just one North Korean plant was producing 15 tons of meth per year.[51]

Law enforcement officials tried to limit this explosion of drugs by controlling the chemical precursors necessary to process it, particularly ephedrine. While this chemical is commonly used in cough syrups, only about 2.5 tons is needed by North Korea, at most, per year. In 1998, the United Nations antidrug smuggling organization discovered that a North Korean company had imported 50 tons.[52] According to a series of news reports, companies in Germany, India, Belgium, France, Australia, and Hong Kong have been supplying North Korea with ephedrine.

With an expanded variety of drugs has come new ways of smuggling. The North Koreans began with the diplomatic pouch because it can't be searched under international diplomatic custom. They also began mixing drugs in with ordinary trade goods coming from North Korea, as with the honey imported by Japan. In a 2001 case, South Korean inspectors found 30 kilos of meth in a shipment of North Korean kidney beans.[53]

Early drug shipments went out of North Korea directly by sea on North Korean ships. Over 1,200 North Korean ships per year dock in Japan alone.[54] As customs inspectors began to look more closely at North Korean ships, the North Koreans turned to Chinese ships and transshipment through Chinese ports. In more recent years, they have transferred the drugs at sea to Taiwanese and Japanese fishing vessels with the North Korean Navy as a conduit. There are many North Koreans working in Russia, and some of them have become drug pushers. In these cases the drugs would come over land.

In the spring of 2003, the U.S. State Department told Congress, "Since 1976, there have been at least 50 arrests/drug seizures involving North Koreans in more than 20 countries around the world."[55] Among the more prominent drug busts involving the North Koreans are the following:

- Japanese police report having confiscated almost 2,000 pounds of North Korean narcotics in 1999, up from 150 pounds just two years before[56]
- In the spring of 2000 a Japanese fishing boat was found to have 500 pounds of North Korean narcotics with a street value of $150 million
- Three hundred pounds of meth were discovered in January of 2002 aboard a Chinese ship destined for Japan[57]
- In the summer of 2002 Taiwanese police found 150 pounds of North Korean heroin aboard a Taiwanese fishing boat. The smugglers had received it from a North Korean Navy vessel hiding behind an island off the North Korean coast[58]
- Then in the spring of 2003 the Australians found almost three hundred pounds of North Korean heroin smuggled in by a North Korean ship and worth $146 million on the street[59]

North Korea doesn't advertise the profits it makes from trafficking drugs. The best guess, by United States Forces Korea (USFK), is half a billion dollars per year, and it is only a conservative estimate.[60] A spring 1999 report by Seoul's National Intelligence Service states:

- "North Korea is believed to be carrying out at the *regime level* such international crimes as narcotics trafficking" [Emphasis added]
- North Korea's narcotics business is "under the direction of Kim Jung Il"

- "The monetary profits from the illicit narcotic trafficking are reportedly used as Kim Jung Il's personal secret funds"[61]

In the spring of 2003, a former high-ranking North Korean official came to the United States to testify before a Senate Subcommittee. He confirmed the findings of the NIS report and estimated that narcotics trafficking accounts for 60 percent of North Korea's yearly foreign exchange earnings.[62] If true, this would make it more valuable than Pyongyang's weapons sales. While this projection is a bit unlikely, the drug trade is of major importance to the Kim dynasty.

In at least one case, authorities have found a connection between North Korean narcotics trafficking and the international arms trade. In late 1998, Russian prosecutors discovered that North Korean agents had used the proceeds from heroin sales in Russia's far east to corrupt Russian generals into selling military helicopters to North Korea. After ten Russian military helicopters were exported to North Korea disguised as "scrap," prosecutors arrested fourteen North Koreans working in a trade office.[63]

KIM'S TARGETS

Certainly the primary motivation behind North Korean regime narcotics smuggling is a simple desire for money. However, a former North Korean KGB official reports that North Korean officials have a political agenda as well—the addiction of young people in South Korea and Japan.[64] This dovetails with the U.S. State Department's view that North Korean drug trafficking targeting Japan is a "state-directed conspiracy." State believes there are more than 2.2 million meth junkies in Japan alone.

The major markets for North Korean narcotics are Japan, Russia, South Korea, China, and Taiwan—although there has been at least one bust of North Korean drugs headed to the Philippines.[65] In the first six months of 2003, Japanese police seized a record number of stimulants from China and North Korea. This was more than all of 2002.[66] Japanese law enforcement officials also report that North Korean amphetamines they have confiscated from Chinese ships are of very high potency.[67]

In the spring of 2003, it was found that street prices of meth in Japan were falling—indicating that the North Koreans and their associates have been able to make substantial deliveries in Japan.[68] The U.S. State Department observed, "The sharp increase in large methamphetamine seizures in Japan after earlier indications of North Korean efforts to import ephedrine strongly suggests a state-directed conspiracy to manufacture and traffic in this narcotic to the largest single market for it in Asia."[69]

The American Drug Enforcement Administration reports that the effects of methamphetamines on the brain as, "Damage to the brain caused by meth usage is similar to Alzheimer's disease, stroke, and epilepsy."[70] North Korean escapees by way of China have told very sad stories of young Chinese women who have had to engage in prostitution to maintain their drug habits. South Korean authorities are also reporting a large increase in drug addicts.[71] According to the U.S Congress' Joint Economic Committee, between three and five million Russians are "regular drug users" and this in turn leads to an increase in violent crime, abandonment of children, and other social ills.[72]

The eighty thousand American service personnel based in Japan and South Korea are equally at risk. According to one report, a Japanese gangster syndicate in league with North Korea had been pushing meth in bars frequented by American sailors assigned to the U.S. naval base at Yokosuka, Japan.[73] In 2002, Japanese police arrested a Yokosuka-based U.S. sailor who was allegedly carrying $10,000 worth of amphetamines and cocaine.[74] During a December 2001 shootout between a North Korean spy boat and the Japanese Coast Guard, the North Koreans were observed jettisoning their cargo, presumed to be narcotics. When the spy boat was raised off the ocean floor, Japanese authorities found a cell phone on board. Tracing the call record, they found that the North

Korean drug smugglers had been in touch with three separate Japanese crime syndicates![75]

THE CHINA CONNECTION

The Chinese have gone to great lengths to disguise their partnership with North Korea in the international narcotics trade. But we know that the first Japanese bust (the honey jar case) involved meth chemically produced in China. Some meth laboratories associated with North Korean trafficking are on the Chinese side of the border. Chinese equipment processes North Korean opium. Chinese gangsters are prominent as middlemen in the trafficking, including the major drug seizure in Australia in spring of 2003. Chinese ships are also the favorite mode of transport for North Korean narcotics at the moment.

There has been one known tip from Chinese law enforcement that led to a successful North Korean bust. It is not known whether this was ordered from higher authority in Beijing or a one-time offering at lower levels. By contrast, there is an unconfirmed report that the North Korean State Security Department and Chinese Ministry of State Security (equivalents in each case to the Soviet-era's KGB) have a "secret agreement" to allow a certain level of drug smuggling across the North Korean and Chinese borders and that this amounts to China's "tacit approval of North Korea's smuggling activities."[76]

What is clear is that there has been no crackdown on the Chinese side. The meth plants in China are still open and Chinese government-owned vessels continue to be the subject of drug busts in Japan. Further, Beijing has made no known effort to restrain North Korean behavior when it comes to narcotics trafficking.

COUNTERFEITING AND ARMS SMUGGLING

Law enforcement officials call them "Super K" notes—the very high quality counterfeit U.S. one-hundred-dollar bills made in North

Korea. Ordinary currency detectors in banks cannot distinguish the real notes from these Super K notes. They have different serial numbers and the printing level is almost up to the level of genuine notes. In the spring of 2003, the U.S. Department of the Treasury sent a report to Congress defending its anti-counterfeit program and revealed the plan to release a new set of notes to replace the old ones in 2003. For the first time, the new notes will include a color other than green.[77] Clearly, there is a major struggle of measures and counter-measures between the U.S. Treasury and Kim Jung Il's counterfeiters.

The North Koreans got their start in 1974 with the alleged sale of some special printing machines by a firm in Lausanne, Switzerland.[78] Whether by coincidence or not, this was the same year that Kim Il Sung named his son, Kim Jung Il, his heir apparent and increased his responsibilities.

In the 1970s and 1980s, the North Koreans only produced medium quality U.S. notes. In 1991, as North Korea's foreign exchange reserves declined precipitously, Kim Jung Il ordered an expansion of the counterfeiting program. Pyongyang ordered the latest equipment from Japan[79]—printing presses, special chemicals, and a very sophisticated currency identification machine. There are at least three locations in North Korea producing counterfeit currency.

By the fall of 1992, extremely high quality bogus hundred dollar bills were beginning to flood into world markets from the Russian far east to Europe.[80] A former Japanese Red Army terrorist who had hijacked a Japanese airliner to North Korea years previously, turned up in Southeast Asia in 1996 allegedly trying to smuggle three million dollars in counterfeit bills.[81] Austria's interior minister accused a North Korean bank, the "Vienna Gold Star Bank AG," of becoming involved "repeatedly in connection with money laundering and circulation of counterfeit money up to the involvement in illegal trade with radioactive materials."[82]

The result was a rapid increase in the number of counterfeiting cases worldwide. Japan's National Police Agency has seized $334,000 worth of counterfeit U.S. currency in 1994 and almost $2 million in a single case in 1997. In 1998, the Russian police arrested a North Korean diplomat who was trying to sell $30,000 counterfeit U.S. dollars in the Russian far east.[83] This particular individual had been deported by the Swedes in 1976 for drug trafficking. He later turned up in Australia aboard a North Korean drug ship busted in the spring of 2003. U.S. Forces in Korea estimated in 2003 that North Korea was generating between 15 and 20 million dollars in profits annually from its counterfeiting operations.[84]

In the late spring and early summer of 2000 it was revealed that the Philippine military had broken up a major North Korean arms smuggling operation. Using former Malaysian military personnel as brokers, three million dollars of Osama bin Laden's money was being funneled to a Philippine armed terrorist group, the Moro Islamic Liberation Front, as payment to North Korea for small arms, ammunition and shoulder-fired anti-aircraft missiles.[85]

"A CULT-BASED, FAMILY-RUN CRIMINAL ENTERPRISE"

In the spring of 2003, Larry Wortzel, vice president of the Heritage Foundation, told Congress, "The Kim Jong Il regime resembles a cult-based, family-run criminal enterprise rather than a government."[86] This is an accurate observation and a useful way to look at North Korea, an outlaw regime whose leadership is cunning, brazen, and absolutely ruthless. To the Dear Leader and his followers, terrorism and any manner of crime have no moral consequences; they are just means to an end.

It is also a regime against which a policy of appeasement, sometimes called a "sunshine" policy, is spectacularly inappropriate. Declaring Kim to be "a man we can deal with" is the height of folly. A democratic politician only reduces his or her own moral authority by being photographed with a major figure of the Kim regime or even Kim himself. In dealing with North Koreans, it is grave mistake to pretend there is mutual good will where none exists. The choice is stark: be firm or become a victim.

Behind all of this is the hidden hand of communist China. North Korea simply could not have become the threat to countries and peoples in Asia that it is without the crucial support of Beijing. The Chinese know what is going on, and, far from stopping it, they have become the Kim regime's enablers, defenders, and often its silent partners. If North Korea is engaged in a "state-sponsored conspiracy," then Beijing is a co-conspirator.

6

A DAGGER POINTED AT JAPAN

I pledge that, in the event I encounter the worst situation, I will offer my physical life not to harm the international dignity of the Great Leader and Dear Leader comrade, to keep the secrets of our revolutionary organization, and let my political life shine eternally.

— Pledge taken by North Korean terrorist and espionage operatives

Takuya Yakota and his twin brother, Tetsuya, were eight years old when their sister Megumi disappeared.[1] She had stayed after school for badminton team practice, then her great passion, and walked home with two girl friends. Sometime around 6 p.m. on November 15, 1977, after the last of her friends safely reached home, Megumi vanished. There were no witnesses. She was thirteen at the time.

Although the Yakota family believes the police in Niigata Prefecture in Japan, where they live, conducted a thorough search, not a single clue was uncovered. The authorities immediately ruled out the idea of a runaway or suicide. Mr. Yakota remembers his sister as an "active girl—a laughing, happy child." The next nineteen years were very difficult for the family—not knowing if she might have been killed or kidnapped by Japanese gangsters.

Then, in late 1996, word began to dribble out from North Korean defectors concerning a young Japanese woman who had been kidnapped by Kim Jung Il's agents. It took a bit of amateur detective work to realize that one of the people described by the North Korean defectors was Megumi. The family immediately raised Megumi's case with the Japanese government, but the government was largely unresponsive. Neither the Japanese politicians nor the Japanese Foreign Ministry wanted to hear about North Korean agents in Japan.

Japanese Prime Minister Junichiro Koizumi, however, had the courage to raise the issue in a September 2002 meeting with North Korea's Kim Jung Il. To everyone's surprise, Kim admitted, "impulsive people who worked for special agencies conducted such activities, motivated by heroism."[2] In mid–October 2002, five Japanese kidnap victims, but not Megumi, were permitted to return to Japan. Their children are still being held hostage in North Korea.[3]

The Yakota family believes that the North Korean agents did not originally intend to kidnap anyone as young as Megumi but, because she was tall for her age and it was dark at that time of year, they made a mistake. Having abducted her, they had to get her away from Japan. The Yakotas believe she was probably first moved to a safe house and then smuggled aboard a large North Korean ship that traveled between North Korea and ports in Niigata.[4]

The North Koreans have told the family that Megumi is dead, a suicide. The North Koreans have, however, produced a fifteen-year-old girl whom they claim is Megumi's daughter; DNA testing has confirmed the family relationship. The child's father might be a North Korean whose family once lived in Japan.[5] The North Koreans will not allow the girl to visit her Japanese family. The Yakotas will be permitted to visit her in North Korea, if they pay enough money and allow themselves to be used for North Korean propaganda.

A Japanese human rights group, the National Association for the Rescue of Japanese Kidnapped by North Korea, has identified at least twenty Japanese citizens who have been kidnapped by North Korea. The group estimates the actual number of victims to be much higher. Defectors claim there are currently more than one hundred Japanese citizens living as prisoners in North Korea.[6] Japanese police are reviewing many past missing persons' cases in light of the new evidence.[7]

While Megumi's capture symbolizes the evil of North Korea's secret abductions, the other family cases are just as heartbreaking. In the summer of 1978, a young mother, Yaeko Taguchi, was kidnapped after leaving her two small children at a Tokyo daycare center. One of the defectors reports having seen her weeping over her lost children.[8] The North Koreans say she, too, is dead.

North Korea first began abducting people by kidnapping its own citizens in the 1950s. After the end of the Korean War, a number of young people were sent to study in Soviet bloc countries. Some of them began to become disaffected with life at home. North Korean agents, sent to watch for any signs of a wavering allegiance, kidnapped anyone who questioned the regime.

Kidnapping foreigners seems to have started in the 1970s, when "Dear Leader" Kim Jung Il assumed more of his father's powers. As we will see, the ugly story that begins with Megumi Yakota and the other kidnapping victims passes through North Korea's unofficial embassy in Japan and touches on the Japanese underworld. And it remains unpunished because of fear of North Korean belligerence, a fear that now includes nuclear weapons.

THE CHOSEN SOREN

During World War II, with millions of Japanese men away at the war front, there was a labor shortage in Japan. As a result, thousands of Koreans were brought to Japan, sometimes willingly, sometimes not, to work in war industries or agriculture. They joined thousands of others who had drifted to Japan beginning in the early 1900s. By the end of World War II, there were more than 2 million Koreans living in Japan.[9] The United States occupation forces repatriated about 1.4 million people, leaving 600,000 Koreans living in Japan by the late 1940s.

Although the vast majority of the Koreans living in Japan were from the area controlled by South Korea, the Japan Communist Party and clever propaganda by North Korea attracted large numbers of Koreans to the "General Association of Korean Residents in Japan" ("Chosen Soren" in Japanese), which was established in 1955. The Japanese communists and North Koreans preyed upon the Korean residents' feeling of discrimination and hardship to feed them into the grip of the Chosen Soren.

For Koreans struggling in postwar Japan, Chosen Soren became an island of Korean identity in a sea of Japanese culture. The organization runs Korean language schools and today even has its own university. Chosen Soren credit unions and banks provide loans that Korean businessmen could not otherwise obtain. Chosen Soren's publishing house produces books, magazines, and newspapers in Korean, mostly propaganda for the North. Chosen Soren also sponsors a Korean opera troupe that travels around Japan giving performances at the local branches.

For decades, Chosen Soren has been North Korea's unofficial embassy in Japan and was treated by the Japanese government with near-diplomatic courtesies. On North Korea's national day, September 9, the North Korean flag flies while Chosen Soren's national and regional headquarters hold large celebrations. In a subbasement of the group's Tokyo headquarters is a lead-lined room where the highest officials of the organization meet for private discussions beyond the prying eyes and ears of the Japanese police.[10] According to a former Chosen Soren official, there are "study groups" within the organization that function as the party committee for the Chosen Soren. All of the top officials of Chosen Soren are members of this shadowy group, and all of them are members of the North Korean Worker's (Communist) Party.[11]

In early 2001, a Japanese magazine published a transcript of Kim Jung Il giving instructions to the Chosen Soren leadership. It is clear that the Chosen Soren is subservient to Pyongyang. Kim is quoted as telling the Chosen Soren leaders to disguise their North Korean affiliation, "In these times we must hide the Red Flag in our hearts and refrain from wearing it on our sleeves."[12]

To Pyongyang, Chosen Soren is primarily a cash cow. No one who actually knows the details is talking, but it seems likely that over the past four-and-a-half decades trillions of Japanese yen, amounting to tens of billions of dollars, have passed from Chosen Soren to the North Korean leadership, all of it in cash.[13] One former Chosen Soren official describes a vault at the Tokyo headquarters, taller than an average man and wider than the breadth of both his arms extended. The vault is filled with cash.[14]

In a May 24, 1994, Senate floor speech, Republican Senator John McCain of Arizona revealed that Japanese Prime Minister Hata had estimated almost two billion dollars per year was flowing from Chosen Soren to the Kim family coffers. This amounted, he said, quoting Hata, to 40 percent of North Korea's yearly foreign exchange and 8 percent of the country's GDP.[15] This river of cash is illegal under Japanese law. Although it has been known to exist for years, the Japanese government has made no effort to stop it until 2003.

Some of the money comes from voluntary contributions by Korean residents in Japan. On special occasions such as North Korean national day, or the birthdays of the Kims, father and son, Chosen Soren extracts large donations out of the Korean community.

Another source of funds is the pachinko parlors run directly by the Chosen Soren or by its members. Pachinko, unique to Japan, is a form of gambling similar to pinball. Until recently it was a completely cash business. Owners of pachinko parlors can adjust the machines in order to increase or decrease the rate of payout. A nighttime stroll through urban areas in Japan would find tens of thousands of Japanese "salary men"[16] sitting on stools, addicted to

the game. Although the customers of pachinko parlors are over-
whelmingly Japanese, the business is considered slightly disrep-
utable and Japanese are generally not owners or managers. Many
Korean residents of Japan, most honest, some not, took over the
industry in the 1950s.[17]

In some cases, Japanese gangsters have a piece of the action.
Japanese gangsters have a particularly close relationship with
prominent members of the Chosen Soren, if not the organization
itself. For example, according to one account, "About 80 percent
of the Hayashi [Japanese gangster] group are Koreans, and most of
them are related directly or indirectly with cadres [officials] of
Ch'ongnyon [Chosen Soren] organizations."[18] Hayashi gangsters
are alleged to be involved in the pachinko business as well as drug
dealing, arms smuggling, money laundering, loan sharking, and
forced prostitution.[19] Illicit funds from the Japanese gangster business reportedly make their way into the Chosen Soren–North
Korea pipeline.[20]

Another lucrative source of money for the Chosen Soren is the
system of credit unions and banks it has established in Japan.
There have been a number of accusations that the Chosen Soren
force borrowers to kickback some of the money they borrow.[21] A
number of the Chosen Soren credit unions have had financial difficulties. A few years ago, one of these credit unions went bankrupt, costing Japanese taxpayers almost $3 billion.[22] By one
estimate, the Japanese government may have laid out as much as
$10 billion to bail out several Chosen Soren-related credit
unions.[23] Japanese taxpayers, forced to save small depositors from
bankrupt credit unions, are very likely funding their own security
threat since the Chosen Soren's money is secretly sent to North
Korea for its advanced weapons and other terrorist programs.

In addition to providing cash, the Chosen Soren has also been
providing Japanese technology to the North Korean military.
According one former Chosen Soren member, "a secret organ was
set up in the early sixties to send up-to-date [military] equipment

and scientists living in Japan to North Korea."[24] Night-vision goggles are among the items sent to Pyongyang. In 1994, a Japanese grinding machine useful for the production of ballistic missiles also went to North Korea, courtesy of a company associated with the Chosen Soren.[25] A satellite photo has established that the North Korean military was using a 30-ton Japanese tractor to move its missiles around on the launch pad. The exporter had told the Japanese government that the enormous tractor would be used for "carrying lumber."[26] There is also suspicion that used Japanese fishing boats have been purchased for their valuable GPS equipment, which is stripped off in North Korea and installed on spy boats.[27]

Illicit Japanese military goods shipments to North Korea have apparently been smuggled out on the passenger ferry between Japan and North Korea. These goods include computers, special materials for missiles, machine tools, scientific gear, and measuring instruments.[28] In 1998, the body of a North Korean infiltrator wearing Japanese military diving equipment washed ashore in South Korea.[29] Japan has been hemorrhaging high technology to North Korea for years, some of which is critical for making nuclear weapons or ballistic missiles. Until recently, the Japanese government has ignored the threat.[30]

At least one senior Japanese police officer has accused the Chosen Soren of having a direct hand in the kidnapping of Japanese citizens.[31] In the "Back to the Fatherland" program of 1959, Chosen Soren officials encouraged more than ninety thousand Korean residents of Japan, including about fifteen hundred Japanese women married to ethnic Koreans, to return to North Korea. Entire families went to live in the North Korean "paradise." Many parents sent their children, in the mistaken belief that they would have a better life in North Korea.

It did not take long for the returnees to discover that they had been duped. North Korea was "the land of no return."[32] Entire families, including children, disappeared into the North Korean prison camp system never to be seen again. The Korean "returnees" of 1959–1960 amount to a giant pool of hostages for Pyongyang to exploit at will. Soon after their departure for North Korea, sad letters, in effect ransom notes, began to appear in Japan. The recipients, mostly family members of the returnees, had no choice but to pay up and keep quiet.[33]

THE SPIDER'S NEST

Kim Jung Il orchestrates the kidnapping of innocents and the training of agents from Pyongyang. When the Dear Leader decided North Korean films needed improvement, his agents kidnapped the leading South Korean movie director and his wife, the leading actress in South Korean films.

The Japanese victims of kidnapping are divided into those who could be useful to the regime and those who would not cooperate. The latter go into the North Korean gulag or are executed.[34] After intense brainwashing sessions, some of the kidnap victims became translators for North Korean news agencies or served other lower-priority functions. Some of these kidnap victims were carefully selected because they do not have close relatives or friends who would actively pursue their disappearance. Professor Yi Yong-hwa of Kansai University in Japan notes, "Another aim [of kidnapping] is to obtain Japanese nationals, who have no relatives, in order to impersonate them for spying activities."[35]

A good example of this happened during the winter of 1980, when a middle-aged Japanese restaurant worker, Tadaaki Hara, was lured aboard a disguised North Korean spy ship with the promise of a job at a Japanese trading company.[36] To the North Korean agent who stole his identity, Hara was the perfect catch: His parents were dead; he had no wife or children, no criminal record, and had never left the country.[37]

The primary purpose of the North Korean kidnapping program is the promotion of Kim Jung Il's grand scheme of terror and espionage, leading to the ability to attack American forces in Japan and sabotage Japanese nuclear power plants in time of crisis.

Several of the first generation of kidnap victims became involuntary instructors at Kim Jung Il University and other training facilities for North Korean terrorist and espionage agents.[38] North Korea is such a closed society that students would have no idea how to operate in a foreign country. So education in foreign languages and culture are vital at Kim Jung Il University. Yaeko Taguchi, the young Japanese mother who was kidnapped in 1978, taught Japanese to Kim Hyon-hui, the North Korean terrorist who blew up KAL Flight 858 in 1987.[39] According to one report, Megumi Yakota might be teaching Japanese to North Korean spies attending a foreign language school run by the North Korean People's Army.[40] According to another account, she teaches Japanese at the Kim Jung Il University.[41]

There is possibly an additional horror to this program: According to one unconfirmed report, Kim intends for the original generation of abductees to become the breeding stock for a second generation composed of "mixed blood" offspring.[42] When these children are very young they are taken away from their parents and immersed in a heavy regimen of brainwashing and indoctrination.[43] If this report is correct, they could become the ideal North Korean "sleeper" agents—able to pass for Japanese and lying in wait until the signal to act.

SPY SHIPS

The popular view of Japan is Tokyo with its large population, huge crowds, and "pushers" stationed at subway stations to pack people together like sardines on the trains. There is also another Japan, an older Japan, of rocky coasts, isolated fishing villages, little hidden bays, and tiny, deserted beaches. This Japan stretches over a thousand miles along the western edge from the northern tip of Hokkaido to the southern island of Kyushu. It faces the Sea of

Japan and beyond it, the Korean Peninsula and the Russian Far East. At night, this Japan has unwelcome visitors.

In October 1990, following a storm, a local fisherman found a heavily damaged wooden boat drifting onto a remote beach about 200 miles west of Tokyo. It was about twenty-seven feet long by nine feet wide. It was clearly no fishing boat—it had three 260 horsepower engines made by the American Outboard Marine Corporation (OMC), giving it perhaps ten times more power than a fishing boat of that size.[44]

Investigating officers from the Fukui Prefectural Police Headquarters quickly determined that it was a small craft from a larger North Korean spy ship. No one in Japan had ever seen one before, but it matched the description that a captured North Korean spy had given to South Korean Intelligence officials a few years earlier.[45] Over the next few days, Japanese police found a pile of espionage-related gear and paraphernalia including codebooks, a rubber raft, and the drowned body of a young male in his twenties or thirties. Two badly decomposed bodies washed ashore in the coming days. In Korean letters, one of the documents had printed on it "Dear Leader Comrade Kim Jung Il" and "Respectfully pray for a long and immortal life."[46] About a month after the small spy boat was found, an underwater scooter was found in some bushes nearby. A defector later reported that one of the graduates of Kim Jung Il University had survived the storm and returned to North Korea a few months afterwards.[47] This was known as "The Mihama Incident," after the location where the spy boat washed up.

In December 2001, the Japanese Coast Guard had a shoot-out with a North Korean spy mother ship off the coast of Japan. The ship was sunk and its crew committed suicide rather than be taken alive. The Japanese have been able to raise the ship and it is now on display in Tokyo along with the items found with it. This ship had a smaller vessel on board almost identical to the one that washed ashore in 1990.

The captured spy ships and gear, together with defector's accounts, give a good picture of how the North Korean spy ship system works.

THE BIG SHIP

Much notoriety surrounds a large passenger ferry that runs between the North Korean port of Wonsan and the Japanese port of Niigata. The "Mangyongbong 92," widely known as the "Big Boat" or the "Big Ship," came into service in 1992, and is the successor of a line of "Big Ships" that have run between North Korea and Japan since the 1960s, making about 30 trips per year.

The "Big Ship" is the principal means of transport for the enormous volume of illegal cash that the Chosen Soren sends to North Korea. "Sturdy youngsters" associated with the Chosen Soren are chosen to carry the heavy bags, of almost one million U.S. dollars each, on the Japanese "bullet train" from Tokyo to Niigata.[48] On arrival in Niigata, a car from the local Chosen Soren headquarters takes the money to the branch office where the money is divided up into smaller bundles, making it easier to smuggle onboard the Big Ship. Under Japan's currency anti-smuggling law, it is illegal to take more than a million yen (roughly $8,500) out of the country without declaring it. Until recently, there were only two Japanese Customs officers on regular duty at Niigata Port and they could not check every handbag. They also knew that their careers would suffer if they found something illegal, not if they failed to find it.

According to at least one report,[49] the Big Ship is used to transport narcotics to Japan. Five times a year, boxes of narcotics arrive at the North Korean port of Wonsan and are loaded on the Big Ship. During the voyage to Japan, North Korean residents of Japan repack the drugs into smaller packets to make it easier to get past Japanese Customs. Once in Japan, criminal gangs take over the distribution.

The Big Ship is the big smuggler for North Korea, carrying from Japan to the communist regime bundles of illegal cash, secret military technology, returnees, and, perhaps Megumi Yakota.[50]

The ship also serves as a command center for Kim's terrorism and espionage operations aimed at Japan and South Korea. In 1974, North Korean agents gave the assassin of South Korea's first lady his orders aboard the current Big Ship.[51] At the time, the ship came in to Osaka. There, a Chosen Soren official wined and dined the assassin and pumped him full of enthusiasm and dedication for the project.

A senior official from North Korea, called a "guidance captain," aboard the Big Ship runs the espionage command post. In the fall of 2002, the Japanese government banned one such "guidance captain" from leaving the ship while in a Japanese port.[52] But this does not prevent Chosen Soren officials from going on board to meet senior officials from North Korea. According to Katsui Hirasawa, a member of the Japanese parliament (or Diet), thirty-six Chosen Soren officials visited the Big Ship in 2002.[53]

North Korean spies come and go via the Big Ship. In one case, under political pressure, the Japanese police were forced to release some infiltrators they had caught red-handed. These spies brazenly walked up the gangplank of the Big Ship, carrying their rubber dinghy, and went home![54]

What the Big Boat does at sea between North Korea and Japan remains unconfirmed. Japanese officials have determined that the ship has a military-class sonar that might be used for underwater espionage activity.[55] Since the Big Ship's route passes through the center of North Korean spy ship operations, Japanese officials believe it has some support role here.

OTHER SHIPS

North Korea also has cargo ships that it uses for spying. In the months of May and September, the Kim Jung Il spy school uses the North Korean ship *Sungni* for graduation exercises. When it docks in Japan, fifty to sixty operatives disguised as crew members come ashore to travel around Japan on a field orientation course.[56]

Until the December 2001 shootout with the Japanese Coast Guard, North Korean spy ships have relied on the speed generated by their great engines to get them away. The trade-off is very high fuel consumption. The Japanese Self-Defense Forces have found North Korean cargo ships lurking suspiciously between North Korea and Japan, often hidden behind one of the many islands in the region. Japanese military intelligence officers believe these cargo ships refuel spy ships at sea and provide other support functions for terrorist and espionage operations.[57]

SPY MOTHER SHIPS

The specifications for the spy mother ships are as follows:[58]

- Length: 90 feet, width: 15 feet
- Four Russian engines of 1,000 horsepower each
- Extensive fuel tanks
- Speed: at least 30 knots
- Weapons: 23mm ZU2 twin barrel anti-aircraft machine gun; B10 recoilless gun; SAM-16 Surface to Air Missile system; RPG-7 rocket propelled grenades; anti-personnel grenades; AK-47 assault rifles; automatic pistols; explosives for ramming other ships
- Other items: Japanese "FURUNO" radar system, spy paraphernalia, "Achilles" brand rubber dinghies, Japanese GPS equipment, SCUBA gear

At the rear of the ship are doors called "French Hatches" that open up the complete stern giving access to a large hold. This is where the smaller spy ship is held before it's launched.

SMALL SPY BOATS

The spy mother ship that the Japanese raised in 2001 held a smaller spy boat that was almost identical to the one that rolled up on a deserted beach in 1990. The major difference is that this smaller spy boat had three Swedish Volvo engines rather than American Outboard Marine Corporation engines.[59] It was a little over thirty feet long by nine feet wide. It had an underwater scooter aboard similar to the one that was found in 1990. The scooter is dark green and has handles for steering.

SPY SHIP OPERATIONS

North Korean terrorism and espionage operations typically begin with an evening oath meeting on the island of Hwangdo-to, off the North Korean port of Wonsan.[60] Standing before the portraits of Kim Il Sung and his son, Kim Jung Il, the operatives and combatants take the following oath: "I pledge that, in the event I encounter the worst situation, I will offer my physical life not to harm the international dignity of the Great Leader and Dear Leader comrade, to keep the secrets of our revolutionary organization, and let my political life shine eternally."[61]

After the oath ceremony, the combatants and operatives head out to sea aboard the spy mother ship. They try to time their trips to the new moon when they have maximum darkness and then try to blend in with the regular fishing boats in the Sea of Japan. It takes about three days to reach Japan. When they approach the coast, they launch the smaller spy ship, which takes some assembly work. About a mile off the coast, they transfer to one of the rubber dinghies or an underwater scooter. In other cases they go ashore in scuba equipment.

On shore they meet up with a "guide," usually from an affiliate of the Chosen Soren. It is the guide's responsibility to conduct an onsite survey to determine appropriate landing spots. Japan has a long and rocky coastline with many small bays and inlets ideal for night landing. The North Korean agents and the guides identify each other with prearranged codewords or sounds. In some cases, the mission is to insert an operative into Japan; in others they are doing an extraction of an agent inserted previously. These missions are very hazardous and the casualty rate is fairly high. A number of bodies have washed ashore in Japan and South Korea including two in 1998 and 1999.[62]

Sometimes, the "guides" are Japanese gangsters and the mission is primarily drug smuggling. Often, when Japanese authorities have spotted a North Korean spy ship, they have also found Japanese gangsters waiting at lonely beaches nearby.[63]

Finally, there are the kidnapping operations. While the Yakota family believes that Megumi went out on the Big Ship, which is certainly possible, it is more likely that she was an involuntary passenger on an outbound spy ship operation. A North Korean defector claims one of his instructors at Kim Jung Il University bragged about being the person who abducted her. According to this account, Megumi walked home along the beach and stumbled on a North Korean spy operation. Rather than kill her to keep her quiet, they locked her below deck for the duration of the return journey to North Korea.[64]

TARGETING AMERICAN FORCES IN JAPAN

Most specialists who have studied the North Korean spy ship operations believe that American forces are their number one target.[65] The United States has about 40,000 military personnel stationed in Japan. The United States Air Force has bases at Misawa, near Tokyo, and Kadena on Okinawa. Also on Okinawa is most of an entire U.S. Marine Division. The U.S. Navy has major bases at Sasebo on the Japanese island of Kyushu and at Yokosuka near Tokyo. The U.S. Army in Japan has a number of units assigned to it including a Special Forces Battalion, Army Logistics Headquarters, and the 500th Military Intelligence Brigade. In addition, there are always American military visitors, particularly when the fleet is in port.

Even before the invasion of South Korea, the Kim regime had agents who "gathered military intelligence on U.S. troop movements and reported the data to North Korea."[66] In the fall of 1951, the Tokyo Metropolitan Police Department rolled up over forty North Korean spies who were targeting American forces. Over the years, the Japanese police have captured North Korean spies who were collecting information about American military bases.[67]

Possible North Korean terrorism against American military personnel is a threat the military takes seriously. Small operations involving the ambush and assassination of American military personnel by North Korean agents are a possibility. But there are also bigger threats. Reportedly, in December 2001, a North Korean spy ship was carrying the Russian-built 9K310 "Igla-2" ground-to-air missile (also known as the SA-16), an advanced, infrared weapon—and a deadly threat to American airmen.[68]

The most lucrative target for Pyongyang would be an American nuclear-powered surface ship or submarine. A number of them are based in Japan and many others frequent Japanese ports. Since the suicide attack on the USS *Cole* in Yemen in 2000 (which killed seventeen American Navy servicemen), Japanese authorities have been concerned about a potential North Korean copycat attack. North Korean agents have had decades to prepare for such an attack. A North Korean suicide bombing of an American nuclear-powered aircraft carrier or submarine has the potential for mass casualties. Even if it produced no radioactive leakage, it could still provoke panic in Japan. American threat analysts are particularly worried about an attack on a U.S. nuclear-powered ship during a visit to Kobe or Osaka because of the threat to Japan's Inland Sea.

TARGETING NUCLEAR POWER PLANTS

Because Japan has limited domestic energy supplies, in the 1960s Japan turned to nuclear power. Today there are fifty nuclear generating plants. Nearly all of them are located along the coast. (See map on page 204.)

Fukui Prefecture is one of several prefectures that face North Korea across the Sea of Japan. The coast is heavily indented with many coves, remote bays, and deserted beaches. It has fifteen nuclear generating units within forty miles of each other. One of these, Mihama, is where the small spy boat washed ashore in 1990. The concentration of nuclear facilities is heavier at Mihama than anywhere else in Japan. It is directly across the Sea of Japan from Chongjin, a common launching point for North Korean spy ships headed for Japan. As Japanese reporter Osamu Eya writes, "The Mihama Nuclear Power Plant on the Tsuruga Peninsula is lighted twenty-four hours a day, and on the western side of the bay, there is a Hayase fishing port lighthouse. A spy vessel, infiltrating Wakasa Bay can easily reach Kugushi-Matsubara Beach if it moves straight through the center of the bay, watching the Hayase fishing port's lighthouse on the right and the lights of the Mihama Nuclear Power Plant on the left."[69]

In a 1999 interview, the former director-general of the Japanese Defense Agency, Fukushiro Nukaga, expressed alarm about the vulnerability of Japan's nuclear power plants to attack from the sea by North Korean agents in spy ships.[70] The discovery of the North Korean spy boat at Mihama is not an isolated incident. In December 2001, as we've noted, the Japanese Coast Guard had a firefight with a North Korean spy ship off the coast of Kagoshima in southern Japan, where several nuclear facilities are located.

Since March 1999, Japanese police and defense officials have conducted an increasing number of disaster drills to prepare for possible North Korean terrorist attacks on nuclear plants or U.S. forces in Japan.[71] To date, North Korean spy ships have been found with relatively light weapons on board. But it would not be difficult to obtain a missile with a sizable warhead and carry it on board a spy mother ship to within a mile of the target.

By some estimates the North Koreans have been able to insert hundreds of "sleeper" agents into Japan.[72] These agents could "pre-position" a weapon at a critical location, ready for detonation after a radio order from Pyongyang.[73] The weapon or weapons could have been brought in by spy ship in pieces, bit-by-bit, over time. If the North Korean weapon were nuclear, it would not have to be that close to the target to be effective.[74]

Mihama is almost due west of Tokyo and within about fifty to seventy-five miles of Nagoya and Osaka. If North Korean agents were able to successfully cause a nuclear incident on the level of the 1986 Chernobyl accident in the Soviet Union, the lives of tens of millions of people would be at risk. Since Japan is an island, there is no place to evacuate large numbers of people, even by sea, in time to minimize the loss of life. Depending on the prevailing winds, a vast expanse of central Japan could be made uninhabitable for generations.

THE CHINA CONNECTION

After the December 2001 spy ship shootout with the Japanese Coast Guard, investigators began to piece together a strong communist Chinese connection.[75] The spy ship had the name of a Chinese homeport written on the stern. The ship had been disguised to look like a Chinese fishing vessel. The crew waved a Chinese flag when they were first intercepted by the Japanese. American spy satellites had also spotted the spy ship being serviced by a North Korean cargo ship off the Chinese coast.

The most damning evidence is the direction the boat was fleeing before it was sunk. It was not headed home to North Korea as other spy boats had done. It was headed towards the Chinese port of "Shipu." The stern of the ship is split down the middle with "French hatches" which, when opened, allow the smaller spy boat to be launched. When the hatches are closed, the stern reads "Shipu," homeport for the North Korean spy ship.

When raised from the bottom, the North Korean spy ship was found to have a number of different coats of paint. Looking at

U.S. Army chaplain performs last rites for dead American soldiers in the Korean War. Tens of thousands of South Korean civilians, including women and children, were found in mass graves. South Korean, American, and other UN soldiers captured by the North Koreans were each executed by a single bullet to the head, their hands tied behind their backs. In one mass grave alone, American troops found seven thousand South Koreans and forty GIs.

The South Korean artillery (above) was no match for North Korean tanks (below). The Soviets supplied North Korea with heavy weapons, including the tanks that played a critical role in the North's initial success in the Korean War. In contrast, it was the U.S. State Department's policy to keep important defensive weapons out of the hands of the South Koreans.

Megumi Yakota, above, was abducted by North Korean agents in November 1977—she was only thirteen at the time. The North Koreans admit to her kidnapping but claim that she is dead, a suicide. They have produced a fifteen-year-old girl who is confirmed to be Megumi's daughter, but will not allow the young girl to visit her family in Japan.

These signs are found in the heavily mined demilitarized zone (DMZ) that separates North and South Korea.

Chinese Chairman Jiang Zemin embraces North Korea's Dear Leader Kim Jung II. A top Chinese military general has likened the relationship between the two countries to "lips and teeth."

This North Korean spy ship (top) was sunk in December 2001 during a shootout with the Japanese Coast Guard. When raised from the ocean, the spy ship was found to have the name of a Chinese home-port written on the stern (above left). The stern of the ship opens to allow a smaller spy boat to be launched (above right).

Kim Jung Il inspects a tank during a visit to China. Beijing has let it be known that its People's Liberation Army has extensive military-to-military consultations with visiting North Korean delegations.

Secretary of State Madeleine Albright's trip to Pyongyang in October 2000, where she was treated to several anti-American and highly militaristic displays by the Dear Leader, became an ugly symbol of the Clinton administration's approach to North Korea.

AP Photo/Xinhua, Liu Jiansheng

In an April 2003 trip to Beijing, North Korean Vice Marshall Jo Myong Rok was greeted by Chinese President Hu Jintao (above). In 2000, Jo wore his military uniform to pose for photos with President Clinton in the Oval Office (below). Only later did Clinton officials realize that some of the medals he bore were awarded for killing American soldiers in combat.

AP Photo/White House, David Scull

photographs, Japanese investigators were able to connect this ship with previous spy ship incidents. Apparently it had been operating out of Shipu for quite some time.

Shipu is located on the edge of Ningbo, the headquarters of China's East Sea Fleet. Ningbo is home to a large military complex spread out much like Norfolk, Virginia, headquarters for the American Atlantic Fleet. The People's Liberation Army has major facilities in the area—ground, air, and especially navy. It certainly stretches the imagination to suppose that Chinese military intelligence did not know North Korean spy ships and their supply vessels were home porting on the edge of one of their biggest military complexes. It is as implausible for the PLA not to have known about North Korean operations in Shipu as it is for the U.S. Navy not to detect a similar operation in Virginia Beach, a resort town on the edge Norfolk.

The evidence suggests that the Japanese Coast Guard inadvertently lifted the rug on a major Chinese–North Korean espionage operation. In this espionage joint venture, the North Koreans have a very large asset to bring to the table—hundreds of thousands of Korean residents in Japan. Until recently, there were very few Chinese in Japan for Beijing to recruit. North Korea, however, had the Chosen Soren. In return for allowing the North Koreans to operate out of the Chinese Navy base, North Korea would share information on the American forces in Japan and other intelligence of interest to Beijing.

The United States has mutual defense arrangements with both Japan and South Korea and the three countries share intelligence every day. Likewise, communist China and North Korea are also military allies sharing information. But being espionage partners with North Korea also makes the Chinese accessories to Kim's other activities, including assassination, drug smuggling, and kidnapping.

This would explain China's strenuous opposition to Japanese efforts at raising the North Korea spy ship sunk in December 2001.

Probably fearing what it would reveal, Chinese foreign minister Tang told a news conference in March 2002 that China had expressed "strong dissatisfaction over Japan's indiscreet use of force in China's exclusive economic zone, which caused the sinking of that boat."[76] Despite Tang's protest, the Japanese government was determined to raise the ship. With the Americans backing up the Japanese, the Chinese caved.

CORRUPTION AND COWARDICE

Through corruption and cowardice, the Japanese political elite has betrayed the Japanese people in the fifty years since the Korean War. When the police raided the home of the Japanese politician Shin Kanemaru in 1993, they found a pile of gold bars without serial numbers. Most of Japan assumed this was part of the bribes he received during his trip to North Korea in 1990.[77] Shortly after Kanemaru's trip to North Korea, he lobbied the Japanese government to give Pyongyang a large aid package. Whispers in Japan suggest Kanemaru was not the only Japanese politician on the take from Pyongyang. Within the last year or so, the press has taken a much more critical look at the North Korean tours made by influential Japanese politicians in the 1990s.[78]

The Japanese politician in the deepest political trouble today is Social Democratic Party leader Takako Doi. She is getting pounded in the Japanese press because her party has long had friendly ties to the Workers (Communist) Party of North Korea.[79] The Japanese Social Democrats liked to brag that they were the "window to relations between Japan and North Korea."[80] Until Kim Jung Il's admission in 2002, the Social Democrats even claimed on their website that the kidnappings and abductions issue was a "fabrication."[81]

A particularly sensitive issue has been the question of taxation of Chosen Soren property. Either through intimidation or political influence,[82] the Chosen Soren has enjoyed a tax-free existence similar to a foreign embassy, courtesy of an agreement with the Japanese tax authorities. This arrangement has made it possible for the Chosen Soren to funnel hundreds of billions of additional yen to the North Korean war machine. At the same time it directly increased the tax burden on the ordinary Japanese taxpayer. Once again, the Japanese taxpayer winds up paying for his own security threat.

During the Cold War, Japanese diplomats working Soviet issues had a well-deserved reputation for toughness, courage, and high integrity.[83] Perhaps they were trying to live up to the record of Japanese diplomat Chiune Shugihara, acting consul in Kaunas, Lithuania, who risked his own life and his career in 1940 to save the lives of over 2,000 Jewish refugees.[84]

In more recent years, those standards seemed to have been forgotten, as was demonstrated during the disgraceful "Shenyang Incident" of 2001. Five members of a starving, desperate North Korean family managed to make their way into the Japanese Consulate in Shenyang, China. But Japanese diplomats allowed armed Chinese police to come onto the consulate grounds and drag the family away. The event was captured on video and shown repeatedly on nearly every TV network in Japan and South Korea. It even appeared on all the major American networks. Reacting to the resulting public uproar in Japan, the Japanese foreign minister ordered two of the offending diplomats home and gave official rebukes and fines to ten others, including the Japanese ambassador to China, Koreshige Anami.[85]

STANDING TALL

If there is any good news to report regarding the increasing threat that North Korea (and its principal sponsor, communist China) poses to Northeast Asia, it is that the Japanese people have decided they are not going to be bullied any more. Today, when the "Big Ship" arrives in Japan there is a crowd greeting it with "Go Away!"

posters and signs. More Japanese Customs officers are now on hand to inspect the ship. At the most recent ruling party election, the politicians competed for who could be more anti-Pyongyang. In the press, Japanese investigative reporters now find their editors smiling on tough North Korea stories. Japan's Defense Agency is getting some of the money it needs for more and faster patrol boats and defense bureaucrats are demanding that the Americans "Stand Firm" against North Korea.[86] The Japanese Maritime Self-Defense Force (Navy) has organized special squads to deal with infiltrators. In the summer of 2003, the Japanese government put up a billion dollars for defense against Chinese and North Korean ballistic missiles. And there are heroes in both the Japanese Diet—parliamentarians like Kiyoshi Ueda, Eriko Yamatani, Shingo Nishimura, Katsuei Hirasawa, Hiroshi Oguma, Shioichi Nakagawa, and Shigeru Ishiba—and in Japanese academic circles—with scholars like Tsutomu Nishioka, Yoichi Shimada, and Yoshitaka Fukui—who understand that North Korea should not be appeased for its barbarity, but restrained. Peace and human rights in Northern Asia will advance if these heroes become the predominant voice in drafting Japan's policy on North Korea.

7

GULAG NATION

There are two worlds in North Korea, one for the
senior military and the elite and a living hell for
the rest.

— German pediatrician Norbert Vollertsen, who spent
eighteen months treating children in North Korea

"**I**t's like another planet." That was the only way one diplomat
could describe North Korea. Consider a visit from the Great
Leader to a foreign dignitary living in Pyongyang: It would
first be determined which particular salon in the forty-room guest
palace the Great Leader would visit. Next, just before the
appointed meeting, an army truck would arrive. A specially trained
team of soldiers would then strip the salon of all furniture, rugs,
and wall hangings—right down to the bare floor. A second truck
would arrive with replacement furnishings. Among these would be
the Great Leader's own desk as well as his personal items and bas-
kets of flowers. In this salon, the Great Leader would exchange ten
minutes of pleasantries with the foreign dignitary and then depart.
Afterwards, the two trucks would come back in reverse order so
that the salon would be returned to its original condition.[1]

North Korean children are taught that Kim Jung Il, the Dear
Leader, was born at a secret military base at the foot of a sacred
mountain in North Korea and that double rainbows appeared at
his birth. In fact, there never was such a secret military base; he

was born at a dismal military post in Siberia where his father was then serving in the Soviet army. In order to make the father into a war hero, the Soviets produced a series of faked documents and even a legend of his exploits.[2] The North Korean propagandists have expanded and extrapolated these lies to give the Great Leader the aura of a god.

According to a North Korean book published in the mid-1990s called *Divine Stories About the Dear Leader,* Kim Jung Il played his first round of golf and scored five holes-in-one. According to another tale, while inspecting the North Korean national pistol team, the Dear Leader took an old model pistol, fired ten shots and got ten bull's-eyes. There are equally fantastic tales of the Dear Leader's literary and scientific skills.[3] The Dear Leader, who never served a day in the military, is called a "heaven-sent brilliant commander [who] will vent our bloody grudge and rage against the U.S. imperialists."[4] He, too, is approaching a god-like stature. North Korean families have a special towel whose only purpose is to keep dust off the portraits of the two leaders.[5]

The people of North Korea are taught to think that since gods lead North Korea, then it must be "paradise on earth." That is an illusion far from the truth. During a round of drinking in Beijing a PLA general bragged to an American diplomat that a number of KPA senior officers have defected to communist China. The general made the rhetorical remark, "Can you imagine what their society must be like if they defect to us?"[6]

U.S. undersecretary of state John Bolton has described North Korea as a "hellish nightmare" and the Dear Leader as a "tyrannical dictator."[7] A French reporter called North Korea a "Kafkaesque Universe," comparing it to absurdities of Franz Kafka's fiction.[8] To a British reporter, a visit to North Korea was "A Journey to the Land that Time Forgot."[9]

North Korea is worse off than the Soviet Union ever was during Stalin's reign. It is built on a foundation of lies—about the country's leadership, North Korea itself, and the world beyond its borders. The cult of personality surrounding the Kims, father and son, seems to have no limits. In a country without enough resources even for children's school supplies, no expense is spared to glorify the Kims. The Great Leader's statue in front of his Memorial Hall is almost eighty feet tall, perhaps the tallest such structure in the world.[10]

In order to keep themselves in power the Kims have consciously drawn on the propaganda techniques of other twentieth century dictatorships. There are unconfirmed stories suggesting that the Hitler regime has been a particular role model. Staged events in Pyongyang, involving tens of thousands of people, are similar to the ones seen in Leni Riefenstahl's Nazi propaganda film, *Triumph of the Will*. This is not surprising since Kim Jung Il has been in charge of North Korean filmmaking and propaganda since the late 1960s.[11] A French reporter, witnessing such an event, described it as "a festival, which would have delighted the Nazis (it will mobilize 100,000 participants in a delirium of propaganda)."[12] Hundreds of these events are done by torch light, making clear comparisons to Nazi Party rallies of the 1930s. According to one defector report, on the evening of September 9, 1988, North Korea's National Day, the Dear Leader arranged for 100,000 people to parade through Pyongyang using their torches to spell out the words "Let us become suicidal units to protect the party!"[13]

Brainwashing begins at an early age. According to a foreign diplomat who visited the countryside, each school has a slogan or statement by one of the Kims written on the wall. Children learn to read by reciting this passage every morning.[14] People are under intense pressure from frequent ideological campaigns. In the fall of 2003, Pyongyang began a new anti-American campaign.[15] The North Korean people are often too battered from the indoctrination to dispute the will of the Kim dictatorship.

THE RED MONARCHY

Nepotism has certainly run rampant in all of the communist countries. But none of the communist regimes except North Korea has dared to turn its political system into a red monarchy.[16] In the 1950s, after the end of the Korean War, the Great Leader purged nearly all of his old comrades, especially those with close ties to Beijing or Moscow. By the 1960s, only those who had demonstrated a fanatical loyalty to Kim himself survived. The question of a successor then became embroiled in family politics as the Great Leader began to lay the groundwork for a hereditary system of dictatorship.

The Dear Leader is the son of the Great Leader's first wife, who some say committed suicide when she found that she was being supplanted by a younger woman. In order to succeed to the throne, the Dear Leader had to defeat his uncle, the Great Leader's brother, as well as his younger half brother by the second wife. This he did through spreading rumors about his uncle, adroit isolation of his brother, and demonstrations of complete loyalty to his father. As the "Short Biography of the Dear Leader Kim Jong Il" notes, "In particular, the revolutionary activity of his father... made the filial piety to his father in Comrade Kim Jong Il's heart sublimate into loyalty to the leader."[17]

The Dear Leader, now aged sixty-one, himself is thought to have had at least four wives and consorts in addition to uncounted short time liaisons. Most North Korea watchers believe that Kim Jung Il intends to appoint a family member as heir. There are at least three sons who are considered contenders for the throne. One of them, long thought to be the anointed successor, is in his thirties and is the son by an early wife now deceased. As his father before him, this son had been groomed by being put in party positions so that he may have a "monarchical" education. That is, he would have been moved from post to post, learning the ropes and how to govern. However, he seems to fallen out of favor when he was caught trying to sneak into Japan in 2001 on a false passport. The cover story claimed he was trying to take his mistress and their son (the Dear Leader's grandson) to visit Tokyo Disneyland. Informed rumors in Tokyo suggest that he was in town to launder the proceeds of North Korean WMD sales through Japanese banks.

These days, this eldest son seems to be spending most of his time in Beijing and Moscow.

His competition for the throne comes in the form of two sons by a later consort of the Dear Leader. One of the boys is in his early twenties and the other in his late teens. Their mother is said to be the current favorite of the Dear Leader. According to one defector report,[18] Kim has started to prepare the older of her two sons to succeed him. But no one outside of a small circle in Pyongyang would know for certain whom the Dear Leader will appoint as his successor.[19] There exists an atmosphere of palace intrigue similar to the contest for successor to the Chinese Emperor or the Turkish Sultan. The winners live in luxury and but the losers have to flee for their lives, if they can.[20]

LIFE OF LUXURY

Until the regime falls, we will not be able to directly compare the palaces and villas of the Kim family to those of Saddam Hussein. There are so many that the Dear Leader sometimes does not get around to visiting them from year to year. There is a family compound of palaces around an artificial lake in Pyongyang. A well-known seaside villa on the east coast is equipped with speedboats. In the northern mountains, Kim has a hunting lodge stocked with deer.

Some of the villas scattered around the country are for use by his official family and in other cases they seem to be hideaways for his passing fancy of the moment. During the time he was officially married to someone else, the Dear Leader stashed a famous actress in one of these villas, out of sight of his father. She bore a child, but it was several years before the Great Leader was told of his grandson, so the story goes. One high-ranking defector claims, "None of the retreats [villas] located throughout North Korea are without one of Kim Jung Il's women, and his children would number seventy in all."[21]

One of the major palaces has a complete projection room for showing movies and a five story garage filled with fancy cars, perhaps as many a hundred. The Dear Leader still has the two armored Cadillac limousines his father received from Colonel Qaddafi of Libya in the late 1980s.[22] Describing just one of the villas, Kim's former bodyguard recalls, "Its interior is beyond imagination. Each floor is fully furnished with high-quality pure wool carpets, many entertainment facilities, workout equipment, shopping items, educational materials, video rooms, bedrooms, kitchens, and satellite communication facilities, which are all top-quality products made in Japan, Switzerland, Sweden, and Norway."[23]

At least some of Kim's various palaces and offices are connected by underground tunnels. One foreign resident of Pyongyang described how the Dear Leader "disappeared" after a function at one of the palaces.[24] According to a defector report, Kim is driven to and from his office in his Lincoln limousine through an underground tunnel that is almost ten miles long.[25] While this may seem implausible, there are tunnels in Beijing that are even more extensive.

"JOY BRIGADES"

Next to the nuclear weapons program, there is probably nothing more secret than the "joy brigades," sometimes known as the "pleasure team."[26] These are exceptionally pretty young women from the countryside who are brought to Pyongyang in their mid-teens. They are taught to sing and dance for the Dear Leader's private parties. Their principal purpose, of course, is to become sex objects for the Great Leader and his closest aides. When he is in a rare magnanimous mood, he is known to pass them out to his subordinates as party favors.

In one instance, after a drinking party he told the male guests they could have any of the young girls they could catch. This led to ludicrous scenes of elderly drunken lechers chasing the girls all over the palace. One defector's account paints the following scene:

[T]he party scene was overtaken by pandemonium. Men and women were rolling over each other near the tables and sofas. Young ladies were shouting, 'Comrade leader!' as they tried to escape. Elderly officials grabbed young ladies that had escaped into the restrooms where they forced them against washbasins to threaten them with comic faces. The scene was overtaken by extreme frenzy.[27]

PAYING FOR KIM'S PLEASURES

It takes a lot of money to keep the Dear Leader in the kind of lifestyle to which he has grown accustomed. Office 39 is Kim's private slush fund. Money from the sale of narcotics and arms deals and counterfeiting operations pour into this office. The funds collected from the Chosen Soren for the Dear Leader's birthday and other holidays also fill the coffers. Office 39 even has its own gold mine.[28] North Korea has a system known as "loyalty" funds or "loyalty payments." These are funds that are voluntarily given by Korean people around the world to show they are loyal to the Kim family. Those who show such loyalty are often rewarded or at least hold the hope that they will be rewarded in the future.

If the funds collected are in foreign currencies, they are often invested abroad. These funds are moved from banks in Singapore to banks in Europe, particularly Switzerland. It is estimated that Kim has two to four billion dollars stashed away abroad. He has highly trusted aides in Europe who handle the money for him. One of them is reported to be the North Korean ambassador to Switzerland.[29]

Office 38 handles the outflow.[30] This is the purchasing office for the Kim family. Everything they want is handled from here—the cars (nearly all Mercedes Benz or expensive sports cars), jewelry, fancy food and clothes, luxury furnishings for the palaces and villas, boats, the latest of anything one could imagine. When his oldest son was a child, Kim gave him a million dollars worth of toys for each of his birthdays. North Korean agents would search Europe and Japan looking for "every electronic game on the market that might be of interest to children, regardless of price."[31]

Office 38 pays for all travel and overseas education expenses for the royal family. Kim's oldest son was educated in Switzerland and Moscow. The North Korean government spent over two million dollars to build a villa on Lake Leman as his residence while he attended school in Geneva. One of Kim Jung Il's nieces describes walking out of the most expensive restaurants in Geneva without paying the bill. North Korean agents told the restaurant they would pay for anything she ordered.[32]

Kim likes to give gifts to those who please him. Very often these are Mercedes Benz cars with the license plate beginning with "216"—signifying his birthday, February 16. Police and guards who see any Benz know that it belongs to a high official. If it has the "216XX" license plate, they know they are close to the Dear Leader.[33]

THE SERFS

While the Kim family and its supporters live like royalty, the bulk of the North Korean population lives like serfs. Survival depends on your rank and circumstances. North Korea has the most rigid class system in the world.

We see this most clearly in public health.[34] At the top is Ward 2 of the Ponghwa Clinic in Pyongyang, which has modern facilities and serves the Kim family and their immediate relatives. The clinic has a "special section" and a "general section." Full politburo members and their families use the first and candidate members the latter. The next level down is the Namsan Clinic, which takes vice minister level patients and foreign diplomats. There are two more levels of modern hospitals for the civilian elite. The military has its own set of graduated hospitals and clinics. From there, the bottom falls out. The healthcare needs of the vast bulk of the population are covered by makeshift clinics at factories and rural areas. In most cases, this means a building or a room labeled "clinic" with no modern medicine.

The best witness is German pediatrician Norbert Vollertsen who spent eighteen months treating children in North Korea.[35] After volunteering his own skin as a graft for a severely burned patient, Vollersten received a medal from the North Korean government and a "VIP passport" to travel around the country. This was a big mistake by the North Koreans because it gave him the opportunity to see what is normally hidden from outsiders.

Vollersten writes of what he found in most hospitals, "In each one, I found unbelievable deprivation. Crude rubber drips were hooked to patients from old beer bottles. There were no bandages, scalpels, antibiotics, or operation facilities, only broken beds on which children lay waiting to die. The children were emaciated, stunted, mute, and emotionally depleted." Vollersten compared this to what he found in military hospitals, "Unlike any other hospital I visited, this one looked as modern as any in Germany. It was equipped with the latest medical apparatus, such as magnetic resonance imaging, ultrasound, electrocardiograms, and X-ray machines."

The doctor's conclusion? "There are two worlds in North Korea, one for the senior military and the elite; and a living hell for the rest." What applies in the case of public health is true for all aspects of life in North Korea. On one side, there are strict restrictions on ordinary people—whether it is food, clothing, housing, or transportation. On the other, as Vollertsen describes it, "The system's beneficiaries are members of the Communist Party and high-ranking military personnel. In Pyongyang, these people enjoy a comfortable lifestyle—obscene in the context with fancy restaurants and nightclubs."

GOVERNING BY GULAG

What sustains this system is the terror. "Gulag" is a Russian acronym standing for the Soviet organization that ran the vast system of political prisons and forced labor camps that existed during the Soviet era, later exposed by Alexander Solzhenitsyn's *Gulag*

Archipelago. We now know that all communist regimes have such systems. The Soviets were the first to institute forced labor camps for political prisoners, followed by the Chinese. In current times, the communist Chinese gulag has been exposed by Harry Wu, a survivor of nineteen years in the Chinese camps, in his book Lao-gai, *The Chinese Gulag*.[36]

North Korea also has such a gulag system.[37] North Korea built on the Chinese model and added a new depravity—child political prisoners. Neither the Soviets nor the Chinese sent children to the concentration camps but the Dear Leader sends the entire family. One of the best accounts of the North Korean gulag is written by someone who was sent to the camps at the age of nine, because his grandfather had offended the system. His sister was only seven; she was also sent to prison.[38] In North Korea, the children of political prisoners are called "seedlings." Official propaganda proscribes the proper treatment of these children, "desiccate the seedlings of counterrevolution, pull them out by their roots, and exterminate every last one of them."[39]

The camps are designed to exploit the prisoners' labor until they die. Prisoners are given difficult and dangerous labor such as mining under unsafe conditions. Children are assigned heavy work as well, such as logging. Even before the famine of the mid–1990s, prisoners, including children, were on rations that would not sustain life in the long run, much less allow for any sort of normal growth. Since the political prisoners are never released, there is no danger of them divulging military secrets; they are assigned to work on missiles and other special weapons.[40] One camp, Camp #14, is notorious for its use of prisoners "as guinea pigs for developing chemical warfare technology," according to information obtained by the Seoul Network for North Korean Democracy and Human Rights.[41]

Since the North Korean secret police send entire families to the labor camps, they have a higher proportion of women imprisoned than even Stalin's gulag or the Chinese concentration camp system today. According to information obtained by a South Korean human rights group, it's bad luck to be an even moderately attractive young woman in the camps. High Communist Party officials troll the camps looking for victims to be used as sex slaves. If the women become pregnant, they are forced to have an abortion without anesthesia. When their usefulness is over, the women are murdered. Their deaths are covered up as "shot while trying to escape."[42] In much the same way, the Nazi "Death Doctor," Josef Mengele, used to comb the arriving trains for an attractive evening companion, only to have her shot the next day.

The prisoners of the North Korean gulags are filthy and disease-ridden. Beatings, torture, and executions are common. There is nothing to check guards from exercising brutality. Perhaps a third of the prisoners survive, for a while, as informers. In the end, death comes to nearly all of them, sooner rather than later.[43]

The Dear Leader's concentration camps are very efficient both for removing any real threat to the regime and in reinforcing the system of state terror. By some estimates, the North Korean gulag currently holds 200,000 men, women, and children. An estimated 400,000 people have perished in the camps over the past several decades.[44] Rumors of the camps-of-no-return circulate in the general population and fear of denunciation prevents an organized opposition from forming.

"ARMY FIRST"

In the 1990s, events began to turn against the Dear Leader's hold on power. The Soviet Bloc countries turned to democracy and free enterprise economics. That meant a sudden halt to the subsidized imports, which had propped up the North Korean economy from its inception. Since the communist Chinese no longer had to compete with Moscow, they too reduced their handouts. Years of agricultural mismanagement were also catching up with Pyongyang. Kim Jung Il's legitimacy to rule was also in question, his father, the

Great Leader, having died in the summer of 1994. Kim Jung Il was forced to execute a number of people, some for disloyalty and others, such as the agriculture minister, as scapegoats for the food crisis. [45] A number of high-level defectors escaped to Seoul with tales to tell about Kim's troubles.

There was a lot of speculation in Washington, Tokyo, and Seoul (and probably in Beijing as well) about the possible collapse of Kim's regime. But cleverly, the Dear Leader found a savior in the military. Communist Chinese leader Mao Zedong is famous for saying "Power comes out of the barrel of a gun," but he also said, "The [Communist] Party controls the gun." Kim has invented a new ideology called "Army-first," which declares that "the [North Korean] regime comes from the barrel of a gun and is maintained by the barrel of a gun"[46] and "the gun barrel should be placed over the hammer and sickle."[47]

North Korea has always been a heavily militarized society. It is one of the policies that drove so many refugees to flee to the South even before the Korean War. During the 1980s, North Korea almost doubled the size of its military establishment. By the end of the 1980s, Pyongyang's defense spending was far beyond the country's ability.

"Army-first" first emerged as a slogan in 1997. Under this policy, the Dear Leader instructed the people of North Korea "to concentrate greater efforts on military activities and strengthen national defense capabilities in every way—no matter how difficult the economic situation and no matter how great the financial burden."[48] According to the official newspaper of North Korea, the Army-first strategy "calls for giving priority to military issues over everything."[49]

This announcement came in the middle of the worst part of the North Korean famine (1995–1998). John Tkacik, Jr., a Heritage Foundation research fellow, notes, "The very legitimacy of 'Dear Leader' Kim Jong Il's regime rests on the so called 'Songun' or 'Army First' policy that Kim personally articulated. . . . This terrifying ideology has made serfs of North Korea's civilian population. They are subservient to a war machine—a move transparently designed by their 'Dear Leader' to ensure loyalty and the support of the military."[50]

At the top of the North Korean power pyramid is the military and the National Defense Commission of which the Dear Leader is the chairman. Next are the secret police and the Worker's Party officials, which include the higher government leaders, amounting to perhaps 1 percent of the population. Together they constitute a gang of ruthless criminals bound together by a common interest in maintaining their privileges over the rest of the population.

"FOOD FOR RELIEF, IN THE NAME OF CHRIST"

Jane Harman is a hard-working congresswoman from California who is now the ranking Democrat on the House Permanent Select Committee on Intelligence. Her district is filled with American defense contractors and she has served on the Armed Services and Intelligence Committees of the House. She has made it her business to know and understand military and intelligence matters.

In August 1997, she made a trip to North Korea to examine the progress of the international aid program. Stopping in Seoul on her return she told a news conference of her concern that "some food aid has probably ended up in the hands of the [North Korean] military and the other elite."[51]

In less than a day, Secretary of State Madeleine Albright's press spokesman, Jamie Rubin, was expressly denying Harman's concern. "I can say that our experts are confident that there is no significant diversion of the assistance we have provided," Rubin told the press.[52]

What Mr. Rubin did not know was that exactly as he was speaking, a U.S. military team inspecting a captured North Korean submarine was finding the remains of tinned food provided by an American church from Virginia. The label on the cans read "Food for Relief, in the name of Christ" and "Donatable food, not for resale." The North Korean submarine had run aground off the east coast of South Korea. Half the crew committed suicide and the other half engaged in a shootout with the South Korean Army and police. By the time it was over, twenty-four North Korean commandoes and fourteen South Koreans were dead. The single surviving commando told authorities his team was on a military reconnaissance and rehearsal mission to probe South Korean defenses.

INTERNATIONAL AID TO KIM'S RESCUE

Here was clear evidence that international food aid to North Korea was being diverted to the military. This leads to some questions about the realities of the North Korean famine and the international food aid that was sent to save the North Korean people.

Was there a famine in North Korea from 1995–1998? Yes, although some observers, including the CIA, doubted it at the time. There is now enough physical evidence of malnourished children to confirm the reports from refugees. The best estimate is that two to three million people died of starvation and diseases related to malnutrition.

Were the reports of people resorting to cannibalism credible? Yes. Refugees streaming into Manchuria reported this.[53] *Washington Times* reporter Bill Gertz obtained a confirmatory Top Secret American intelligence document, which he included in an appendix to his book *Betrayal*.[54]

What was the cause of the famine? Only about 20 percent of North Korea's land is suitable for agriculture. Communist-style collectivization and mismanagement made the situation worse. Prior to 1990, North Korea was exchanging its low-quality industrial goods with China and the Soviet Bloc for food at subsidized prices. When that ended, famine was almost inevitable.

How did the North Korean government respond to the food crisis? Kim Jung Il ensured that the military and the Communist elite were fed and left the rest of the population to fend for themselves. The North Korean government then appealed for international food aid under the excuse of a natural disaster—severe flooding. While there was some truth to that claim, the famine was mostly man-induced. The Imjin River runs through the DMZ to the sea on the western side. Standing on the south bank of the river, in South Korea, and looking across the river into North Korea, one immediately notices that the northern bank and the hills beyond have been completely stripped of trees and shrubs. This kind of practice has led to extreme environmental damage in North Korea and loss of agriculture.[55]

What was the international response to the North Korean famine? The World Food Program, an arm of the United Nations, organized an international program that included major donations from the United States, Japan, South Korea, and the European Union. The World Food Program is currently soliciting donations for 2003–2004.

Was it necessary for the North Koreans to seek international aid? A high-ranking North Korean defector reported that the Dear Leader spent almost a billion dollars on a Memorial Hall glorifying his dead father.[56] These sorts of projects continued unabated throughout the worst of the famine. In 1996, the Agency for International Development, an arm of the State Department, hired an experienced researcher, Sue Lautze, to examine the food situation in North Korea. She traveled over much of the country including the border region. When her draft report concluded that the Kim regime had the foreign currency reserves to pay for its own food imports but that these financial reserves had been spent on weapons instead, the State Department, then headed by Secretary Albright, ordered a revision of the report before releasing it.[57]

Was the international food aid diverted for illicit purposes? The diversion of international food aid in North Korea is much more serious than a few cans of American food found in a submarine. The World Food Program lacked any management or control of the distribution. In 1998 a number of highly respected international aid groups, including Medecins sans Frontieres (Doctors without Borders) and the International Federation of Red Cross Societies, "decided not to supply any food aid to the communist state because this food had often been turned over to the military of its own use."[58] In one instance, the North Korean military commandeered five thousand tons of food aid at gun point right in front of WFP officials.[59] In 2001 another UN agency, the UN Commission on Human Rights, received a damning report from Jean Ziegler, the UN Special Rapporteur on the Right to Food, stating that it "gradually became clear that most of the international aid was being diverted by the army, the secret services, and the [North Korean] government."[60]

A North Korean army defector has pointed out just how easy it was to fool the WFP. He told a South Korean magazine that because of the "military-first" policy, the KPA has carte blanch for whatever it wants at the ports.[61] His unit simply put on civilian clothes and changed from military to civilian license plates whenever the WFA inspectors were around. "Since South Korean rice was of high quality, it all went to high-ranking figures," he said with regard to a 1999 shipment. The defector recalls that, "Soldiers also ate all of that rice. North Korea is based on military-first politics. . . . There is no need to pay attention to the residents."

There is also the question of whether North Korea became a food exporter during this famine period. A Japanese visitor to the Kim palaces reports seeing a letter of thanks for food aid donated to an African country. There were also unconfirmed rumors of North Korea trading food for arms.

What effect did the famine have on the Kim family and its supporters? Almost none at all. In the summer of 2003 the memoirs of the Dear Leader's Japanese chef were published in Japan. The chef revealed that Kim and his children (who were known as "Princes" and "Princesses") continued to live the high life while his subjects starved. His menu includes the most expensive delicacies from around the world. He had 40,000 bottles of imported wine in his cellars. When his jet ski wasn't fast enough, he ordered a bigger and faster one. When he wanted to get around one of his extensive estates, he just picked out a Honda motorcycle from a catalogue and it appeared as if by magic. For entertainment there was fishing, horseback riding, bowling, billiards, satellite TV, and films in the private screening rooms.

The Communist elite did all right as well. The Korean Bar-B-Que restaurants in Pyongyang were constantly filled. An American observer noted that a high school for the elite had healthy children "comparable with those in South Korea or Japan."[62]

Some of the food aid did manage to find its way to children and average North Koreans. But substantially fewer North Koreans received aid than the World Food Program claims.

What did communist China do during the famine? The communist Chinese were total opportunists in this tragedy. They refused to cooperate with the UN so no one really knows how much food aid they actually gave. China secretly admitted to the UN that their aid was specifically designed to keep the North Korean military happy so they would not overthrow the Kim dynasty.[63]

Did the international relief effort moderate North Korean behavior? No. The international food aid program and North Korean aggression against others existed in parallel universes. While the massive effort to help the North Korean people was in full swing, the following occurred:

- Two submarine-launched espionage operations were detected in South Korea
- North Korea fired a ballistic missile across the Japanese islands
- North Korea continued to traffic narcotics trafficking to Japan and South Korea
- North Korea continued to send nuclear weapons and missiles to terrorist countries

- North Korea continued to engage in espionage and sabotage rehearsals in Japan and South Korea
- The North Korean secret uranium enrichment program prospered

The amount of physical and mental suffering that occurred during the North Korean famine is more than we can really imagine.[64] A substantial portion of the older generation simply disappeared. An American observer passing through a North Korean city noted the total absence of older or even middle-aged people. The reason? Grandparents and parents had given their rations to their children while they, themselves, either starved to death or died of malnutrition-related illnesses. When they could get it, people drowned themselves in alcohol.

Sadly, it may be that the international food aid program saved the North Korean regime at a moment when it was most vulnerable. If there had been no international food aid at all or if the United Nations officials had demanded openness and an equitable distribution for the food, Kim's regime may have collapsed. Andrew Natsios, the American administrator of the Agency for International Development, offers the following analysis:

> Had the ration even in these very lean years been evenly distributed among the entire population, people might have been able to use their coping mechanism to avoid famine. Such an egalitarian ration, however, would have shaken the tenuous foundations of the state. It would have caused panic among the party cadres, internal security apparatus, and the military who might have seen themselves starving as the rest of the population did, and it was on these three groups that the survival of the Kim dynasty depended.[65]

But the UN made no such demands. Likewise, the Clinton administration did not demand an end to North Korean aggression as a condition for sending American food aid, nor did it pressure the Chinese to use their leverage on Pyongyang. By utter ruthlessness in Pyongyang, aided by weakness in Washington and at the UN, Kim's regime remained in place. The hypocrisy continues today. In the fall of 2003, an American government official had a meeting with a senior North Korean diplomat in New York. His mission was to try to persuade Pyongyang to be more open on the distribution of recent shipments of international food aid to North Korea. The North Korean diplomat dismissed him with contempt. Nothing has changed.

DEMOCRACY AND HUMAN RIGHTS

The Kim family has ruled over North Korea for fifty-eight years. These have been years of unremitting state terror directed at the population, famine, and an exploding political camp system. The people of North Korea are worse off than they were even under Japanese colonialism. In the same fifty-eight years, South Korea has moved from authoritarian rule to full, and often raucous, democracy. The people of South Korea live far better than Koreans have ever lived in their homeland before.

Communist China has been the guarantor of the North and the United States has been the guarantor of the South. It's worthwhile looking at the stewardship of each. The Americans recognized that South Korea was under unremitting internal and external aggression generated by North Korea, but felt that the key to success for the South was democratization and respect for human rights. Throughout the 1960s–1980s, the leader of the Republic of Korea was always an army general. But most officials, including at the cabinet level, were civilians.

Beginning in 1987, the U.S. began a major push on the South Korean leadership to achieve democracy and human rights.[66] President Ronald Reagan felt the time was right to move. He appointed Gaston Sigur the top State Department official on Asia and James

Lilley as the U.S. ambassador to South Korea.[67] Sigur began with a public speech in New York calling for constitutional reform aimed at regaining civilian control over the South Korean military. In June, President Reagan sent a personal letter to then-South Korean President Chun Doo Hwan pointedly supporting "democratic institutions" in South Korea. To reinforce the point, Ambassador Lilley personally delivered the letter after meeting with U.S. military commanders in South Korea. He was able to tell South Korean officials that the entire United States government was united behind the idea of democratic reform in Seoul.[68] The message was received and understood. Free and fair elections were held within a year.

Not surprisingly, communist China has not attempted to promote democracy or human rights or even halt the North Korean programs in weapons of mass destruction or nuclear proliferation. Rather, it has been an enabler of Kim's regime. Beijing has not even shown the most basic humanitarianism toward the North Korean people. Every day, PLA guards turn back dozens of North Korean refugees to their tormentors.[69] With the early help of Joseph Stalin, Beijing created North Korean regime, supported its aggressions, rescued it from the United Nations, nurtured it for decades with subsidized food so it could spend its money on weapons, and today keeps it from collapse. The tyranny in Pyongyang has so far suited Beijing's purpose, and its continued existence depends on China's support.

8

LABORATORIES OF DEATH

Based on North Korean actions to date, DIA assesses that North Korea will continue its nuclear weapons program despite any agreement it signs to the contrary.[1]

— Lt. Gen. James Clapper, Jr.,
Director of the Defense Intelligence Agency

O n December 1, 1994, the U.S. Senate Foreign Relations Committee was holding an important hearing on the Agreed Framework on nuclear matters between the United States and North Korea. North Korea had agreed to give up its nuclear weapons program and, in return, the United States had agreed to pay for substitute forms of energy in North Korea. Though the treaty did not need Senate confirmation, implementing it would require hundreds of millions of taxpayer dollars from Congress. President Clinton had sent Ambassador Robert Gallucci to the Senate to defend the Agreed Framework. The underlying issue was this: Could the North Koreans be counted on not to cheat on the agreement?

Senator Larry Pressler, a thoughtful Republican from South Dakota, was no novice on these issues. Indeed, when it came to arms control and nuclear matters, he was probably the most knowledgeable senator on the committee. As the former chairman of the Foreign Relations Committee's arms control subcommittee, it was he who demanded accountability in a similar situation with Pakistan, as the author of the "Pressler Amendment." In an effort to prevent the spread of nuclear weapons, this amendment included conditions that American foreign aid to Pakistan would only be given if the country remained free of nuclear weapons. Despite these efforts, Pakistan crossed the "red line" toward nuclear weapon production and the aid was cut off. As Pressler entered the committee hearing room that day, he knew full well the pitfalls of nuclear agreements and verification.

Senator Pressler addressed the committee, noting in his opening remarks that North Korea is a "hostile power" and that the terms of the Agreed Framework did not provide the International Atomic Energy Agency (IAEA) with the "go anywhere in North Korea, go anytime" inspection authority needed to detect cheating.[2] Ambassador Gallucci agreed that was an "accurate" characterization. Senator Pressler then asked Ambassador Gallucci if he agreed with, or was even aware of, the following statement made earlier that year to Congress by Air Force Lieutenant General James Clapper, Jr., the director of the Defense Intelligence Agency: "Based on North Korean actions to date, DIA assesses that North Korea will continue its nuclear weapons program despite any agreement it signs to the contrary."[3]

Ambassador Gallucci was visibly surprised.[4] Clapper's statement flatly predicted the inevitable failure of the Agreed Framework, the Clinton's administration's entire approach to North Korea. Gallucci was placed on the defensive. He replied, "I cannot tell you, Senator, that North Korea is going to abide by this agreement." But the ambassador went on to gamely predict that the terms of the inspections, though limited, would still allow the United States to detect any cheating by the North Koreans. Senator Pressler, clearly at odds with this point of view, declared he would not vote to fund the Agreed Framework with taxpayers' money. Unfortunately, Senator Pressler was outvoted. Over the next several years, billions of taxpayer dollars from the United States, South Korea, and Japan flowed to North Korea to provide heating oil and to construct two nuclear power plants in North Korea for electrical production.[5]

President Clinton clearly thought the implementation of the Agreed Framework was a major foreign policy success of his administration. At the time of the signing, he stated, "This agreement will help achieve a long standing and vital American objective, an end to the threat of nuclear proliferation on the Korean peninsula."[6] Two years later, at the 1996 Democratic National Convention, Clinton again declared, "In the last four years, we have frozen North Korea's nuclear weapons program."[7] In the final days of the Clinton administration, his boasts were echoed by then Secretary of State Madeleine Albright, who told PBS that with the "Agreed Framework that we worked out in '94, we were able to freeze their fissile [nuclear] material programs."[8] These were indeed strong guarantees.

As it turned out, Ambassador Gallucci and the rest of the Clinton administration were tragically wrong. The Agreed Framework was designed to halt one type of nuclear weapons program, the one based on plutonium. But by summer of 2002, all relevant America intelligence agencies concluded that North Korea had for several years been embarking on a secret program to produce highly enriched uranium.[9] Senator Pressler and Lieutenant General Clapper were proven correct in their distrust of trust Kim Jong Il to abide by the agreement. (As noted in Chapter 1, when the U.S. State Department confronted the North Koreans about their violation of the Agreed Framework in October, they shot back, "Not only YES, but HELL, YES and you tell that to your president!"[10])

Back in 1994, North Korea had enough plutonium to make one or possibly two crude nuclear devices. By the end of 2003, North Korea was simultaneously running two state-of-the-art nuclear weapons programs and rapidly developing ballistic missiles with the capability to strike any point in the United States. Former Secretary of State James Baker said it best when he noted that, "This is exceedingly dangerous and enormously troubling. What it is not, however, is surprising. Rather, it is the natural and foreseeable result of the 1994 Framework Agreement between the United States and North Korea."[11]

Both the Republicans and the Democrats who were on the Senate Foreign Relations Committee in December 1994 thought that the Agreed Framework was defective. It was in fact the Democrats who had tipped off Senator Pressler, their Republican colleague, to General Clapper's prediction—a prediction he had given to another senate committee. The Democrats were in a difficult position: They had to show loyalty to their president, but they also suspected the agreement would make the American government hostage to Kim Jung Il's inevitable cheating. More cynical observers, mostly Democrats, were taking private bets on how soon the Agreed Framework would blow up in the White House's face.

A RUSSIAN START

Pyongyang had long had help in developing its nuclear program. In the mid–1950s, the Soviets set up the Dubna Atomic Energy Research Institute to train scientists from other communist countries in nuclear physics. As part of this, the Soviets and North Koreans signed an agreement in 1956 to cooperate on the peaceful use of nuclear energy.[12] In Pushkin Square,[13] a short walk from the Kremlin, a retired but still active nuclear scientist from the Soviet era confirmed to me, "[W]e trained North Korean scientists at the Dubna Atomic Energy Research Institute but it was only for peaceful purposes."[14]

In the mid–1960s, the Soviets helped North Korea establish a small five-megawatt nuclear research reactor at Yongbyon, sixty miles north of Pyongyang. About a dozen years later, in return for assistance from the International Atomic Energy Agency in uranium mining, Pyongyang put this reactor under safeguards and allowed the inspectors to visit. A reactor this small can produce a tiny amount of plutonium but it would take several years to produce enough plutonium for one bomb.

BEIJING TAKES OVER

A crucial moment in the North Korean nuclear weapons program occurred in the spring of 1975. The capitals of Indochina—Phnom Penh, Vientiane, and Saigon—were falling to communist armies, and fear swept through the other Asian governments allied at that time with Washington. American prestige in Asia was at an all-time low. It did not go unnoticed in Northeast Asia that there had been no retribution when North Korea killed an American sailor aboard the USS *Pueblo* in 1968 and thirty-one American servicemen aboard a U.S. Navy aircraft in 1969. President Nixon's speech on Guam in 1969 had signaled that American allies in Asia would have to look more to their own devices for their security. The total takeover of Indochina by communist forces had also made everyone wonder if the Americans were retreating across the Pacific.

The Great Leader of North Korea, thinking the time was right for another Korean War, rushed to Beijing to seek a joint blitzkrieg on Seoul with the communist Chinese. But it was an inopportune moment for Beijing. China was still being torn apart by Mao's ten-year Cultural Revolution (1966–1976). Military modernization of the People's Liberation Army had been neglected in the state of political ferment. The Sino–Soviet split of 1960 had cut off Beijing from its main arms supplier for a decade and half. Mao Zedong had just recently been diagnosed with Lou Gehrig's disease.[15] The communist leadership in China was not ready for another military adventure on the Korean peninsula. Besides, although the Americans may have been weakened, Seoul was not. South Korea's President Park Chung Hee had begun a major military modernization program. Having lost their beloved "National Mother" in 1974 to a North Korean assassin, South Korea was on the alert for another attack from the North. Beijing knew a second Korean War would not be a walkover.

Faced with such North Korean aggression and a weakening American presence, President Park began a highly secret nuclear weapons program. The Americans had tactical nuclear weapons in South Korea; in theory, the South was under the U.S. nuclear umbrella but that protection could be withdrawn at short notice.[16] Building South Korea's own nuclear weapons program would take years and President Park thought it was best to start early.

Two particular events seem to have triggered President Park's decision—a humiliating defeat of the South Korean Navy at the hands of the North and the decision by President Nixon to withdraw the American Seventh Division from South Korea.[17] President Park kept his nuclear program secret from the Americans and worked with the French and other suppliers. However, by the end of 1974, the American Embassy in Seoul alerted Washington that a South Korean nuclear weapons program was underway.[18] Over the next year and half, Washington and Seoul struggled with the issue. Finally, according to *Washington Post* reporter Don Oberdorfer, Donald Rumsfeld, then on his first tour as secretary of defense, threatened that the United States would "review the entire spectrum of its relations with the ROK [South Korea]" if the program did not cease.[19] President Park reluctantly gave into American demands and ended South Korea's nuclear weapons program. Today, South Korea is a signatory to the Nuclear Non-Proliferation Treaty and all of its nuclear power stations are under international safeguards.

United States policy towards South Korea is certainly open to reasonable criticism, but it must be acknowledged that in general it has been a successful policy. Washington has helped the people of South Korea, who, despite living under constant threat from the Kim regime, are prospering and taking their rightful place in the international community. The United States has made certain that

South Korea is not a threat to its neighbors, no matter how much we sympathize with the daily aggression it must live under.

In contrast, Beijing helped launch the Great Leader's nuclear weapons program. They expanded training for North Korean nuclear scientists in weapons production. Within two years, a top member of the North Korean government was the guest of honor at a nuclear weapons test in western China. On the same visit, this North Korean official had a sit-down with the Seventh Ministry of Machine Building, which was then in charge of Beijing's ballistic missile program.[20]

During the 1980s, the North Korean regime began to build three newer and larger nuclear power reactors. As allied intelligence watched the construction progress, it soon became obvious that these reactors were built for the production of plutonium. Although North Koreans claimed that these were designed to produce electricity for civilian use, the reactors were not hooked up to the power grid. Allied intelligence also discovered that the North Koreans were building an enormous plutonium reprocessing plant, also at Yongbyon. Plutonium from a power reactor has to be reprocessed before it can be turned into weapons-grade nuclear explosive materials. Putting the new nuclear power reactors together with the plutonium reprocessing plant made it clear that a serious nuclear weapons program was underway in North Korea.

It was at that time, in 1985, that Moscow reasserted itself.[21] That spring, Mikhail Gorbachev became general secretary of the Communist Party of the Soviet Union. Moscow was as suspicious of what the North Koreans were doing (possibly with Chinese help) as the Americans. In December, a senior North Korean official came to Moscow to ask for a continuation of the subsidized trading system that kept Pyongyang afloat. Moscow told the North Korean that in order to continue receiving aid, Pyongyang would have to sign onto the Nuclear Non-Proliferation Treaty and put the new reactors under international inspection. Thus pushed, Pyongyang signed.

There is much speculation as to why the Soviets suddenly began to use their leverage on North Korea. Gorbachev was attempting reforms to make the Soviet Union a more responsible party in the field of arms control. Perhaps also, as Moscow now claims, the Soviets felt that because of their earlier work with the North Korean nuclear program, they would be blamed if Pyongyang were to launch a full nuclear weapons program.[22] They also were receiving intelligence proving their fears to be valid. In 1990 the head of the KGB, Vladimir Kyuchkov, told Soviet Communist Party bosses that North Korea had an unknown number of nuclear weapons. (Currently, the KGB is reported to believe that North Korea is pursuing nuclear weapons but doesn't have them yet.[23]) The Soviets were finally acknowledging that Kim's regime did its best to deceive the world. Since joining the international nuclear inspection system, North Korea has continued to engage in nineteen years of lying, cheating, and wrangling.

Unraveling the nuclear crisis in North Korea means taking a look at the dark underbelly of international arms smuggling. Motivated by greed and a lust for power, corrupt politicians, scientists, and businessmen wield previously unimaginable powers of destruction. This "mutual aid society" of nuclear warmongers deals in training, parts, technology, machine tools, and other components in the production of nuclear weapons. Its members export their expertise and import what they need, and do so with the utmost secrecy.

Sitting at the center of all this is the Chinese Communist Party in Beijing.

CHINA–NORTH KOREA MISSILE COOPERATION

When the Chinese agreed to jumpstart North Korea's nuclear weapons program in 1975, Kim Il Sung wanted short-range ballistic missiles capable of striking South Korea. The Communist Chinese did not have a missile matching Kim's requirements, but they agreed to help him develop one. This missile would have had a 360-mile range and a one-ton payload, just enough to bring all of South Korea under nuclear threat. This missile was probably never built—canceled due to political upheaval in China—but the North Korean engineers were able to learn much about engine design and missile production from the Chinese.[24]

In 1980, the North Koreans obtained some Soviet Scud rockets from Egypt. With Chinese help, North Korean scientists improved the Scud's engine design, metallurgy, and airframe design. The Chinese also provided more training for North Korean missile engineers and some critical high-tech machine tools. North Korea's improved Scuds were sold to Iran for its war with Iraq, thus making Iran a financial partner for the next generation of missiles.

At the end of the decade, the North Koreans began to build the Nodong series of missiles—the Nodong (810 mile range) and the Nodong 2 (900 mile range)—both of which are still based on improved Scud designs. As many as five hundred of these missiles might have been produced already.[25] North Korea also began work on a new class of longer-range, multistage rockets, the Taepodong and the Taepodong 2. This is surprising since moving from a single-stage to a multistage missile system requires a significant leap in technology. Multistage rockets require stronger materials, more powerful engines, and more precise design tolerances to weather the stresses of launch. Crucial knowledge is needed to control the stage separation without sending the second stage flying out of control. For these reasons, a third-world country with limited resources like North Korea would have faced immense difficulties in trying to produce a multistage rocket.[26]

But in 1994, according to the *Wall Street Journal*, the U.S. Defense Intelligence Agency discovered the North Koreans already had a mockup of a multistage rocket. The first stage of this rocket was almost identical to that of the Chinese CSS-2 intermediate range ballistic missile. A DIA official concluded, "Presumably, the

only way they [North Korean engineers] would know how to build
something the size of the CSS-2 is either physical transfer of the
beast or of engineers familiar with the program."[27] This mockup
eventually became the Taepodong 2.

North Korea has no qualms about being a profit-sharing proxy
of Chinese missile makers and sellers. Already ostracized from the
civilized world as international pariahs, the North Koreans have
little fear of being caught either selling a (Chinese or
Chinese–North Korean) missile system or cooperating with other
members of the infamous "mutual aid society."

ISLAMABAD, BEIJING, PYONGYANG TRIANGLE

Perhaps that is why, in 1998, an Indian diplomat dining at a
Korean barbecue restaurant in the Koryu Hotel—reputed to be the
best such place in Pyongyang—spotted Abdul Qadeer Khan, father
of Pakistan's nuclear programs, eating there as well without any
attempt at disguise.[28] Indeed, a North Korean defector reports that
dozens of Pakistani nuclear engineers went to North Korea and an
equal number of North Korean missile specialists have been working in Pakistan.[29]

According to U.S. Army Intelligence, Chinese assistance to the
Pakistani nuclear weapons program began in 1974 when Chinese
scientists were assigned to train Pakistani researchers. Army intelligence also reported that Chinese were providing secret assistance
to a Pakistani nuclear weapons facility near Islamabad.[30] Gary Milholin, director of the University of Wisconsin Project on Nuclear
Arms Control, is one of America's leading experts on the spread of
nuclear weapons. He once told Robert Windrem of NBC News, "If
you subtract China's help from Pakistan's nuclear program, there
is no nuclear program."[31]

In 1996 there were several discoveries of China–Pakistan
nuclear collaboration over the years. The State Department admitted to Republican Senator Robert Bennett of Utah that Chinese

military companies had transferred critical nuclear materials-making equipment to Pakistan as well as having provided "other cooperation" in the nuclear field. With further prodding, the State Department reluctantly admitted that "other cooperation" indeed meant "weapons development." It turned out that Beijing had provided not only the nuclear materials, but also the technology to make them explode.[32] Later in the same year, Bill Gertz of the *Washington Times* obtained a top secret CIA document revealing that the Chinese were smuggling sophisticated equipment useful for producing nuclear weapons into Pakistan.[33] U.S. intelligence concluded that the Chinese military was taking elaborate measures to "deceive" the United States about the extent of its assistance in building the Pakistani bomb.[34]

At this point, the only thing Pakistan lacked was a delivery system for their bomb. In 1990 India and Pakistan had come very near to an all out nuclear war. Thankfully, the crisis passed, primarily because Pakistan did not have a missile delivery system for its nuclear device. Shortly thereafter, in 1991, China sold Pakistan solid fuel M-11s, a short-range ballistic missile capable of carrying a nuclear weapon. President George H.W. Bush's administration exacted sanctions on both the Chinese and the Pakistanis for this smuggling operation. In the short time between the 1992 election and the inauguration of President Bill Clinton, another batch of M-11s were delivered to Pakistan from Beijing, leading to another round of U.S. sanctions. Despite Beijing's solemn promises to various American politicians, the Chinese were repeatedly caught selling missiles, missile technology, critical parts, and even an entire missile-producing factory to Pakistan throughout the 1990s.[35]

Enter Beijing's proxy, the North Koreans. In 1993, while the Clinton administration was placing sanctions on the Chinese for the second batch of M-11s to Pakistan, the North Koreans and the Pakistanis christened their missile collaboration. In the mid–1990s, North Korea supplied Pakistan with a number of Nodong missiles, (which the Pakistanis call the Ghauri) which use Chinese guidance systems.

This continued into the next decade, when, just one month after the U.S. confronted North Korea about its uranium program in October 2002, David Sanger of the *New York Times* dropped a front-page story in the Sunday paper.[36] American intelligence had discovered that Pakistani Air Force C-130 cargo planes were flying back and forth between Islamabad and Pyongyang, exchanging North Korean missiles and missile technology for Pakistani nuclear weapons-making technology. What Sanger did not report is that the C-130 Hercules cannot fly nonstop between North Korea and Pakistan. It had to stop to refuel on each trip—at a Chinese Air Force base in western China.

Here was a crystal-clear depiction of the three-way smuggling operation between Pakistan, communist China, and North Korea on weapons of mass destruction and ballistic missiles. From North Korea, Pakistan gets the longer-range multistage missiles. In return, North Korea gets technology and critical parts for its highly enriched uranium program. Both the North Korean multistage missile program and the Pakistani nuclear program are based on Chinese models and contain critical Chinese parts. It seems likely that the C-130 jet stopovers in western China are more than just refueling stops.

In the spring of 2003, German intelligence caught a North Korean diplomat assigned to the International Atomic Energy Agency headquarters in Vienna trying to purchase 200 metric tons of a special, restricted, aluminum tubing sufficient to make 3,500 to 4,000 gas centrifuges for uranium enrichment. The dimensions of the aluminum tubing were identical to those used in Pakistan's uranium enrichment program, strongly suggesting that the North Koreans are using a Pakistani design. The aluminum tubing was loaded aboard a French ship for delivery to a branch of the Shenyang Aircraft Company in China. The German exporter had a letter on the aircraft company's letterhead, explaining that the aluminum tubing was going to be converted to airplane fuel tanks.[37] Shenyang Aircraft Company, one of the largest aircraft makers in China, is a player in China's defense industrial complex and is under the direction of the People's Liberation Army. The branch assigned to receive the tubing is located in the city of Dandong, just across the Yalu River from North Korea. German prosecutors say that this particular branch has a history of being used as a cover for "evasive deliveries"—arms smuggling.[38]

Mark Hibbs, of the respected journal *Nucleonics Week*, concluded that if the North Korean smuggling operation had been successful, "North Korea would have been able to produce close to 90 kilograms of weapons-grade high-enriched uranium per year, enough for about a half-dozen nuclear explosive devices."[39]

The North Korean diplomat to the IAEA has since disappeared. Strangely enough for a North Korean diplomat assigned to the IAEA headquarters in Vienna, his mailing address was an apartment in an upscale neighborhood in Beijing. Investigators noted expensive SUVs and Audi sedans parked in his garage.[40] His story illustrates the fact that communist Chinese authorities have often looked the other way when North Korean companies set up shop in China and use Chinese addresses for arms smuggling operations.

POISON GAS AND GERMS

In 1992 Pyongyang handed out gas masks to every member of the North Korean population. This sent alarms throughout national security circles in the United States, Japan, and South Korea. A dozen years later, it's still not clear what triggered the distribution of gas masks. However, the incident has drawn useful attention to North Korea's chemical and biological weapons program.

Although it is the nuclear and missile programs that receive the most international publicity, North Korea also has advanced chemical and biological weapons programs, their origins going back several decades. In 1954, China and the Soviet Union provided North

Korea with chemical agents and the technology to make poison gas.[41] According to a South Korean "defense white paper," North Korea is estimated to have a stockpile of 2,500 to 5,000 tons of various lethal chemical weapons. By most accounts, North Korea has the capability to produce common chemical weapons—nerve agents, blood agents, and mustard gas—in large quantities. The South Korean Foreign Ministry estimated that just two tons of North Korean poison gas would murder 100,000 civilians on the peninsula.[42] (South Korea has an extensive chemical and biological weapons defense system.)

Allied defense planners in Seoul predict that any North Korean attack on U.S. and South Korean forces will begin with a poison gas attack delivered by artillery shells, rockets, and even aircraft. This would render airbases, airfields, and ports unable to receive reinforcements. The U.S. House of Representatives advisory group on North Korea noted, "the concept of international abhorrence regarding chemical and biological warfare carries little weight in the DPRK [North Korea]."[43] A South Korean specialist recently remarked, "The KPA [North Korean Army] has traditionally viewed chemical and biological weapons as an integral part of any military offensive. . . . It is well understood that North Korea will use chemical weapons . . . in order to generate casualties of 10,000 to 20,000 among the American forces stationed in South Korea so that anti-war sentiments may rise across the board in the United States."[44]

Pyongyang also has a large germ warfare program. According to undersecretary of state John Bolton, "the U.S. government believes that North Korea has one of the most robust offensive bioweapons programs on earth."[45] North Korea is suspected of having the military capability to inflict a dozen infectious diseases, including plague, smallpox, and anthrax. As noted in the previous chapter, this apparent willingness to inflict horrendous infectious diseases on a population is underscored by reliable reports that North Korea has used political prisoners as subjects for testing biological weapons.

The North Korean chemical and biowarfare threat is not limited to South Korea. Japan and the American forces stationed there are within easy range of North Korean missiles. Poison gas and deadly infectious diseases also make excellent weapons for terrorism and sabotage. It seems very likely that the North Korean agents who have come and gone at will in Japan for the past several decades have been rehearsing a chemical and biological weapons attack. Even after the trauma caused by the 1997 Sarin gas attack by the Aum Shinrikio cult that murdered twelve of civilians in the Tokyo subway, Japan is still not adequately prepared to handle large numbers of chemical and biological weapons casualties.

TARGETING AMERICA

Ever since President Ronald Reagan inaugurated an American missile defense program almost twenty years ago, it has been the most contentious issue of national defense. With some exceptions, Republicans have continued to support a strong missile defense program, while Democrats have expressed more skepticism. In the 1990s, with Republicans controlling the Congress and President Clinton, a democrat, holding the White House, it was constant "push-pull."

In July 1998 a congressionally mandated commission, headed by Donald Rumsfeld, concluded that "rogue nations could acquire an Inter-Continental Ballistic Missile capability in a short time and the intelligence community may not be able to detect it." The Clinton administration swatted away this intelligence, replying in a letter from the chairman of the Joint Chiefs, General Hugh Shelton, to Republican Senator James Inhofe of Oklahoma, "We remain confident that the intelligence community can provide the necessary warning of indigenous development and deployment by a rogue state of an ICBM threat to the United States."[46] General Shelton's letter was dated August 24, 1998; Six days later North Korea fired off a three-stage missile that literally flew in the face of the Clinton administration response, hurtling across the world to land at the doorstop of the United States.

This landmark journey progressed as follows. The first stage successfully separated and fell into the Sea of Japan, between Japan and the Korean Peninsula. The second stage flew directly over the Japanese islands, passing not far from the U.S. Air Force base at Misawa. The third stage failed to launch a satellite but the warhead reached Alaska.[47] North Korea had demonstrated the theoretical potential of lofting a 440-pound warhead as far as the Mississippi River and a 220-pound warhead anywhere on the East Coast.[48]

Tokyo was stunned. The U.S. intelligence community was as embarrassed as General Shelton. They certainly did not expect the North Koreans to drop a warhead on the United States, much less on Alaska, a state represented by the chairman of the Senate Defense Appropriations Subcommittee.[49] Opponents of missile defense, at home and abroad, ran for political cover.

What the intelligence community had missed, and what was the crucial piece of the puzzle, was the China connection. Yet, there were plenty of clues along the way:

- According to Gary Milholin, as early as the 1970s, the Chinese were assisting the North Koreans with "technology for rocket engine design and production, metallurgy, and airframes"[50]
- By the mid-1990s, it was known that two hundred North Korean missile engineers had traveled to China for training[51]
- In 1994, the U.S. Defense Intelligence Agency had already discovered the connection between the Chinese CSS-2 intermediate range ballistic missile and the North Korean Taepodong
- Semi-annual proliferation reports to Congress regularly covered Chinese and North Korean missile cooperation
- Republican Congressman Chris Cox of California had revealed that the North Korean satellite was a carbon copy of a Chinese satellite[52]

But what the intelligence community really missed was the traveling "X-man,"[53] General Xiong Guangkai, the PLA's deputy chief of staff for intelligence and Beijing's point man on North Korean–Chinese military-to-military relations. He visited Pyongyang in early August of 1998. Soon thereafter, the North Koreans startled the world with its three-stage missile launch. It is widely assumed in Washington that Xiong gave the North Koreans the "Go!" signal.

On North Korea's side of its border with China there is a network of deep underground bases to serve as missile storage and launch areas. In 2001, a defector reported twelve such underground bases and it appears the North Koreans are building more of them.[54] Their location is well chosen. These bases are high priority targets in the event of a war or crisis, but one would have to think carefully before striking so close to the Chinese border. The Chinese should have enough leverage with Pyongyang to have forced the missile bases away from the border. By acquiescing to their establishment there, the Chinese are giving the North Koreans a subtle measure of cover.

In September 2003, as Pyongyang prepared to "celebrate" fifty-five years of rule by the Kim family, American spy satellites detected a new missile in North Korea. U.S. officials described the missile as "a completely new and different missile system, an intermediate range missile system based on improved different technology."[55]

The new North Korean missile looks like the R-27/SS-N-6, a submarine-launched missile designed by the Makayev Engineering Bureau during Soviet times. This missile has certain features[56] and a longer range that make it a serious threat to Japan and even Guam. Its discovery is sure to escalate the arms race in Northeast Asia. As of this writing, the new missile has not been tested or even displayed in public. It is unclear whether North Korea successfully acquired the technology by sneaking right under the noses of the Russian security services or whether Moscow knew and approved. If it was indeed an official sale or transfer, then Washington must reevaluate its estimates of where the Russian Federation fits into the North Korean equation.

By contrast, there are no questions about Beijing's involvement in North Korea. Beijing has initiated and fostered these deadly weapons systems for decades:

- Without help from Beijing, North Korea could not have started its nuclear weapons program
- Without a Pakistan nuclear program, North Korea would not have been able to violate the Agreed Framework
- Without help from Beijing, North Korea could not have completed its long-range missile delivery program. And without a North Korean long-range missile program, there would be no Pakistani long-range liquid-fueled[57] missile program
- Without help from Beijing, North Korea could not have started its poison gas program as early as it did
- In early 2003, the CIA caught the Chinese shipping a special chemical to North Korea's nuclear weapons program[58]

The Chinese Communist Party has initiated and promoted weapons of mass destruction and ballistic missile programs in North Korea knowing full well that there is no legitimate defensive need for these weapons. The CIA reports that in late 2000 communist China made a public pledge "not to assist, in any way any country in the development of ballistic missiles that could be used to deliver nuclear weapons." But China is doing just that with North Korea, Pakistan, Iran, and Libya.[59] Beijing is clearly lying when it declares its desire for a nuclear weapons-free Korean peninsula.

9

MERCHANTS OF DEATH

China Shields North Korea on Atom Issue

—Headline from the *New York Times*

The Indian Customs and Revenue Intelligence officials[1] call it the "Kandla Catch" after the busy port on India's west coast where the bust was made. What they found was a complete missile factory aboard a North Korean ship bound for Libya. Allied intelligence and law enforcement officers had been chasing the Chinese arms merchants and their partners for almost twenty years, with only limited success. The "Kandla Catch" was a big break, dramatically increasing allied material intelligence on the Chinese–North Korean arms trade in WMDs.

In late June 1999, the Kuwolsan, an ordinary-looking merchantman flying the North Korean flag, docked in Kandla to deliver a load of sugar. Acting on "specific information about suspicious cargo" (code words for allied intelligence information), Indian officials demanded access to the ship. This led to a fistfight between the North Korean crew and the Indian officers who were, at this point, unarmed. The North Koreans even tried to seal the hatch while the Indian inspectors were inside. Not about to be bullied by the North Koreans, the Indians came back with arms. The cargo declaration stated that the wooden boxes onboard were water purification equipment destined for "Malta Economic Joint Corporation." Instead of water purification equipment, the Indians found that these boxes contained missile-making equipment and related parts labeled "SCUD B" and "SCUD C."

The boat also contained an almost complete assembly line for missiles, including blueprints for missiles and pages of technical drawings and descriptions. The centerpiece of this catch was an "integrated machining center" with "MADE IN CHINA" stamped on it with twenty-five tons of milling, grinding, bending, and other large tools all on one platform. If Qaddafi wanted SCUD Bs and Cs, he can buy them completely made up or in a kit. But if he wanted to build his own ballistic missiles in Libya, he had to have this integrated machining center from China.

Along with the integrated machining center, there was also a variety of machinery used to make missiles and critical components—a hydraulic press, special alloy steel tubing, metal bending machines, forged steel bar stock for rocket motors, sheet metal to encase the outside of the missile, metal rings that appear to be rocket motor casings, air bottles used to guide missile warheads, nosecones, and instrumentation for testing and calibrating missile components.

Steve Engleberg and Michael Gordon, writing in the *New York Times*, first revealed Qaddafi's interest in WMDs in 1989.[2] They found he was building a massive chemical weapons plant with equipment provided by German firms. Over the years, other poison gas plants were discovered to be under construction in Libya. Chinese military firms were named as the key suppliers.[3]

Qaddafi had plenty of poison gas but no delivery system. Because he was based in the southern shores of the Mediterranean, he couldn't reach his prime targets, U.S. military bases in Europe. He had purchased some early model SCUDs and fired one at an American base on the island of Lampedusa. It fell short. Then, in the early 1980s, he recruited some renegade German engineers to work on an Intermediate Range Ballistic Missile project. Washington, having discovered this, was able to persuade the German government to close the project.[4] By the 1990s, Libya was under UN sanctions because of the PanAm bombing, and even shady companies were weary of dealing with Qaddafi.

The communist Chinese–North Korean partnership was the perfect setup for Qaddafi. As the CIA told the Congress, "North Korea has no constraints on its sales of ballistic missiles and related technology."[5] The Chinese became missile suppliers to Qaddafi both directly and in partnership with North Korea and others.

In the summer of 1991, allied intelligence services picked up reports that a North Korean military delegation was in Libya conducting preliminary discussions with Qaddafi on the sale of the 620-mile range Nodong missile.[6] North Korean specialist Joseph S. Bermudez, Jr. had reported that the North Koreans had already developed chemical warheads for their SCUD Bs a year earlier.[7] In 1995 the Chinese and the North Koreans were discovered working together to deliver a longer range SCUD to Libya through an Iranian firm for the payment of $31 million.[8] During the mid- to late 1990s Qaddafi continued to import missiles and missile parts from China and North Korea.[9] But Qaddafi's primary ambition has always been to manufacture either his own poison gas or a ballistic missile.

To the allied intelligence officers, to study international arms smuggling operations like that of Qaddafi is almost like searching for the path of a cold, dark river. They know where the river originates and ends, but very little about its meandering path. What they do most often find is the occasional small fish—in one case, for example, a Taiwanese businessman passing through the Zurich airport bound for Libya with North Korean missile parts in his backpack.

The "Kandla Catch" is a significant example because it reveals exactly how the international arms smuggling system operates. International investigators have also been able to gain some understanding of how a missile factory is assembled. This particular seized cargo had dozens of microelectronic components labeled "Made in Japan," that were probably destined for missile guidance systems. Did these components come aboard the "Big Ship" that travels between Japan and North Korea? Did they come through communist China? Since the cargo contained almost, but not a complete assembly line, investigators followed up on questions such as: Were some critical parts due to come directly from China or indirectly through Iran or Syria? Had they already arrived or were they delayed somehow?

The investigators also recognized that there is a great deal of money to be made in a secret missile transfer operation—assembly, calibration, service, training, and development. As evidence of that fact were the "personal items apparently intended for North Korean workers, including cookbooks in Korean, Korean spices, pickles and acupuncture sets" found aboard the Kuwolsan.[10] Presumably, Qaddafi was paying North Koreans to set up the facility. According to a later report, Libya is also paying the Chinese to train their own Libyan military personnel to operate North Korean missiles.[11]

What is particularly striking about this missile factory is that it is for SCUDs, not the longer range Nodongs. It appears that the North Koreans drive a hard bargain: Qaddafi gets a domestic factory, but only to produce the older model missile; he still has to buy the new model, the Nodong, directly from North Korea. The Chinese drive the same deal with North Korea: What became the Taepodong, is based on an older Chinese missile. The Chinese are by no means selling the production rights to their newest and best models to everyone.

Like clockwork, every six months the CIA reports to Congress that there is continued missile trading among North Korea, China, and Libya. The CIA warns that "Libya's capability is improving and with continued foreign assistance it will probably achieve a Medium Range Ballistic Missile capability—a long desired goal— or extended-range SCUD capability."[12] In addition to the Taiwanese businessman caught at the Zurich airport, in January 2000 British police stopped thirty-two crates of missile parts at a London airport, bound for Libya.[13] The following March, an American spy satellite spotted a large cargo of missile components on the dock at Nampo in North Korea. Since the shipment contained "chemical weapons-related warheads," American officials believed it was destined for Libya.[14] Later that year the American National Security Agency reported that the Chinese had agreed to supply Libya with a hypersonic wind tunnel, a critical item for modeling and simulation in missile development.[15] London's International Institute for Strategic Studies estimates that Qaddafi has between 450 and 500 surface-to-surface missiles including SCUD Bs and Nodongs.[16] Israeli intelligence believes the Nodongs began to arrive in 2000.[17]

All this amounts to an overwhelming flood of evidence documenting the intricate relationship between these countries. It is clear that the North Koreans and communist Chinese are both wide and deep in partnership to supply Qaddafi with the capability to kill American forces in Europe, attack Israel, and murder tens of thousands of European civilians as "collateral damage."

By now, the chances are high that Colonel Qaddafi has an operating missile factory for long-range SCUDS and that his SCUD and Nodong missiles can carry poison gas at least as far as Rome. If he gets his medium-range missiles, he will be able to hit every American base in Italy.[18] For the North Koreans, it's a win-win deal—they rake in the cash while creating a new and critical threat to American forces.[19]

MORE THAN TIT-FOR-TAT

In one of its last foreign policy decisions, the Reagan administration slapped a curiously timed travel restriction on PRC diplomats assigned to the Chinese consulate in Chicago.[20] They could only leave Cook County, Illinois, if they took public transportation. The Chinese diplomats could use their private cars, but only in Cook County. Why cause a row with China as you're leaving office?

Because the Chinese had imposed an identical restriction on American diplomats assigned to the U.S. consulate in Shenyang.

The American consulate in Shenyang covers the area of Manchuria. The Chinese had stopped American diplomats in Shenyang from using the highway between Beijing and the city of Dandong on the North Korean border in order to prevent trained observers from confirming in greater detail what satellite images were already showing. From this particular highway, one can see the main rail line connecting communist China with North Korea. It is this rail line that is used to transport Chinese missiles and other WMDs to North Korea and beyond.[21]

The Reagan administration was particularly concerned with the missiles' destinations beyond North Korea. For several years American intelligence had watched Chinese cruise missiles go to North Korean ports and thence to Iran, which was at war with Iraq. Chinese officials had issued numerous denials followed by solemn promises to stop doing it each time they were caught. The Americans were frustrated. (The chairman of the House Armed Services Committee, a Democrat, called China's denials a "flim-flam.") When an Iranian ship was spotted taking on Chinese missiles at a North Korean port, this news was broadcast to the world, thanks to a tip from the Reagan administration to ABC News and the *Washington Post*.[22]

The communist Chinese have been partners with the North Koreans on WMD and missile sales to Iran for at least sixteen years. In many cases, North Koreans serve as a transshipment point, no doubt for a fee, so that the Chinese can issue a credible denial. In other cases the cooperation is more complex.

NATANZ

Within the last year allied intelligence, acting on a tip from an Iranian dissident group, pointed the International Atomic Energy Agency inspectors towards the dusty Iranian town of Natanz, two hundred miles south-southeast of Tehran. There the inspectors found two giant underground complexes under construction. In them, the Iranians were secretly building a massive uranium enrichment facility. IAEA inspectors told confidants that the layout of the facility was an exact duplicate of a uranium enrichment facility in Pakistan. But there was no workshop needed to build the actual equipment to go in the buildings. They suspected that the workshop was in North Korea.

Once Natanz was discovered, the IAEA intensified its spotlight on the full range of Iranian nuclear activities. The Iranian dissident group who had tipped off the IAEA also revealed the existence of a previously unknown heavy water factory, which is needed to process enriched uranium, near Arak. (During World War II the Allies bombed a Nazi-controlled heavy water facility in order to keep Hitler behind the nuclear curve.) The IAEA also discovered that the Iranians secretly received a shipment of uranium from China and turned the Chinese uranium into uranium hexafloride gas for use in their uranium enrichment facility.[23]

In addition, Iran was working on nuclear weaponization. In the summer of 2003, Japan's *Sankei* newspaper reported that Iran and North Korea had a secret program for "joint development of nuclear warheads."[24] With the price of oil holding up, Iran can afford to pay the North Koreans the substantial costs associated with a nuclear warhead program. China would be the logical place the North Koreans and Iranians would go to for technical backup.[25]

The final requirement for a strategic weapons strike force is the delivery system. Iran was a very early customer for the North Korean SCUD B and SCUD C programs with heavy input from Communist China. A number of them were fired at Iraqi cities during the Iran–Iraq War of the 1980s, causing heavy casualties. The International Institute for Strategic Studies estimates that Iran still has 300 North Korean SCUDs as well as 175 short-range Chinese missiles.[26] Iran was probably the major source of funding for the North Korean Nodong missile, which the Iranians named

"Shahab-3" to disguise its origin. The North Koreans have agreed to transfer the production know-how to Iran and the initial run is expected at any moment.[27] Once the assembly line is moving we can expect Nodong/Shahab-3s to be added to the Iranian inventory and then to be sold to Libya.

Even more ominous are recent reports that the Iran and North Korea are now collaborating on a new longer-range missile, which the Iranians call the Shahab-5, and is based on the North Korean Taepodong-1. Iranian IL-76 heavy transports have made at least six round-trip visits to North Korea between April and June of 2003 to pick up missiles and missile components (and perhaps uranium enrichment equipment as well).[28] Late in the summer of 2003, *Sankei* reported that the North Koreans and Iranians are working together on the 6,000 mile Taepodong-2 Inter-Continental Ballistic Missile.[29]

According to *Sankei*, Iranian "nuclear affairs specialists" visited North Korea three times in the spring of 2003 in order to "receive know-how from North Korea on how to respond if a nation accepts an international inspection team."[30] The usual international political wrangle ensued. The Iranians went into a stalling, lying, hiding mode. The Americans hardliners inside the administration pushed for sanctions. The Chinese and the Europeans, looking after their commercial interests, found excuses to say that Iran had made "progress." The IAEA was split with the inspectors taking a tough line and the headquarters less so.[31] Paragraph 52 of an August 2003 IAEA report on new information provided by the Iranians contains an amusing observation that "some of the information was in contrast to that previously provided by Iran,"[32] which is UN agency-speak for "They lied until we caught them at it."

The Israelis have been making it clear that they do not like the nuclear weapons and missile trends in Iran. They believe the Iranians are two years away from having a functioning nuclear weapon.[33] The Iranian Shahab-3/Nodong can already reach Israel from launching points in Iran. Prime Minister Ariel Sharon used a late July 2003 meeting with President Bush to brief him on the issue—the president was reportedly impressed by the potential Iranian danger. In 1981 Israeli fighter-bombers destroyed Saddam Hussein's first nuclear weapons plant. If the international community does not deal with the Iranian threat, the Israelis may take matters into their own hands. The Iranians know as much, which is perhaps why the concrete walls at Natanz are eight feet thick.

DAMASCUS

Syria has all of the ambitions of the others but it does not have the oil revenues of Libya or Iran nor, for political reasons, does it have a supplier who wants to transfer WMDs as Pakistan and North Korea have with communist China.[34] Since Damascus has to live within a budget, it has more a modest, but still deadly, WMD and missile program.

Undersecretary of state John Bolton has told the Congress that Syria has one of the most advanced chemical weapons programs in the Arab world and that it includes the deadly nerve gases Sarin and VX.[35] Communist China, in a move well rehearsed from past endeavors, jump-started the Syrian nuclear program with a research reactor in 1991. In theory this reactor was under international inspection, but by the fall of 2003 undersecretary Bolton was telling the Congress that Syria "may use a Chinese reactor" to build nuclear arms.[36] Syria was also a customer for North Korean SCUD Bs. The International Institute for Strategic Studies estimates that Syria now has about 850 surface-to-surface missiles, a mix of Soviet and North Korean models.[37] Even worse, some of these missiles may have chemical weapon warheads.

The great unsolved mystery of Syria that continues to baffle investigators, is the Chinese M-9 story of the early 1990s. China had agreed to sell the M-9 missile to Syria, with some of them to be shared with Libya. The M-9 is a solid-fuel missile and much more accurate than the SCUDs. The first Bush administration pleaded with Beijing and, allegedly, the deal was cancelled. However, *New York Times* columnist William Safire reported that the Chinese did indeed flaunt this agreement with the U.S. and went ahead to build two underground factories in Syria to produce the M-9.[38] There was, it should be noted, a conflicting story reported two years later by NBC's Robert Windrem that while one of the factories was built by the Chinese, the other was built by the North Koreans.[39]

The Syrians, for their part, have been keeping a tight lid on their missile program. They don't announce anything and they don't test missiles where spy satellites can see them. Nevertheless, there is evidence to prove that their course of action has not changed. In the mid-1990s the Washington Times revealed that Beijing had shipped missile guidance systems to Syria.[40] In 1999 ABC News reported that Syria was receiving missile technology through a complex Iran–Pakistan–North Korea deal with communist China in the mix.[41]

HAVANA

There is also the unanswered question of Cuba. The CIA has told an American television network that there is an inordinate amount of shipping traffic between Cuba and North Korea.[42] These might be conventional weapons deliveries from North Korea to Cuba. It is interesting that North Korean defector stories tend to get the most dramatic whenever Cuba is mentioned.[43] What we do know for sure is that the communist Chinese military is in Cuba in a substantial way.[44] We also know that Cuba has a first class biological warfare program and it would not take much to share that with North Korea. If allied intelligence knows anything more, they are not sharing it with the public.

TERRORIST GROUPS

There is no doubt that, among international terrorist groups, there are many willing buyers. It's hard to imagine any of the international terrorist groups turning down an offer for WMD, if they have the money. Would North Korea, and its Chinese partner, become willing sellers? At least one person confirms that the answer is yes. Terrorism expert Yossef Bodansky claims that a single deal has been completed between Osama bin Ladin and the North Koreans. He writes, "lethal anthrax samples (toxic living body used worldwide as a weapon) were brought in from North Korea at comparatively cheap prices."[45] This story has not been confirmed.

But existing evidence points to a strong likelihood that North Korea has supplied terrorist groups, including al Qaeda, with weapons. According to the 1999 edition of the State Department's *Overview of State Sponsored Terrorism–Types of Global Terrorism*, "North Korea maintained connections with Usama bin Ladin and his organization." According to a defector report (recounted in Chapter 5), North Korea is training terrorists and has connections to other groups, not just bin Laden's. During a heated discussion with a State Department officer in the spring of 2003, North Koreans threatened to begin selling nuclear weapons. This threat seems meaningless for the very reason that, looking at the past record, North Koreans, in partnership with the Chinese, have never hesitated to sell any weapons system they have ever developed. The U.S. government has even brought sanctions against China for selling poison gas equipment to a terrorist country, Iran. There is little reason to think that Pyongyang and Beijing will discriminate between a terrorist state and a terrorist group.

If the North Koreans and the communist Chinese have not already completed a WMD transaction with a terrorist group, is probably because the various conditions of the deal—money, deniability, availability—have not been right. When these elements come together, there will be a deal.

SHIELDING PYONGYANG

About a decade ago, the *New York Times* produced a headline that read: "China Shields North Korea on Atom Issue."[46] For years,

Beijing has been the prime protector of Pyongyang, staving off numerous efforts by the United States to form an international consensus to stop North Korea's WMD programs and exports. Without Beijing running interference over the past decade, Pyongyang might not have succeeded in become a global nuclear and missile threat.

IN THE HEADLINES:

- "China Stalls Anti-Atom Effort on Korea"—*New York Times*, November 15, 1991
- "China Opposes U.N. Over North Korea"—*New York Times*, March 24, 1993
- "China Resists U.N. Resolution on North Korea, U.S. Aides Say"—*Washington Post*, March 30, 1994
- "China Blocks U.N. Statement Condemning North Korea"— *Washington Post*, April 9, 2003

The effects of Beijing's diplomatic defense of North Korea can be seen in three American administrations. In 1991, the first Bush administration removed American nuclear weapons from South Korea in hopes that this unilateral action would lead to international pressure on North Korea to reciprocate by ending its nuclear weapons program. However, communist China dealt a setback to U.S. efforts by objecting to pressure on Pyongyang.[47] In 1993, the new Clinton administration was faced with North Korean refusal to allow international inspections of its nuclear facilities. As the Clinton administration scrambled to make its case before the UN Security Council, Chinese foreign minister Qian Qichen declared Beijing's opposition to "any sanctions" against North Korea, dealing, as the *New York Times* noted, "a major blow to international efforts to force North Korea to give up its nuclear weapons program."[48] A year later, Clinton administration officials correctly voiced their concerns that China "may become an obstacle" to international efforts to contain North Korea's nuclear weapons program.[49]

The current administration of George W. Bush has had the same problem with Beijing shielding North Korea. In February 2003, Beijing blocked a U.S. attempt to censure Pyongyang for having withdrawn from the Nuclear Non-Proliferation Treaty.[50] Then, in early April, Chinese diplomats stalled an effort by the Bush administration and the British to have the UN Security Council criticize North Korean plans to start plutonium production. The *Washington Post* noted that China's move "diminished the prospects of the council's playing a central role in managing the nuclear crisis." With the UN system hopelessly blocked by Beijing, the Bush administration began to organize in the summer of 2003 an international maritime program to interdict North Korean missile shipments at sea. This again led to a series of complaints from Beijing.[51]

When another round of diplomatic talks with North Korea went nowhere this past summer of 2003, the Chinese vice foreign minister declared, "America's policy toward the DPRK [North Korea] ... is the main problem we are facing."[52] The largest problem facing American diplomats on the North Korean issue is Beijing.

By removing the threat of sanctions, Beijing has rendered the UN powerless to resolve any North Korean problems. Beijing and Pyongyang have successfully defined the issue as "North Korea's way" or war. That is, Americans are forced to chose between a leaky deal like the Agreed Framework, or going to war.

LACK OF STEWARDSHIP[53]

Former Secretary of State Madeleine Albright begins a chapter of her memoirs with a note on North Korea, "Much of what the Clinton administration attempted in its Korea policy has unraveled since I left office, opening scenarios for the future ranging from the restoration of stability to a nuclear-armed North Korea, to war."[54]

In the summer of 2003, Secretary Albright and her associate Wendy Sherman participated in a *New York Times*–Discovery Channel television production that was deeply critical of the George W. Bush's North Korean policy.[55] It appears that Clinton administration alumni are seeking to make North Korea an issue in the 2004 election.

During the Clinton administration, top officials only seriously addressed North Korean proliferation twice, once at the beginning of Clinton's term and once at the end of his second term. In between, the North Korean issue was put on hold, with the administration hoping that the Agreed Framework would stick. Former Secretary of State James A. Baker, III, warned that it wouldn't. Writing in 1995 and addressing the Agreed Framework, then one year old, Secretary Baker predicted, "Given their track record, there's substantial reason to question whether the North Koreans will keep their side of the current agreement. The worst part of it is that a dangerous message has been sent to other would-be proliferators in capitals such as Tehran [Iran], Tripoli [Libya] and Baghdad [Iraq]: sometimes crime pays."[56]

It became apparent that the Clinton administration would have to address the issue of North Korean missile sales to other terrorist countries. Starting with the Taepodong launch in 1998, there was increasing evidence of North Korean missile technology flowing to Pakistan and Iran; the North Korean role in the missile threat was public.

Clinging to the Agreed Framework, the Clinton administration sent Secretary of State Albright to Pyongyang just before the 2000 election to try to obtain another agreement from North Korea to restrain its missile program. That trip became an ugly symbol of the Clinton administration's approach to North Korea. It originated from a meeting in the summer of 2000 between Secretary Albright and the North Korean foreign minister at a conference in Southeast Asia. During this exchange, North Korean Vice Marshall Jo

Myong Rok was invited to visit Washington. Jo, a tough North Korean soldier and the chief political commissar of the North Korean Army, arrived in early October. He wore his military uniform to pose for photos with President Clinton in the Oval Office. Only later did the Clinton officials realize that some of the medals he bore were awarded for killing American soldiers in combat. North Korea reciprocated Jo's visit by inviting Secretary Albright to visit Pyongyang—a journey she should never have taken.

ON THE SLIPPERY SLOPE

Albright's party arrived in Pyongyang on a cold gray dawn. Her first mistake was agreeing to visit the Mausoleum of the Great Leader.[57] Although her assistants were careful to keep the American press away ("bad optics," as one of them opined privately),[58] the North Korean propaganda machine trumpeted her visit across Asia. The American secretary of state was respectfully visiting the mausoleum of the man who started the Korean War and was responsible for the deaths of tens of thousands of U.S. soldiers.[59]

From the Mausoleum, Albright visited a kindergarten where she spontaneously joined the children in a song and dance routine. Only later did Albright discover that the song she was singing was an anti-American tune and the long banner in the background, written in large Korean letters, was a similar propaganda attack. TV audiences across the world, especially in South Korea and Japan, saw the footage and understood the insult. Later that afternoon, Albright accepted an invitation from the Dear Leader for further evening entertainment.

THE "AMBUSH"

The Americans arrived at the Pyongyang stadium filled with 125,000 people standing silently in the stands.[60] The Albright party was greeted with total silence, but thunderous applause exploded as the Dear Leader made his entrance. For the next seventy minutes, North Korea put on a highly militaristic display. Steven Mufson, a reporter for the *Washington Post* covering the Albright trip commented, "Choreographed as it may have been, it was a stunning display of a fervor that evoked chilling reminders of the mass rallies of the Third Reich."[61] In the middle of the extravaganza the card section in the stands presented a reenactment of the launch of the Taepodong. Fireworks spelled out "Down with Imperialism" in big glowing red Korean characters. When the performance ended, North Korean television showed Secretary Albright, her assistant Wendy Sherman, and Kim Jung Il rising and clapping their hands to a cheering crowd of performers, with smiles on their faces. North Korean television fed this propaganda coup to outlets around the world.[62]

Secretary Albright's trip was severely criticized in the American press and ridiculed overseas, primarily on human rights grounds.[63] A *Washington Post* editorial had particularly harsh words for the secretary, "When Ronald Reagan called the Soviet Union an 'evil empire,' we now know that the word traveled from cellblock to cellblock across the taiga, giving courage to dissidents throughout the gulag." By contrast, the *Post* declared that Secretary Albright's "silence on this repression diminished U.S. credibility."[64]

The Clinton administration's silence on the dismal state of human rights in North Korean was not an accident or a misinterpretation of intentions; it a was matter of deliberate policy. The *Post*'s Steve Mufson wrote at the time, "A senior State Department official, acknowledging a lower U.S. priority on human rights issues in North Korea, said last week that different priorities are appropriate for different countries."[65] After a spring 1999 Senate hearing on North Korea, the Voice of America decided to blast the North Koreans for human violations but its programming was vetoed by the State Department that had declared a "moratorium" on criticism of the Kim regime.[66] Clinton's policy towards North

Korea was "engagement"—a position that would not work if the U.S. government were publicly criticizing Kim Jung Il.

While American cabinet officers are forced to meet with unsavory foreigners from time to time, there is a strict protocol appropriate for handing these difficult situations. For example, in the fall of 2003, Secretary of Defense Donald Rumsfeld met with Chinese Defense Minister Cao Gangchuan. Cao's career has been built on buying, building, and selling weapons. Rumsfeld held formal discussions with Cao in his office, but he and all of his top officers declined to attend the Chinese Embassy dinner in Cao's honor. The Chinese got the message when this snub hit Washington's major newspapers.[67] Secretary Albright took the opposite tack—she accepted all invitations to ceremonies glorifying communist rule in North Korea. One had to wonder if the American secretary knew or cared that her host was throwing entire families, including women and children, into the death camps.

Nothing substantive came of her Pyongyang visit. There were discussions of a possible missile no-export deal in return for a billion dollars a year from American taxpayers. But at the end of the day, the North Koreans weren't prepared to enter an agreement. That was that.[68]

In the end, the Clinton administration's policy of classic appeasement on North Korea was a failure on nuclear, missile, and human rights grounds. The Agreed Framework was little more than self-delusion. The Clinton administration stood by and watched for eight years as the North Korean–Chinese missile export joint venture prospered. Remaining silent on human rights in North Korea earned them nothing but contempt from Pyongyang and confusion abroad.

The Clinton administration might have begun with good intentions but the journey ended in an embarrassing fiasco. Secretary Albright told the Associated Press' diplomatic correspondent George Gedda that she had been, in effect, "ambushed," by the Dear Leader in Pyongyang.[69]

A CRIMINAL CONSPIRACY

The WMD and missile trade among communist China, North Korea, and their vile customers is a vast and immensely profitable criminal conspiracy. Deception is a major part of these operations. Arms traders engage in a battle of wits against customs inspectors and allied intelligence in the back alleys of the world. The struggle between the authorities and the mutually supporting arms trading gangs is akin to efforts to stamp out the narcotics cartel. Corruption is also a major factor, as the profits generated from illicit arms sales keep the Dear Leader and his cronies in luxury.

In some cases these arms deals are simple buy-sell-delivery-close operations. But as in the "Kandla Catch," they can also be complex operations involving a machining center, upgrades, parts, service, and training. The net result is a much more dangerous world. Every weapons delivery and every technology transfer brings us closer to the day one or more of these weapons will be used. The result will be catastrophic.

The question is whether the United States, or anyone else, can stop this criminal conspiracy before it kills millions. At a minimum, the United States needs to hold China fully accountable for its role in spawning the horrors of the future.

10

NORTH KOREA: CHINA'S KNIFE

When the communist Chinese Army attacked UN forces in the fall of 1950, many North Korean Christian families feared for their lives. UN forces had swept North Korea clean of Kim's secret police but now the UN was retreating from the onslaught of Chinese soldiers. The people of Pyongyang had celebrated their short-lived freedom from the Kim regime and they feared that swift retribution would follow behind the advancing Chinese. A flood of refugees began to flee south. But without means of transportation, most of them would not be able to outrun the troops.

In Pyongyang, a woman opened her door to find her brother whom she had not seen or heard from in years. He was dressed in South Korean uniform and he had a truck. The woman, her husband, and her two small children ran to the truck with nothing but the clothes on their backs and what they could carry with their two hands. The woman had received the miracle for which she had prayed.

Unfortunately, for every "Miracle of Pyongyang" there are thousands who have been less fortunate—executed, assassinated, starving, thrown into prison camps, tortured, abused, and kidnapped at the hands of the Kim family. This is not a closed chapter in history. Pain and suffering in North Korea continues, as does North Korea's threats against its neighbors and America as well. With every day that passes, the Dear Leader gets closer to nuclear weapon capability and the means to deliver them. And standing behind him is the People's Republic of China, the "Shield of Pyongyang."

DAMNING QUESTIONS FOR CHINA

North Korea is China's knife, doing the violent bidding of its master.

Does the communist Chinese government know what is going on in North Korea? Yes. The two communist countries share a border as well as long-standing defense and intelligence contacts. North Korean refugees have been crossing the Yalu and Tumen Rivers into China by the thousands, easily accessible to Chinese debriefing officers. China knows about North Korea's aggression against its neighbors and its weapons of mass destruction programs.

Can the Chinese government intervene to stop dangerous North Korean behavior? Yes. Beijing controls 70 percent of North Korea's energy supply, an enormous leverage over Pyongyang. But rather than intervening to prevent dangerous rogue state behavior, Beijing has helped to advance Kim's weapons of mass destruction programs, turns a blind eye to North Korea's aggression against its neighbors, and often is a fully profiting partner in North Korea's illicit arms deals.

Is Beijing a willing participant? Yes. Beijing is at least an "enabler" if not an accomplice and partner in these illicit activities. It is simply not logistically possible to fly a C-130 from Pakistan to North Korea without refueling. Nor would either Pakistan or North Korean have had the level of WMD and missile programs they have today without critical Chinese assistance.

Is the Beijing elite making personal money on the North Korean weapons of mass destruction deals? Yes, in all probability. An analogous case can be seen in China's missile deals with Pakistan. Former Secretary of State James Baker shed light on this in his memoirs. In fact, he insisted that this passage remain in his memoirs despite State Department efforts to have it deleted because of the embarrassment to China: "I suspected why [the effort to halt Chinese missile sales to Pakistan had failed]; the Chinese had signed lucrative contracts to deliver missiles to Pakistan. In all probability, several senior government and party officials or their families stood to gain from the performance of those contracts."[2]

Given the corruption and rapaciousness of the elite in Beijing, logic would suggest that, "in all probability," party officials would profit as much from the Beijing–Pyongyang illicit arms smuggling trough as they do from the Beijing–Islamabad WMD connection.

THE BORROWED KNIFE

In 1950 Moscow, Pyongyang and Beijing had an ambitious world view: They were the driving forces of a global communist aggression. These days Moscow is democratizing and has no ambitions beyond its own borders. Pyongyang still wishes to conquer the south but the force of circumstances makes regime survival the first order of business.

Communist regimes have obviously been in trouble since the fall of the Berlin Wall. For now, regime survival is paramount. In 1989 ordinary citizens challenged many of the world's communist regimes. In Eastern Europe and the Soviet Union, the people prevailed. In China, the regime triumphed by massacring Chinese students at Tiananmen Square but it knows that the Chinese people would end dictatorial rule if they had the opportunity.

For Beijing, regime survival means above all keeping the democracy virus away from its borders. Therefore, the communist Chinese want to keep the regimes in North Korea, Vietnam, and Burma as they are. China also does not want democracy to return to Pakistan. Rather than trying to spread communism around the world, Beijing these days wants to keep the world a safe haven for dictatorships. This explains their deep political relations with the countries on the State Department's terrorism list—Iran, Syria, Libya, and Cuba, among others. By spreading weapons of mass destruction to these countries, the terrorist countries become "strategic proxies" for Beijing, helping to keep the United States occupied.[3]

Beijing also has territorial ambitions. It wants to keep the vast Tibetan Plateau it conquered in 1950 as well as to conquer Taiwan. In both cases, keeping the United States out of the picture is a high priority—either by having one of its strategic proxies occupy the United States' attention elsewhere or through direct deterrence.

DANGERS OF A ROGUE NORTH KOREA

What are the dangers inherent in allowing the North Korean issue to fester without solution? First, there is the continued misery and privation of the people living in North Korea. Unless there is a regime change, there is little or no likelihood it will evolve into something less hideous. The Dear Leader and his cronies are making small changes to the economy but they will not make the major changes that would materially improve the lives of the people because such a breath of fresh air would threaten the regime. International aid and aid from China keeps the regime afloat now and will do so into the indefinite future.

Second, there is the prospect of continued aggression against South Korea and Japan, where there are tens of thousands of U.S. service personnel and their dependents. The Dear Leader, if he chose, could launch his million man army in a poison gas-led attack against Seoul, order his secret agents to wreak havoc in Japan, or anything in between. As late as November 2003, his navy was crossing into South Korean waters to test the South Korean Navy's resolve.

Third, there is every reason to believe that North Korea continues to be a WMD and missile proxy for Beijing's proliferation activities. The danger is that every illicit transfer puts the day closer when a terrorist state or group will set off a nuclear explosion that could destroy an American or Japanese city, or spread an incurable disease that will sweep the world as fast as passenger jets can deliver the unwitting carriers.

Finally, North Korea has proven that it could hit American soil (Alaska) with a North Korean–Chinese hybrid missile. That happened five years ago. There is every reason to believe that it has made progress since then and will continue to do so until any point in the United States could be targeted for nuclear destruction within minutes. Considering how porous American borders are, despite recent improvements, it is also not beyond the realm of possibility that North Korea could be planning to set off a so-called "dirty bomb" (radiological explosion) on American soil.

The People's Republic of China and the Chinese Communist Party deserve an enormous amount of blame for the threats and horror that the Kim regime presents to the people of North Korea, the Northeast Asian region, and the world at large.

A rogue North Korea makes a perfect Chinese proxy. Over the last fifty years, Beijing has secretly nurtured and shielded Kim's regime:

- By supporting its North Korean proxy in a war that destroyed the Korean Peninsula, killed a million people, and left hundreds of thousands of people homeless and tens of thousands of children orphaned
- By sending the Chinese army on a surprise attack against the United Nations in defense of North Korea
- By allowing North Korean spy ships to operate from Chinese shores
- By allowing North Koreans to use Chinese ships to transport narcotics to Japan

- By directly and indirectly giving North Korean (as well as other terrorist states and groups) poison gas, nuclear weapons, and the ballistic missiles to deliver these weapons
- By doing nothing as three million North Koreans starved and entire families were thrown into death camps

DEALING WITH NORTH KOREA: RECOMMENDED ACTIONS

The international response to the North Korea threat has been fragmented and ineffectual. Moscow has been reasonably helpful but tended to looking after its own interests. It is deeply concerned that any nuclear event in North Korea will result in radioactive fall out on the Russian Far East, particularly on Vladivostok. On the other hand, positive changes in North Korea would allow Russia to construct a railway connecting the Trans-Siberian Railway with the South Korean port closest to Japan. Though the South Korean government is grudgingly following America's lead in responding to Kim's threats, it suffers from internal divisions. The Japanese have made the most progress, but they are reluctant to confront Beijing. The Chinese themselves are playing the usual duplicitous game, trying to participate in the process of reform but not the substance. Most importantly, Beijing continues to disguise its true influence over North Korea.

For its part, the Kim dynasty has shown itself to be incorrigible. In late November 2003 the North Koreans murdered a South Korean guard at a nuclear power plant financed by the U.S., South Korea, and Japan. The same week, the North Korean Navy made an intrusion into the South. This is just one example among many. The U.S., South Korea, Japan, and Russia should not tolerate further regional aggression from Kim—absolutely no more kidnappings, murders, spy boats landing, or saboteurs.

Putting an end to this regime must be the ultimate goal for the U.S., South Korea, Japan, and Russia. This group of four will have to use its combined diplomatic talents to put the North Korea issue on the regional agenda and, more important, convince Beijing to put pressure on Pyongyang. (China can even offer a comfortable exile to the Dear Leader.) As a sweetener for China, the U.S. can promise not to deploy troops to North Korea following a regime change in Pyongyang. With the Kim regime gone, there would be less need for the United States to keep the level of troops it has so far maintained in South Korea. These troops could be redeployed, in the same way the United States has redeployed the forces once stationed in Germany.

USING RICO. The North Korean regime acts like a criminal gang and should be treated like one. The United States has the "Racketeering Influenced and Corrupt Organizations Act" (RICO) statute, which has useful provisions that can be applied to North Korea's drug and arms trafficking and other criminal activities.[4] The RICO statute also has conspiracy provisions that might be applied to accomplices to North Korean crimes. This is something the Bush administration should explore.

The Bush administration has been holding inter-agency meetings on North Korean narcotics trafficking, money laundering, and other illegal activities. But these issues remain a low priority for the administration. That needs to change.

CONGRESSIONAL ACTION. "The Comprehensive Anti-Apartheid Act of 1986"[5] contained sanctions designed to end the practice of apartheid in South Africa. Congress could use this statute as a model or precedent to pass comprehensive sanctions legislation aimed at North Korea. The South Africa legislation's secondary boycott provisions—those who continued to have prohibited dealings with South Africa would be denied access to the American market—gave it real teeth. The same provisions could be enforced against North Korea and its accomplices with devastating effects on Kim's regime.

A PROGRAM FOR JAPAN. It's difficult to suggest a program for Japan because in recent years, Japanese public opinion has driven the government to take more aggressive action toward Kim Jung Il's rogue behavior. The Japanese government would do well to consider reassigning those Japanese diplomats who remain appeasement-minded toward Beijing and Pyongyang. Japan is ahead of the United States, South Korea, and Russia in dealing with North Korea. The Japanese have:

- Put human rights on the agenda through the kidnapping issue
- Tightened restrictions on the Chosen Soren's operations
- Tightened export controls to prevent leakage of Japanese technology to North Korea
- Increased taxpayer spending to develop a missile defense system with the United States

A PROGRAM FOR SOUTH KOREA. South Korea is at the other end of the spectrum from Japan. Its current government might be the weakest, least competent, and least popular in the entire history of the Republic. Further, South Korean popular opinion is completely fractured, with realists on one side and those who have been pandered to by corrupt politicians on the other. With an almost 50–50 split, any significant change in policy from South Korea would be extremely difficult to extract. The current government is wedded to its "sunshine policy," a propaganda slogan identifying what is in reality a policy of appeasement in its most raw form.

What could be done, however, without the current South Korean government losing face, would be a renewal of the "Team Spirit" military exercises with the United States to remind Pyongyang (and Beijing) that aggression from the North will meet with a powerful military response.

A PROGRAM FOR THE INTERNATIONAL AID COMMUNITY. North Korea is still on the dole. President Bush has declared that food will not be used as a weapon and U.S. aid continues to flow to North Korea. During the first ten months of 2003, the United States taxpayers contributed over $31 million worth of food aid to North Korea—making America the leading international donor to North Korea, behind only communist China in 2003.[6] American and UN officials are trying to ensure that more of the food gets to the intended recipients (and not the North Korean Army), but progress is limited at best.

For 2004, the director of the UN World Food Program in Pyongyang has appealed for $221 million, claiming that North Korea is still in a "chronic emergency . . . without a clear end in sight."[7] Kim is still starving the children. The UNICEF representative in Pyongyang claims that 40 percent of North Korean children are chronically malnourished and 70,000 children were at risk of dying from inadequate medical care.[8]

Beijing does not participate directly in the aid program and there is no independent verification of what aid it is supplying. According to Japanese sources, Chinese aid exports of grains in 2003 were up over 200 percent from the previous year. Grain exports passing through one city in Manchuria to North Korea was up more than 50 percent in 2003.

In September 2003, the U.S. tried to get Pyongyang to be more open about the distribution of international aid, but was stonewalled by the North Koreans as usual. The international aid community can make a significant contribution to solving the North Korean problem by demanding increased truthfulness. In the past, the international aid community has not always been completely forthcoming regarding the distribution of aid to North Korea for fears that donors would stop giving if they knew what was really going on. As noted in Chapter 7, the UN World Food Organization's attempt to suppress a report to the UN Human Rights Commission in 2001 was disgraceful and counterproductive. Finding "progress" where there is none will not improve the lives of North Koreans.

NOT AN ELECTION ISSUE. Neither the Republicans nor the Democrats should make the other side's handing of the North

Korean problem a 2004 election issue. The North Korean propaganda machine widely distributed films of Secretary Albright and
her aide, Wendy Sherman, standing beside the Dear Leader and
applauding the Nazi Party-like performance in Pyongyang. Given
what we know of the nature of the regime and the Dear Leader himself, that doesn't seem to be something the Democratic National
Committee would like to see appear in a Republican TV ad. With
North Korea still unfettered to cause what trouble the Dear Leader
wills, the Republicans don't have a lot of North Korea-related
accomplishments to crow about, either. North Korea should be an
issue both parties address in cooperation, not competition.

A PROGRAM FOR THE WHITE HOUSE. The Bush administration has formed a number of principles in dealing with North
Korea, but at present there is no sign that the administration is
ready to permanently put an end to Kim's regime.[9] In an interview
with Bob Woodward of the *Washington Post*, President Bush said
that he loathed the Dear Leader. While the president is clearly concerned about the dismal state of human rights in North Korea,
there is no indication that the administration has been able to
translate these concerns into a coherent, active policy. The administration's policy toward North Korea borrows some elements from
previous administration policies. But some fundamental differ-
ences stand out. No high level official from the Bush administration will be duped into taking an Albright-like trip of humiliation
through Pyongyang. And President Bush will not be inviting any
North Korean general for a photo op at the Oval Office.

Most importantly, the Bush administration recognizes the
inevitable failure of the Agreed Framework and will not sign any
phony deals where the North Koreans are given free reign to cheat.
Instead, Washington is demanding that North Korea must forego
and dismantle—completely, verifiably, and irreversibly—its current
nuclear program and any future nuclear ambitions. Without a substantive plan, however, the administration officials have become
bogged down in the negotiating process.

One initiative that has been launched is the Proliferation Security Initiative, an international interdiction scheme created by undersecretary of state John Bolton. The goal of the initiative is to allow like-minded countries and allies—such as Australia and Japan—to work together in developing legal mechanisms and strategies to identify and interdict North Korean shipments of WMD items. This has promise, if for no other reason than that it will point out culpable Chinese middlemen and other accomplices. As might be expected, China vigorously opposes undersecretary Bolton's idea.

At this point, the unfortunate truth is that the Bush administration is still doing more talking about the regime's criminal behavior than actually taking aggressive action to attack the problem. Too many of the bad old habits have carried on:

- There is no endgame strategy
- North Korean aggression and provocations still go unpunished
- American food aid still feeds the North Korean Army
- North Korean human rights violations are not on the table for discussion
- The North Koreans and their Chinese "shield" seem to have successfully bogged any process in endless diplomatic meetings and conferences while North Korea's nuclear research marches on

Most importantly, the highest ranks of the Bush administration are still blind to the role of communist China. They do not know or want to know that China is a major part of the problem and not yet any measurable part of the solution. It is not surprising that Washington officials are reluctant to come to such a conclusion. However, recognizing Beijing as the mastermind behind its North Korean proxy could fundamentally change the nature of the relationship between the U.S. and China.

But so long as the issue remains isolated to North Korea, it is unlikely that a solution will be found. Redefining the issue as

North Korea coupled with communist China is a necessary first step. Those in Washington must recognize Beijing's critical role in North Korea's rogue state behavior. Beijing's leverage with Pyongyang gives it both the ability and the responsibility to take action. Only when this "borrowed knife" concept is understood will the White House be able to respond with an appropriate strategy to end the suffering of the North Korean people and the dangers that the Kim dynasty poses to all the people.

The Kim regime is inherently weak. It is possible to tear down Kim's throne without war, but only *if* the Bush administration can show communist China that it is in Beijing's interest to do so.

APPENDIX

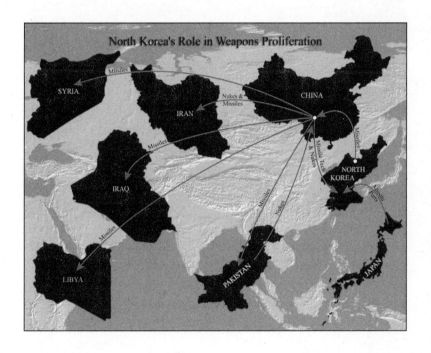

North Korea's Role in Weapons Proliferation

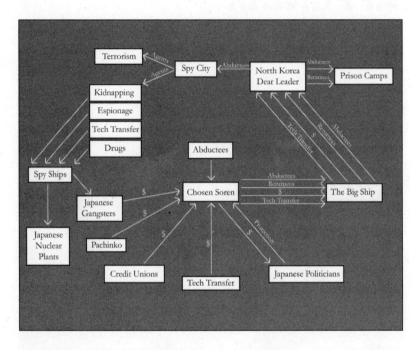

The Chosen Soren, an organization of ethnic Koreans living in Japan, has extensive connections with Japanese gangsters and funnels $2 billion per year to the Kim family coffers.

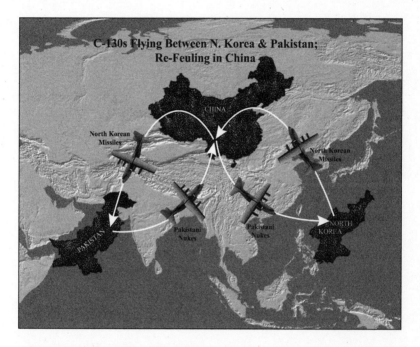

Pakistani Air Force C-130 cargo planes fly between Islamabad and Pyongyang, exchanging North Korean missiles for Pakistani nuclear weapons technology. These planes stop to refuel in western China.

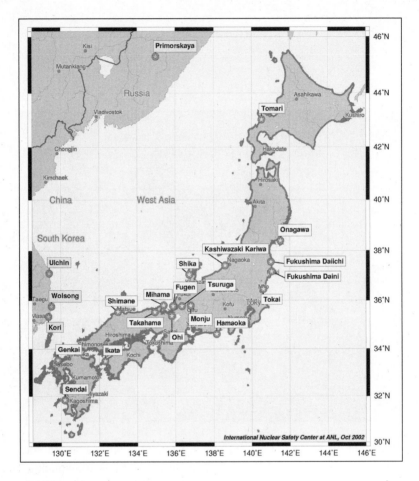

Nuclear Power Reactors in Japan
Source: International Nuclear Safety Center (Department of Energy)

Many of Japan's nuclear power plants, located on the island's coast, are vulnerable to sabotage by Kim's agents approaching from the sea. In 1990, a North Korean spy ship was found near Mihama, where the concentration of nuclear facilities is higher than anywhere else in Japan. It is directly across the Sea of Japan from Chongjin, a common launching point for North Korean spy ships headed for Japan.

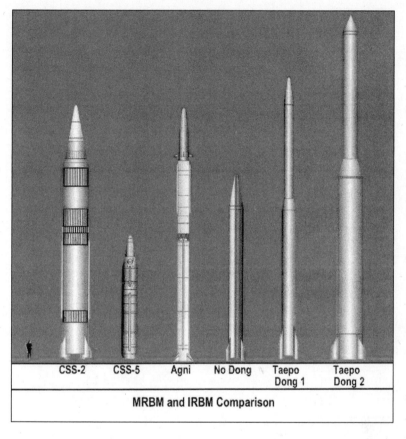

| CSS-2 | CSS-5 | Agni | No Dong | Taepo Dong 1 | Taepo Dong 2 |

MRBM and IRBM Comparison

A comparison of Chinese and North Korean medium- and long-range ballistic missiles

Name	DF-61	Hwasong 5	Hwasong 6	Nodong 1/2
Year	1978 ??		1989	1991
Target Objective	ROK; U.S. bases in ROK	ROK; U.S. bases in ROK	ROK, U.S. bases in ROK	ROK; Japan; U.S. bases in ROK, Japan, Okinawa
Stages	1	1	1	1
Range	600km	320km	500km	1,350km/ 1,500km
Warhead	1,000kg	1,000kg, HE	770kg, HE,;chem.; cluster	1,200kg/1,000kg believed nuclear capable; HE; Chem
Number in North Korea	Designed by PRC but not built, but PRC began to train NK missile engineers	@600 total; up to 150 w/ chem. warheads		Estimates: 100- 200; up to 500
Foreign Cooperation		Modificanton of Russian SCUD from Egypt; shared tech with Egypt	Funded by Iran; PRC tech assistance	Iran funding; possible Pakistan funding; Russian and PRC technical support
Sales	None	Iran, 90-100; UAE: 25	Iran, 60; Vietnam; Egypt; Yemen, Syria: 150, co-production; Libya attempts co-production	Made in Iran as Shahab-3; made in Pakistan as Ghuari; about 36 sold to Libya; possible sale to Egypt

Source: Joseph S. Bermudez, Jr.; *Jane's Missiles and Space;* various press reports

TD 1	TD SLV	TD 2	TD ?/R-27
Unkown	1998	Unknown	2000-2003
Japan, U.S. bases in Japan, Okinawa, Guam	Demonstrate three-staging to build later ICBMs	U.S.A.	U.S.A.
2	3	2	1
1,500-2,500km	3,800-5,900km	6,700km	3,600km
700-1,000kg, estimate; possible nuclear; chem	Space launch vehicle; one satellite; debris reported to have hit Alaska	700-1,000kg, estimate	Russian versions:1 nuclear, 650kg; some version up to 3 warheads; one version reported for long-range anti-ship strikes
Unknown	Unknown	Unknown	1-3 possible
Said to benefit from Iran, Pakistan funding; likely Russian, PRC tech assist	PRC assistance to make satellite stage, which requires validating total missile	In 1994 the U.S. DIA said PRC DF-3 is basis for TD-2, but disputed by CIA	Modified copy of Russian Makeyev R-27 SLBM; product of Makeyev engineers working in North Korea; possible acquision of one missile from Russia
None known to date; possible basis for future Iran and Pakistan missiles	None known to date; possible satellite launch cooperation with Iran, though this could come from PRC too	None known to date; technology likely to be shared with Iran, Pakistan	None known to date; but technology likely to be shared with Iran, Pakistan

NOTES

1: ROGUE STATE

1. Interview with senior American diplomat, June 2003, location undisclosed. Some interpretation and poetic license taken in this description, but not much.
2. Korean Central News Agency, December 2, 1998.
3. Account of Hwang Chang-yop, the highest ranking defector. *Choson Ilbo*, June 15, 1998.
4. Stratagem Number 3 has four characters that read "Borrow. Knife. Kill. Person." One translator illustrates its application as, "Eliminate an opponent using an outside agency (the 'strawman' stratagem); harm someone else indirectly without exposing oneself ('alibi' or 'substitute' stratagem)." See Harro Von Senger, *The Book of Stratagems* (Penguin 1991), translated from German by Myron B. Gubitz, 41.
5. Private communication, fall 2003.
6. For example, author Michael J. Mazarr presents the North Korean nuclear program as a response to American nuclear threats. See his *North Korea and the Bomb* (New York: Macmillan, 1997), 16.

2: THE MOSCOW CONSPIRACY

1. Coronwy Rees, *A Chapter of Accidents* (New York: The Library Press, 1972), 185.
2. The British nuclear scientist Alan Nunn May, later convicted of giving nuclear secrets to the Soviets, was a classmate and friend of Maclean at Cambridge.

3. Norman Polmar and Thomas B. Allen, *Spy Book* (New York: Random House, 1997), 98.

4. Andrew Boyle, *The Fourth Man* (New York: The Dial Press, 1979), 333.

5. Christopher Andrew and Oleg Gordievsky, *KGB: The Inside Story* (New York: Harper Collins, 1990), 393.

6. Ibid.

7. Polmar and Allen, *Spy Book,* 348.

8. Visit in 2001 and 2003.

9. Kim Philby, *My Silent War* (New York: Modern Library, 2002), 148.

10. Ibid., 167.

11. On the day Burgess and Maclean fled to Moscow, another of the Cambridge spies, Anthony Blunt, told a British writer that Burgess' "violent anti-Americanism was an attitude shared by many liberal-minded [British] people" and that if Moscow took in all such persons it "would be besieged by defectors seeking asylum." The writer did not dispute this—such were the times. See Rees, *A Chapter of Accidents*, 208.

12. Andrew and Gordievsky, *KGB*, 395.

13. *The Sunday Telegraph*, [London] March 27, 1983, and the *Observer*, March 27, 1983.

14. Ibid.

15. Ibid., 394.

16. Strobe Talbot, ed.,*Khrushchev Remembers* (New York: Bantam, 197), 262.

17. Ibid., 302.

18. Herbert Romerstein and Eric Breindel argue that if the Soviets had not become a nuclear power, Stalin would not have dared unleash Kim's attack on the South. See Herbert Romerstein and Eric Breindel, *The Venona Secrets* (Washington, D.C.: Regnery, 2001), xv.

19. Reportedly, Stalin personally selected Kim over other contenders. See Sergei N. Goncharov, John W. Lewis, and Xue Litai, *Uncertain Partners* (Stanford, CA: Stanford University Press, 1993), 132.

20. Bernard Fall, *Street Without Joy* (Mechanicsburg, PA: Stackpole Books, 1961), 16.

21. Ibid., 382.

22. Ibid., 27.

23. Ibid., 17.

24. Chen Jian, *China's Road to the Korean War* (New York: Columbia, 1994), 104.

25. Strobe Talbot, ed., *Khrushchev Remembers*, 400.

26. This has led some scholars to doubt that Kim was present in Moscow in

this time frame. See Goncharov, Lewis, and Xue, *Uncertain Partners*, 318. Mao appears in the birthday picture with Stalin and the other communist leaders but Kim does not. However, recent research based on newly released documents and analysis by Chinese mainland scholars based in the West gives support to Khrushchev's account. See Jian, *China's Road to the Korean War*, 86. Apparently all of the communist leaders then in power had gathered in Moscow for the birthday celebration. Since Kim was by this time the head of North Korea, his absence would have been unusual.

27. The dacha was originally a simple affair of only one story. In honor of Mao's visit, Stalin directed that a second story be built so the two communist leaders could have some private time together. For reasons now unknown, Mao rejected the offer and stayed in a Moscow hotel. Author interview with son of former Soviet politburo member in Moscow, August 17, 2003.

28. Strobe Talbot, ed., *Khrushchev Remembers*, 403.

29. "There are no documents on the decisions leading to the Korean War in either the Soviet Ministry of Foreign Affairs or the Soviet Ministry of Defense archives." See Goncharov, Lewis, and Xue, *Uncertain Partners*, 131n5. Also, "Members of the Russian declassification committee for Korean War documents have reported that further records regarding the preparations for the military offensive against South Korea in the spring of 1950 are not in the presidential archive and have not been located." (Woodrow Wilson International Center for Scholars, Winter 1995/1996), 35.

30. *The Cold War in Asia*, 88n99.

31. Interviews, Moscow, summer 2003.

32. See Shu Guang Zhang, *Mao's Military Romanticism* (Laurence, KS: University of Kansas Press, 1995), 55n1.

33. "Mao–Stalin meetings produced a Chinese–Soviet green light for Kim's plans to attack the South." From Jian, *China's Road to the Korean War*, 90.

34. Strobe Talbot, ed., *Khrushchev Remembers*, 401.

35. In November 1957, Mao and Kim went to Moscow for another communist summit, but this meeting was known for its disharmony among the international communist leadership.

36. Goncharov, Lewis, and Xue, *Uncertain Partners*, 90 and 104.

37. Ibid., 127.

38. Ibid., 151.

39. Jian, *China's Road to the Korean War*, 106.

40. Goncharov, Lewis, and Xue, *Uncertain Partners*, 132.

41. William Stueck, *Rethinking the Korean War*, 66.

42. Author interview, Seoul, August 2003.

43. Bruce Cumings, *The Origins of the Korean War, Vol II* (Princeton, NJ: Princeton University Press, 1981), 358–359.

44. Jian, *China's Road to the Korean War*, 108.

45. William W. Whitson, *The Chinese High Command* (New York: Praeger, 1973), 304 and Chart H.

46. *The Korean War: Vol. II*, Korea Institute of Military History (Lincoln: University of Nebraska Press, 2001), 7.

47. Goncharov, Lewis, and Xue, *Uncertain Partners*, 140–141.

48. Jian, *China's Road to the Korean War*, 107.

49. Ibid., 109. According to ROK materials, this seems to have been a follow-up meeting to three-way talks sponsored by the Soviet Ministry of Defense in Moscow the previous month. See *The Korean War: Vol. One*, 102.

50. Jian, *China's Road to the Korean War*, 69.

51. Ibid., 109.

52. Ibid., 87n91.

53. Ibid., 133.

54. Ibid., 150.

55. *The Cold War in Asia* (Woodrow Wilson International Center for Scholars, Winter 1995/1996), 9.

56. The Tibetan homeland includes all of the Tibet Plateau and other areas of several Chinese provinces.

57. Goncharov, Lewis, and Xue, *Uncertain Partners*, 79n15.

58. Jian, *China's Road to the Korean War*, 94.

59. The Federation of Malaya was a partially independent territory under British protection. The Malayan Communist Party formed and began a guerrilla uprising against the British that became known as the Emergency. Malaya achieved independence in 1957. Sabah, Sarawak and Singapore combined with Malaya to establish Malaysia in 1963, but two years later Singapore withdrew from the confederation.

60. Jian, *China's Road to the Korean War*, 95.

61. Bernard D. Cole, *The Great Wall at Sea* (Annapolis, MD: Naval Institute Press, 2001), 18.

62. Jian, *China's Road to the Korean War*, 77.

63. Ibid., 84.

64. Cole, *The Great Wall at Sea*, 19.

65. Author has made visits on many occasions over a long period of time, most recently in 1999.

66. Whitson, *The Chinese High Command*, 244.

67. Dengbu island, see Jian, *China's Road to the Korean War*, 99.

68. Qiang Zhai, "China and the Vietnam Wars 1950–1975," in *The New Cold War History*, John Lewis Gaddis, ed., (Chapel Hill, NC: University of North Carolina Press, 2000), 11.

69. Fall, *Street Without Joy*, 32.

70. Ibid.

71. Ibid., 20.

72. Douglas MacArthur, *Reminiscences* (New York: McGraw-Hill, 1964), 327.

73. Ibid., 335.

74. S.L.A. Marshall, *The River and the Gauntlet*, (New York: Time, 1953), 5.

75. MacArthur, *Reminiscences*, 5.

76. Ibid., 320.

77. William Stueck, *Rethinking the Korean War*, (Princeton, NJ: Princeton University Press, 2002), 52.

78. *U.S. News and World Report*, May 6, 1950.

79. Stueck, *Rethinking the Korean War*, 73.

80. Cumings, *The Origins of the Cold War, Vol. II*, 420.

81. Ibid., 408.

82. Jian, *China's Road to the Korean War*, 120.

83. For example see, Ibid., 75.

84. Goncharov, Lewis, and Xue, *Uncertain Partners,* 136.

85. *The Cold War in Asia*, 25. According to another account, Herbert Norman, the Canadian ambassador to Tokyo in 1950, also a Cambridge spy, "went far to contribute to Moscow's decision to give the North Koreans the green light to invade South Korea in June 1950." When exposed, Norman threw himself off the roof of his apartment building. Chapman Pincher, *Too Secret Too Long* (New York: St. Martin's Press, 1984), 418.

86. Ibid., 177.

3: BEIJING'S WAR

1. Harry S. Truman, *Years of Trial and Hope* (New York: Doubleday, 1955), 334.

2. Clay Blair, *The Forgotten War* (New York: Anchor, 1987), 58.

3. T. R. Fehrenbach,*This Kind of War* (New York: Macmillan, 1963), 14.

4. First Lieutenant Hamilton, later Major Hamilton, would see more than his share of combat in Korea. See Roy E. Appleman, *South to the Naktong, North to the Yalu* (Washington, D.C.: Center of Military History United States Army, 1961), 23.

5. By at least one speculation, the attack may have derived from lessons taught at an academy that former German Field Marshall Ferdinand Schoerner established in Moscow after World War II. See Charles Whiting, *Battleground Korea* (Glouchestershire, UK: Sutton Publishing, 1999), 9.

6. In an effort to save first the South Koreans and later the American 24th Division, FEAF pilots repeatedly ran great personal risks during these desperate hours and days but the weather was such that FEAF could not really throw its full force at the battlefield until about mid-July in 1950. See Robert F. Futrell, *The United States Air Force in Korea, Revised Edition* (Office of Air Force History, 1983), 66 and Robert Leckie, *Conflict: The History of the Korean War* (New York: DaCapo Press, 1996), 75.

7. Captain Darrigo would demonstrate his heroism again, leading an attack on the KPA during the struggle for Pusan. Appleman, *South to the Naktong, North to the Yalu*, 326.

8. Blair, *The Forgotten War*, 60.

9. Appleman, *South to the Naktong, North to the Yalu*, 20.

10. According to one source, the North Koreans and the Chinese signed a defense agreement in 1947, over two years before Mao had triumphed over the Nationalists. See Bruce Cumings, *The Origins of the Korean War, Vol II* (Princeton, N.J.: Princeton, 1990), 359.

11. Ibid., 362.

12. Leckie, *Conflict*, 39–40.

13. During the first days of the invasion "ROK [South Korean] artillery fired on the tanks, scoring some direct hits, but they were unharmed and, after halting momentarily, rumbled forward." Appleman, *South to the Naktong, North to the Yalu*, 30.

14. Ibid., 16.

15. Author, as a young soldier.

16. Fehrenbach, *This Kind of War*, 109.

17. Leckie, *Conflict*, 50.

18. Appleman, *South to the Naktong, North to the Yalu*, 32.

19. Fehrenbach, *This Kind of War*, 76.

20. Leckie, *Conflict*, 58.

21. Cumings, *The Origins of the Korean War, Vol. II*, 660.

22. Ibid., 75.

23. Visitors to the State Department's main diplomatic entrance on C St. NW in Washington, D.C., can look on the wall to their left to see the list of FSOs who have made the final sacrifice for their country.

24. See unfortunate series of Muccio cables quoted in Blair, *The Forgotten War*, 56.

25. Ibid., 71.
26. Fehrenbach, *This Kind of War,* 72.
27. James F. Schnabel, *Policy and Direction: The First Year*, (Washington, D.C.: Center of Military History, United States Army, 1990), 35–36.
28. Blair, *The Forgotten War*, 7.
29. Fehrenbach, *This Kind of War*, 128.
30. Schnabel, *Policy and Direction*, 61.
31. Interview August 1, 2003, See also John K. Singlaub, *Hazardous Duty* (New York: Summit Books, 1991).
32. William B. Breuer, *Shadow Warriors* (New York: Wiley, 1996), 40
33. Cumings, *The Origins of the Korean War, Vol II*, 609–610. General Singlaub indicated [August 1, 2003 interview] that the reports of his Korean agents [a CIA operation] passed through General MacArthur's G2 in Tokyo and the analysts there tended to disparage them. There was at the time a competition between CIA and G2 so that by the time the Singlaub network reports arrived in Washington, they might have had a designation of untrustworthiness. Therefore, the warning might have arrived on June 19th but been dismissed, especially since it went against the prevailing theories of no war in Korea.
34. Truman, *Years of Trial and Hope*, 334.
35. Ibid., 628.
36. Ibid., 647.
37. The Taiwan announcement was made in the guise of preventing either side of the Taiwan Strait from attacking the other; but given the relative military strengths at the time, it had only one effect.
38. Blair, *The Forgotten War*, 88.
39. There were many problems with the 8th Army that were beyond senior commanders' control. However, there was no excuse for not having a proper PT program. Too many soldiers went to Korea out of shape and died because of it. Some troops just didn't have the stamina to climb hills and keep fighting. The 8th Army leadership failed in this prime responsibility.
40. Blair, *The Forgotten War*, 91. There is no disguising the fact that the 24th Division has been ill-treated by historians of the Korean War. However, the division's initial difficulties in battle derive more from being the first American unit into combat in Korea than anything specific to the 24th. The problems of the 24th Divisons were Army-wide. Over time, incompetent leaders were removed, training and equipment were provided, and, in the end, these troops were able to hold the line at the critical moment of the war.
41. Leckie, *Conflict*, 70.

42. The regimental commander of 34th Infantry was attempting to stop T-34s with the useless 2.34 inch bazookas when he was cut in half by an 85mm tank round. See Leckie, *Conflict*, 73.

43. Fehrenbach,*This Kind of War*, 166.

44. Ibid., 204.

45. Leckie, *Conflict*, 95.

46. Ibid., 117.

47. Shu Guang Zhang, *Mao's Military Romanticism,* (Laurence, KS: University Press of Kansas, 1995), 73.

48. These consisted mostly U.S. Marines, the Army's Seventh Division, some Army Field Artillery Battalions, and 2,786 South Korean marines. See Appleman, *South to the Naktong, North to the Yalu*, 503.

49. The Inchon landing took place on September 15. On September 13, 2003, a massive typhoon struck South Korea, causing over a hundred deaths and billions in property damage.

50. North Korean 19th Infantry Regiment.

51. Cumings, *The Origins of the Korean War, Vol II*, 664.

52. Ibid., 704.

53. Fehrenbach, *This Kind of War*, 172.

54. Ibid., 672.

55. See Kang Chol-Hwan's account of his confrontation with leftist South Korean students in *The Aquariums of Pyongyang*, (New York: Basic Books, 2001), 228.

56. The poll showed that South Korean young people claim to prefer North Korea (53%) and communist China (49%) to the United States (42%). *Yonhap*, Seoul, in English July 3, 2003.

57. The standard interpretation derives from Alan Whiting, *China Crosses the Yalu* (London: Macmillan, 1960).

58. See, for example, Rosemary Foote concluding, "Beijing's entry [into the Korean War] could have been averted and the war could have been concluded in the autumn of 1950 if the United States had refrained from crossing [the 38th Parallel]" in "Making Known the Unknown War: Policy Analysis of the Korean Conflict in the Last Decade" in *Diplomatic History* (Summer 1991), 411–413.

59. As of this writing Dr. Chen teaches at the University of Virginia and Dr. Shu at the University of Maryland.

60. Chen Jian, *China's Road to the Korean War* (New York: Columbia, 1994), 3.

61. Shu Guang Zhang, *Mao's Military Romanticism*, 9.

62. *The Cold War in Asia, Issue 6, Winter 1995/1996*, (Washington, D.C.: Woodrow Wilson International Center for Scholars), 40.

63. Ibid., 42.

64. Ibid.

65. Ibid., 43.

66. These war preparations are discussed extensively in *China's Road to the Korean War*, *Mao's Military Romanticism*, *The Cold War in Asia*, and Sergei N. Goncharov, John W. Lewis and Xue Litai, *Uncertain Partners: Stalin, Mao and the Korean War* (Stanford, CA: Stanford University Press, 1993).

67. Shu Guang Zhang, *Mao's Military Romanticism*, 85.

68. Ibid., 80.

69. Lin Biao and Su Yu.

70. As reprinted in Goncharov, Lewis and Xue, *Uncertain Partners*, 177.

71. November 8, 1950, from Mao to Stalin as reprinted in *Cold War in Asia*, 48.

72. Schnabel, *Policy and Direction*, 212.

73. Ibid., 221

74. S.L. A. Marshall, *The River and the Gauntlet* (New York: Time Books, 1955), 18.

75. Appleman, *South to the Naktong, North to the Yalu*, 718.

76. Ibid., 708.

77. Representative samples among thousands too numerous to recount here.

78. Memoirs of General Hong Xuezhi, excerpts translated in Xiobing Li, Allan R. Millett, and Bin Yu, eds., *Mao's Generals Remember Korea* (Laurence, KS: University Press of Kansas, 2001), 121.

79. Peng escaped. He was hiding in a nearby cave. Ibid.

80. Conversation with author.

4: THE NEW KOREAN WAR

1. Korean Central Broadcasting Network, (Pyongyang, in Korean), February 4, 1999.

2. Author has made numerous official visits to South Korea over the past twenty years. Neither General Carpenter nor I can recall precisely when this one occurred but it had to have been approximately 1990 considering what assignments the general had during his last Korean tour of duty.

3. Author wishes to thank the South Korean military for their assistance.

4. American tactical nuclear weapons were withdrawn from Korea over a decade ago.

5. In Vietnam, American troops tied empty tin cans from their C-Rations to the wire. The DMZ noisemakers are similar to tin cans but uniform, indicating some commercial product.

6. While traveling around the DMZ in August 2003, I saw snakes wander onto the road.

7. Estimates made by a retired South Korean military officer.

8. UN Camp Bonifas, located four hundred meters south of the southern edge of the DMZ, is named after the murdered American officer.

9. *Far Eastern Economic Review*, February 28, 1984, 28.

10. After his election, President Carter did try to withdraw American troops from Korea but even though his party controlled the Congress, Congress stopped this idea in its tracks. President Ronald Reagan eventually ended the proposal. It is not known who suggested this to candidate Carter.

11. The American Second Infantry Division deployed in alert positions and the U.S. brought in B-52s as an additional show of force. Source: an American officer present at the time.

12. This section is largely based on interviews with General Singlaub, fall 2003. For more details of this incident, see John K. Singlaub, *Hazardous Duty* (Summit Books, 1991).

13. Lloyd Bucher, *Bucher: My Story* (Garden City, NY: Doubleday, 1970), 316.

14. Ibid.

15. "*Banner* had touched there [coast of North Korea] on a couple of occasions and been totally ignored by the KORCOMS [Korean Communists]." Bucher, *Bucher*, 107.

16. Peter Braestrup, *Big Story* (Garden City, NY: Anchor Press, 1978), 111.

17. *Far Eastern Economic Review*, April 26, 1969.

18. Ibid.

19. April 25, 1969.

20. *Washington Times*, November 18, 2003.

21. As of summer 2003, it was General LaPort.

22. As of summer 2003, it was General Shin.

23. *Yonhap*, June 11, 2003.

24. Interview in August 2003.

25. 5027 was established before the recent deployment of American forces to Iraq.

26. Elmendorf's assets include one squadron of F15 Strike Eagle fighter-bombers, two squadrons of F-15C air-superiority fighters, and one squadron each of A-10s and F15Cs.

27. *Bungei Shunju*, in Japanese February 2003, 126–133.

28. Article 9 of the Japanese Constitution, in particular.

29. After the People's Republic of China, the U.S., and Russia, counting active and reserves. If only active duty forces were counted, North Korea would rank third in the world, ahead of Russia.

30. The North Korean Air Force has forty modern MIG-29 *Fulcrums*, plus fifty-six relatively modern MIG-23 *Floggers* and about two hundred older Soviet and Chinese-made MIG-21 *Fishbed* fighters. The former Soviet Union also sold North Korea about twenty-five SU-25 *Frogfoot* antitank attack aircraft.

31. *Yonhap*, in Korean, February 16, 2002.

32. *Kin Seinichi no Himitsu Heiki Kojo*, in Japanese, November 25, 2001.

33. *Yonhap*, in Korean, February 16, 2002.

34. Interview in Asia, summer 2003.

35. *Yonhap*, in Korean, April 29, 2002.

36. "North Korea Prepares for Digital War," by Joseph S. Bermudez, Jr., *Jane's Intelligence Review*, October 2003.

37. See Chapter 7.

38. There may be underground military facilities of the same or similar size that have not been detected by Allied intelligence.

39. *Choson Ilbo*, in Korean, May 9, 2002.

40. Ibid.

41. It is certainly possible that the PRC has a secret military alliance with another country or countries.

42. It is not known whether these munitions were destined for the KPA itself or whether they were to be exported from North Korea to a third country. As we shall see, the PRC often uses North Korea as a cutout in its proliferation activities and these may have included missiles for Iran.

43. Kyodo, July 11, 1997.

44. Korean Central Broadcasting Network, Pyongyang (in Korean), February 4, 1999.

45. Interview, Washington, summer 2003.

46. Kyodo, December 1, 1997.

47. Unlike his favorable treatment during Clinton-era visits to Washington, his December 10, 2002, visit had to be something of a trial. Many Bush administration officials do not care for him and don't mind showing it. National

security advisor Condoleezza Rice gave him a severe lecture and then called in the *Washington Times*' Bill Gertz to tell him she had done it. Xiong did not meet with or get his picture taken with the president, the vice president, the secretary of state, the deputy secretary of state, or the secretary of defense—certainly a major disappointment, given Xiong's known ambitions.

48. U.S. government source, fall 2003.

49. First there is the initial cost of the vehicle itself since an APC is a lot more expensive than a truck. Then there are the additional after-sale costs related to mechanization. For example, mechanized units now require a repair unit that is expensive and tracked vehicles use more fuel so they need more fuel and more tankers. The list goes on and on. (I am indebted to an American specialist for these observations. He also notes that the spare parts for tracked vehicles are more expensive that parts for trucks and tracked vehicles need a larger training area. E-mail September 24, 2003.) There is never enough money for everything a defense establishment would want and every defense dollar or Yuan spent on tanks and other heavy ground items is a dollar or Yuan taken away from the military space program or the potential Taiwan operation, etc. After the Soviet Union dissolved, Russia removed its heavy tank units previously stationed near Manchuria. Since there is no longer a threat coming from Russia, logic would suggest that Manchuria would be at the bottom of the defense dollar or Yuan priority list *unless* Beijing's highest leaders think they might have to fight the Americans again in Korea.

50. PLA group armies will typically have some mix of infantry [usually three divisions], armor, artillery, and air defense. Whether a group army should be considered as "heavy" or "regular" or even "light" depends on whether the infantry units are completely mechanized and whether the armor or artillery forces are present at brigade of full division strengths.

51. The 38th is headquartered at Baoding, Hebei Province. The 39th is headquartered in Liaoyang, Liaoning Province.

52. *Jiafangjun Bao*, Huabao, in Chinese, December 1, 2002.

53. *Jiefangjun Bao*, January 23, 2003.

54. General Xu Caihou is the chief of the General Political Department of the PLA.

55. August 2003.

56. General Zhang, in particular, has packed the PLA senior leadership with former associates. General Liang Guanglie later went on to command the Nanjing Military Region opposite Taiwan.

57. August 4, 2003.
58. This author is personally acquainted with Mr. Woolsey and holds him in the highest regard.

5: TERRORISM AND CRIMES

1. President Park was not a man to show emotion in public. His grief was widely known but mostly whispered about during his lifetime and confirmed ten years after his death when his diary was produced. From "Blue House Diary," *Minju Ilbo*, November 24, 1989, in Korean, translation by Carter Eckert in Don Oberdorfer, *The Two Koreas* (New York: Basic Books, 2001), 55–56.
2. Her name was Yook Young-soo. Korean women do not take the name of their husbands at marriage. On her passing she left three grown children.
3. August 16, 1974.
4. This account is based on the confession of the assassin who was later executed.
5. The Korean national dress for women is not particularly practical but it is very elegant and beautiful.
6. *New York Times*, August 20, 1974.
7. The fastest way to take the air out of a conversation in Seoul and turn it to deadly seriousness is to mention her passing. Interviews, Seoul, August 2003.
8. Osamu Eya, *Tainichi Boryaku Hakusho*, in Japanese (Tokyo: Shogakkan, 1999)
9. Ibid.
10. *Tokyo Shimbun.*
11. Kim Hyon-hui took the one-year course.
12. Ibid.
13. Ibid.
14. *TV Asahi*, in Japanese, December 9, 2002.
15. Eya, *Tainichi.*
16. Ibid.
17. *Gendai.*
18. This account is derived from discussions with foreign government officials over time and the account of An Myong-chin, a North Korean defector, in his autobiography, *North Korean Kidnapping Operative*, published in Japanese by Tokuma Shoten in 1998. *Asiaweek* reported in 1998 that no South Korean publisher had the courage to publish it.

19. Eya, *Tainichi*
20. *Wolgan Choson*, in Korean, November 1, 2002.
21. Ibid.
22. Ibid.
23. *Far Eastern Economic Review*, October 27, 1983.
24. *Far Eastern Economic Review*, October 20, 1983.
25. Ibid.
26. *Far Eastern Economic Review*, January 5, 1984.
27. *Far Eastern Economic Review*, January 26, 1984.
28. *Far Eastern Economic Review*, November 17, 1983.
29. *Far Eastern Economic Review,* January 26, 1984.
30. *Far Eastern Economic Review,* February 2, 1984.
31. For example, in the summer of 1983, Beijing refused a visa for a South Korean official to attend a geological training program of the UN Economic and Social Commission for Asia held in the Chinese province of Shandong. See *Far Eastern Economic Review*, July 28, 1983, for this and other examples.
32. The Libyan bombing of Pan Am Flight 103 was thirteen months later. Considering the demonstrated successful use of consumer electronics to bring down a jetliner by North Koreans, Pan Am should have been more alert.
33. *Asiaweek* also reports her autobiography was published in Japanese because no South Korean publisher would touch it.
34. *Far Eastern Economic Review*, November 10, 1983.
35. State Security Department
36. *Wolgan Choson*, in Korean, July 1, 2002.
37. *Wolgan Choson*, in Korean, May 1, 2000.
38. *Sindong-a*, in Korean, September 1, 2002.
39. *Pukhan*, in Korean, April 1999.
40. *Yonhap*, in Korean, May 16, 2002.
41. *Choson Ilbo*, in Korean, April 8, 2003.
42. *Chungang Ilbo*, March 12, 1999.
43. *Pukhan*, in Korean, April 1999.
44. *Yonhap*, in Korean, April 4, 2000.
45. At Nanam and Hongnam.
46. *Chungang Ilbo*, May 22, 2003.
47. Confession of North Korean KGB drug traffickers apprehended in Russia. *Tokyo Shimbun*, in Japanese June 4, 1996.
48. *Yonhap*, November 8, 1998.
49. AFP, July 10, 1998.
50. *Sisa*, in Korean, April 12, 2001.

51. *Choson Ilbo*, May 10, 1999.
52. *Chungang Ilbo*, May 7, 1999.
53. *Yonhap*, May 16, 2001.
54. *Sentaku*, in Japanese, March 2003.
55. Testimony of William Bach, U.S. State Department, to the Senate Committee on Governmental Affairs, May 20, 2003.
56. Kyodo, February 17, 2000.
57. Kyodo, January 8, 2002.
58. AFP, July 3, 2002.
59. AFP, May 27, 2003.
60. *Choson Ilbo*, in Korean, May 13, 2003.
61. *Pukhan*, in Korean, April 1999.
62. *Yomiuri*, in Japanese, May 20, 2003.
63. *Choson Ilbo*, January 20, 1999.
64. *Sankei Shimbun*, August 3, 2002.
65. *Yonhap,* December 28, 2001.
66. Kyodo, August 7, 2003.
67. Kyodo, January 12, 2002.
68. Jiji Press, May 25, 2003.
69. Testimony of William Bach, U.S. State Department, to the Senate Committee on Governmental Affairs, May 20, 2003.
70. DEA website description of the effects of narcotics on the brain.
71. *Sisa Jornal*, in Korean, April 12, 2001.
72. "Russia's Uncertain Economic Future," Senate Printing 107–50, December 2001, 313.
73. *Sindong-a*, in Korean, October 1, 2001.
74. Kyodo, February 3, 2002.
75. NHK Television, July 10, 2003.
76. Statement by defector from North Korean State Security Department to the *Sankei Shimbun*, in Japanese, August 3, 2002.
77. U.S. Department of the Treasury press release, March 14, 2003.
78. *Choson Ibo*, March 2, 1999.
79. There is an unconfirmed report that at least one special printing press was procured from Russian ex-KGB personnel left over from a late Cold War project that never got started. *Forecast,* in Japanese, April 18, 2003.
80. *Sankei Shimbun*, June 28, 1997, and August 12, 1997.
81. Yoshimi Tanaka, acquitted by a Thai court.
82. *Format*, in German, October 12, 1998.
83. *Novyye Izvestiya*, April 21, 1998
84. *Yonhap*, May 13, 2003.

85. This story was covered extensively in the Philippine and Japanese press in June and July 2000. For example, see *the Manila Business World*, June 23, 2000.

86. Testimony before the Senate Governmental Affairs Committee, May 20, 2003

6: A DAGGER POINTED AT JAPAN

1. Interview with Takuya Yakota and Professor Yoshita Fukui, Tokyo, August 2003.

2. *Wolgan Choson*, in Korean, November 1, 2002.

3. This unfortunate situation has limited the returned kidnap victims from speaking about their experiences in North Korea.

4. There is hearsay from a defector that Megumi Yakota was taken to North Korea by a spy boat.

5. *Gendai,* in Japanese, July 2003.

6. Ibid.

7. Interview in Tokyo, September 2003.

8. *Tokyo Shimbun*, in Japanese, September 20, 2002.

9. Motoi Tamaki, *History of Chosen Soren,* in Japanese, 1999.

10. Han Kwang-hui, *The Crime and Punishment of My Ch'ongnyon*, in Japanese, 2002.

11. *Tokyo Shokan*, in Japanese, July 2, 2003.

12. *Modern Korea*, in Japanese, January, 2001.

13. By one estimate, the Chosen Soren has provided between 600 million and 800 million dollars annually to North Korea (a seemingly conservative figure). *Sankei Shimbun*, in Japanese, 1995.

14. Han Kwang-hui, *The Crime and Punishment of My Ch'ongnyon*, in Japanese, 2002.

15. *Congressional Record*, May 24, 1994 page S6245 et. seq.

16. White-collar employees of big companies.

17. In Japan, pachinko is known as "Korean business." Interview with a Japanese academic, summer 2003.

18. *Sindong-a*, in Korean, October 1, 2001.

19. Ibid.

20. Ibid.

21. Han Kwang-hui, *The Crime and Punishment of My Ch'ongnyon*, in Japanese, 2002.

22. 315.9 billion yen. See *Shukan Toyo Keizai*, in Japanese, February 13, 1999.

23.   *Shokun*, in Japanese, July 2002.

24.   *Yomiuri Shimbun*, June 5, 2003.

25.   *Sankei Shimbun*, February 13, 2003.

26.   *Yomiuri Shimbun*, June 7, 2003.

27.   Ibid.

28.   *JiJiWeb*, in Japanese, June 7, 2003.

29.   Atsuyki Sassa, *Enigmatic Dictator, Kim Chong-Il*, 1999. Sassa is a former high-ranking Japanese police official.

30.   *Sankei Shimbun*, January 16, 2000.

31.   "But, it is very obvious that GAKRJ [Chosen Soren] officials were involved in the kidnapping operations." *Shokun*, December 1, 2002.

32.   Seoul Network for North Korean Democracy and Human Rights, in English, May 22, 2001.

33.   Ibid.

34.   *Bungei Shunju*, in Japanese, January 1998.

35.   *Tokyo Shimbun*.

36.   Details of the Hara story are known because his abductor was later captured in South Korea and confessed. North Korea says Hara is dead.

37.   *Kyodo*, in English, September 23, 2002.

38.   AP, September 16, 2003.

39.   *Tokyo Shimbun*, in Japanese, September 20, 2002.

40.   *Gendai*, in Japanese, July 2003.

41.   *Wolgan Choson*, in Korean, November 1, 2002.

42.   Ibid.

43.   Ibid.

44.   Atsuyki Sassa, *Enigmatic Dictator.*

45.   Osamu Eya, *Tainichi Boryaku Hakusho*, in Japanese (Tokyo: Shogakkan, 1999)

46.   Atsuyki Sassa, *Enigmatic Dictator.*

47.   Eya, *Tainichi.*

48.   100 million yen each. Han Kwang-hui, *The Crime and Punishment of My Ch'ongnyon.*

49.   *The Daily Yomiuri*, in English, August 21, 2003.

50.   Speculation by her family.

51.   *Sentaku*, in Japanese, March 2003.

52.   Ibid.

53.   *Shokun*, in Japanese, April 2003.

54.   Atsuyki Sassa, *Enigmatic Dictator.*

55.   *Daily Yomiuri*, in English.

56.   An Myong-chin, *Megumi Yakota is Alive*, in Japanese, (Kodansha, 2003).

57. *Daily Yomiuri,* June 6, 2003, and *Weekly Yomiuri,* June 8, 2003.

58. What follows is a description based on a number of Japanese press sources.

59. *Kyodo,* October 21, 2002.

60. What follows is an amalgamation of defector's stories mostly based on *Tainichi.* The spy ship sunk by the Japanese Coast Guard in December 2001 seems to have begun its journey from the North Korean port of Nampo on the western side of the Korean Peninsula (*Sankei Shimbun,* in Japanese, December 27, 2001) rather than Wonsan on the eastern side. In some cases, the spy ships also leave from Chongjin (*Bungei Shunju,* in Japanese, May 1999). But the general, overall pattern of spy ship activities holds.

61. Eya, *Tainichi.*

62. *Yomiuri Weekly,* in Japanese, April 21, 2002.

63. NHK Television, July 10, 2003.

64. *Wolgan Choson,* in Korean, November 1, 2002.

65. For example, see *Tainichi* and *Sentaku.*

66. Atsuyki Sassa, *Enigmatic Dictator.*

67. Ibid.

68. *Sankei Shimbun,* September 24, 2002.

69. Eya, *Tainichi.*

70. *Kankai,* in Japanese, June 1999

71. *Yomiuri Shimbun,* in Japanese, March 14, 2003.

72. *The Daily Yomiuri,* in English, January 29, 2003.

73. "Pre-positioning" is a particular nightmare for defense planners and was the subject of a Frederick Forsyth novel, *The Fourth Protocol,* and a later movie starring Michael Caine.

74. There are also other possibilities such as chemical weapons, biological weapons or so-called "dirty bombs," i.e. radiological weapons. See *Yomiuri Weekly,* in Japanese, March 16, 2003.

75. See *Bungei Shunju,* in Japanese, September 2002.

76. *Xinhua,* March 6, 2002.

77. *Far Eastern Economic Review,* June 10, 1993.

78. For example, see TV Asahi, in Japanese, December 1, 2002.

79. *The Daily Yomiuri,* in English, July 23, 2003.

80. *Asahi Shimbun,* in Japanese, October 10, 2002.

81. *Daily Yomiuri,* in English, July 23, 2003.

82. Diet Member Katui Hirasawa reports that the decision to give the Chosen Soren a forty-year tax holiday was the result of a decision by a leftist governor of Tokyo and the influence of the Japan Socialist Party. See *Shokan,* in Japanese, April 2003.

83. Based on the author's personal experience working with them on the 1983 KAL-007 shoot down.

84. *AERA*, in Japanese, May 27, 2002.

85. Kyodo, July 4, 2002.

86. Personal experience, Tokyo, September 2003.

7: GULAG NATION

1. Interview in 2003 with someone who personally observed this.

2. Moscow TV documentary described by *Shukan Posuto*, February 3, 2003.

3. Interview in 2003 with European member of a nongovernmental organization who served in Pyongyang in the 1990s.

4. *[North] Korean Central Broadcasting Station*, in Korean, October 7, 2003.

5. *Wolgan Chosan*, in Korean, June 1, 2001.

6. Private communication, 2003.

7. Kyodo, July 31, 2003.

8. *Le Figaro*, in French, April 3, 2002.

9. *The Land that Time Forgot* is a famous novel by early twentieth-century English writer Edgar Rice Burroughs. *The Times*, September 17, 2003.

10. *Wolgan Choson*, in Korean, June 1, 2001.

11. There has been at least one report of North Korean ties to German neo-Nazi organizations. See *Sapio*, in Japanese, July 9, 2003.

12. *Le Figaro*, in French, April 3, 2002.

13. Ko Yong-hwan, *P'yongyang at 25 O'Clock*, in Japanese (Tokuma Shoten, 1997). Ko was a North Korean diplomat who defected in the 1990s.

14. Interview, 2003.

15. *Yonhap*, in English, September 24, 2003.

16. It seems possible that there was such a trend in Romania, but the army executed the country's leader and his wife, and imprisoned their son in 1989.

17. From the DPRK (North Korea) official website.

18. *Gendai*, in Japanese, August 2003.

19. In the fall of 2003 there was an unconfirmed report that this consort had suffered a serious auto accident. Reuters, October 7, 2003.

20. The sister of the Dear Leader's current favorite escaped to the United States in 1998 out of fear that she would be murdered for knowing too much about her brother-in-law's slush funds. *Bungei Shunju*, in Japanese, February 1998.

21. Kang Myhong-to, *Pyongyang Dreams of Exile*, in Korean (*Chungang Ilbo*, 1995). Kang is the son-in-law of former North Korean premier Kang Song-san.

22. Interview with an Asian diplomat, 2003.

23. By Yi Yong-kuk, in Korean, published by Sidae Chongsin, 2002.

24. Interview, Asia, 2003.

25. *Gendai*, in Japanese August 2003.

26. When the South Korean Broadcasting Service, KBS, tried to air a drama describing Kim's "pleasure groups," Radio Pyongyang threatened to blow up the station. See *The Korea Herald*, in English, January 7, 1998.

27. Ko Yong-hwan, *P'yongyang at 25 O'Clock*. There are other defector accounts of the "joy brigades" that are similar to this account.

28. *Wolgan Choson*, in Korean, November 1, 2000.

29. Ibid.

30. There is an unconfirmed report that Offices 38 and 39 have been combined as of 2000, *Gendai*, in Japanese August 2003.

31. *Wolgan Choson*, in Korean, November 1, 2000.

32. *Bungei Shunju*, in Japanese, February 1998.

33. *Wolgan Choson*, in Korean, November 1, 2000.

34. What follows is an account by defector Ko Yong-hwan. Ko Yong-hwan, *P'yongyang at 25 O'Clock*.

35. What follows is an article the doctor contributed to the *Chungang Ilbo*, in English, April 30, 2001. He has repeated this testimony in congressional testimony.

36. Westview, 1992

37. Of necessity, this is the short course on the North Korean gulag. For the long course, Kang Chol-Hwan, *The Aquariums of Pyongyang* (New York: Basic Books, 2001) and "Gulag Nation," a special report by *U.S. News and World Report*, June 23, 2003.

38. Kang Chol-Hwan, *The Aquariums of Pyongyang*.

39. Ibid., 79.

40. Ibid.

41. Website, in English, May 22, 2001.

42. Seoul Network for North Korean Democracy and Human Rights website, in English, May 22, 2001.

43. Under unique circumstances a very few families were released in the 1980s but since the Dear Leader took over from his father, these seem to have ended.

44. "Gulag Nation," *U.S. News and World Report*.

45. Defectors report that during the 1990s there were a number of cases of almost-revolts and coups. See Yun Tae-il, *The Inside Story of the State Security Department* (Wolgan Choson, 2002).

46. *Minju Choson*, in Korean, September 20, 1998.

47. *Nodong Sinmun*, in Korean, March 21, 2003.

48. *Nodong Sinmun*, in Korean, July 2, 1997.

49. *Nodong Sinmun*, in Korean, March 21, 2003.

50. Private communication, October 2003.

51. *The Korea Herald*, in English, August 14, 1997.

52. Yonhap, in English, August 15, 1997.

53. Before he was fired by the *South China Morning Post* for being too critical of communist China, reporter Jasper Becker did some excellent old-fashioned press digging along the China–North Korea border. He broke the famine story with a brilliant series of articles. On the question of cannibalism, see *South China Morning Post*, October 1, 1997.

54. Bill Gertz, Betrayal (Washington, D.C.: Regnery, 1999).

55. Author, summer 2003.

56. *Choson Ilbo*, in Korean, June 15, 1998.

57. Andrew S. Natsios, *The Great North Korean Famine*, (United States Institute of Peace Press, 2001), 173–174. This book was published before Natsios became administrator of the Agency for International Development under the Bush administration.

58. *Choson Ilbo*, in English, December 29, 1998.

59. *Choson Ilbo*, in Korean, June 1, 1997.

60. *Yonhap*, in English, February 28, 2002.

61. *Wolgan Choson*, October 1, 2003.

62. Natsios, *The Great North Korean Famine*, 35.

63. Ibid., 125.

64. What follows is based mostly on Natsios, *The Great North Korean Famine*.

65. Natsios, *The Great North Korean Famine*, 183.

66. What follows is principally based on an extensive interview with Ambassador James R. Lilley, Washington, D.C., October 2003.

67. In his career, Ambassador Lilley was a career CIA official, ambassador to South Korea and the People's Republic of China, as well as the U.S. representative to the Republic of China, Taiwan.

68. The foregoing was based on an interview with Ambassador Lilley, October 2003.

69. According to some analysts, when communist Hungary opened its borders in 1989, allowing tens of thousands of East Germans to pass through to Austria, this helped destabilize the East German regime and contributed to the fall of the Berlin Wall. Beijing would not want to have a repetition in North Korea and this may explain why it is cracking down on North Korean refugees.

8: LABORATORIES OF DEATH

1. Statement made to the Senate Select Committee on Intelligence, March 22, 1994.
2. The following is based on the transcript of "Implications of the U.S.–North Korea Nuclear Agreement," hearing before the Senate Foreign Relations subcommittee on East Asian and Pacific Affairs, December 1, 1994.
3. Statement made to the Senate Select Committee on Intelligence, March 22, 1994.
4. Author was present in the room.
5. As of this writing, construction on the two light water reactors has halted at about 30 percent completion.
6. Quoted by Baker in the *Washington Post*, Oct 27, 2002.
7. President William Jefferson Clinton, "Address to the 1996 Democratic National Convention."
8. Interview by Jim Lehrer of the Lehrer News Hour, October 30, 2000.
9. Interview with senior member of the Bush administration in July 2003, Washington, D.C.
10. Interview with senior American diplomat in June 2003, location undisclosed. Some interpretation and poetic license is taken in this description, but not much.
11. *Washington Post*, October 27, 2002
12. *Segodnya*, in Russian, June 15, 2003.
13. These days, as Russia becomes a normal country, Pushkin Square, named for the nineteenth-century poet Alexander Pushkin, is the place to see and be seen. On the southwest corner is the "Cafe Pushkina," popular with the "New Russians" crowd and so elegant it was featured by *National Geographic*. Across the tree-lined Tverskoy Boulevard is the other end of the scale—an enormous McDonald's. Scattered around are stylish restaurants and blues clubs. These places compete for the prettiest Russian college girls as waitresses and in the summer, when it's crowded and the light lingers until very late, it's easy to have a private conversation without attracting unwelcome attention.
14. This interview took place in 2003.
15. "Amyotrophic lateral sclerosis" would ultimate prove fatal for Mao. Dr. Li Shisui, *The Private Life of Chairman Mao* (New York: Random House, 1994), 9.
16. This is what essentially happened in 1991.
17. Don Oberdorfer, *The Two Koreas* (New York: Basic Books, 2001), 68.
18. Ibid., 69.
19. Ibid., 72. Oberdorfer cites the *Monthly Chosun*, of August 1995.

20. See also "North Korea's Nuclear Programme," by Joseph Bermudez, *Jane's Intelligence Review*, September 1991.

21. Communication, Russian official, 2003.

22. Ibid.

23. *Novoye Vremya*, in Russian, January 19, 2003.

24. "A History of Ballistic Missile Development in the DPRK," *Occasional Paper No, 2,* Joseph S. Bermudez, Jr. Center for Nonproliferation Studies, Monterey Institute, November, 1999.

25. *Yomiuri Weekly*, June 1, 2003.

26. Anyone watching the American missile and space programs in their early years could have wondered if Warner von Braun's engineers would ever be able to get it right. The Japanese are good engineers and they went through years of failure after failure and the expenditure of billions before they were fully able to master the needed techniques.

27. March 15, 1994.

28. Former Clinton administration State Department official Robert Einhorn once quipped, "If the international community had a proliferation most wanted list, A.Q. Khan would be the 'most wanted' on the list!" "Nuclear Scientific Community of Pakistan: *Clear and Present Danger to Nonproliferation,*" by Dr. Rajesh Kumar Mishra, South Asia Analysis Group, Paper no 601, July 2, 2003.

29. *Gendai*, in Japanese, December 2002.

30. Materials provided to the author by Mikio Haruna of Kyodo News Service

31. "China gave Pakistan design data, training and nuclear material," *Indian Express*, June 9, 1998. In 1990, India and Pakistan came very near to an all-out nuclear war. Robert Kerr, then the deputy director of the CIA, declared that this "was the most dangerous nuclear situation we have faced since I have been in government." *New Yorker*, March 28, 1993.

32. Communication to Senator Bennett, August 6, 1996.

33. October 9, 1996.

34. Ibid.

35. This is described in detail in Edward Timperlake and William C. Triplett, II, *Red Dragon Rising* (Washington, D.C.: Regnery, 2000), Chapter 12.

36. November 24, 2002.

37. *Der Spiegel*, in German, September 22, 2003.

38. Ibid.

39. May 22, 2003.

40. Ibid.

41. www.fas.org/nuke/guide/dprk/cw

42. *CBW Chronicle, Volume III, Issue 1 (February 2000)*, Henry L. Stimson Center.

43. Report to the Speaker, November 1999.

44. *The Korean Journal of Defense Analysis*, Spring 2002, 92–93.

45. Speech given to Korean–American Association, Seoul, August 29, 2002.

46. Quoted by Frank Gafney, in "Don Rumsfeld's Heroic Legacy," *Washington Times*, October 7, 1998.

47. *Korea Times*, March 4, 2003.

48. Bermudez, op. cit.

49. In the mid 1990s the American Intelligence Community had produced a National Intelligence Estimate [NIE] predicting that nothing of this nature would occur for the next fifteen years. In 1998 the NIE was still operative.

50. From unpublished manuscript shared with the author.

51. *Yonhap*, September 12, 1995.

52. The 1999 Cox Report on Chinese espionage contained a photo of the North Korean satellite placed next to a photo of the first Chinese satellite, which showed that the North Korean satellite was an almost exact copy of the Chinese satellite.

53. This is a Washington nickname for the general. He is sometimes called "General Bear" because "Xiong" means "bear" in Chinese.

54. *Gendai*, in Japanese, December 2002.

55. AP, September 10, 2003.

56. The R-27 uses storable chemical fuel, making it a candidate for silos. SCUD-based missiles must be fueled just prior to launch, making them vulnerable to discovery and attack.

57. Communist China has been assisting Pakistan in a long-range *solid-fueled* missile program but this missile has not been tested as yet. Pakistan has displayed this missile twice at military parades but it is not certain if it is a working model or a mock-up.

58. *Washington Times*, January 22, 2003.

59. "CIA Unclassified Report to Congress on the Acquisition of Technology Relating to Weapons of Mass Destruction and Advanced Conventional Munitions, 1 January through 30 June 2002."

9: MERCHANTS OF DEATH

1. Author acknowledges the kind assistance of Indian officials.

2. January 1, 1989.

3. For a more complete account, see Edward Timperlake and William C. Triplett, II, *Red Dragon Rising* (Washington, D.C.: Regnery, 2002), Chapter 7.

4. See William Burroughs and Robert Windrem, *Critical Mass*, (New York: Simon and Shuster, 1994), 213.

5. "Unclassified Report to Congress on the Acquisition of Technology Relating to Weapons of Mass Destruction and Advanced Conventional Munitions 1 July through 31 December 1998." One possible reason for this lack of constraint could be because the Korean War ended with a ceasefire rather than an armistice, the communist Chinese and North Koreans could easily still consider themselves at war with the United States and the United Nations, and certainly wiling to ignore U.S. and UN protests.

6. *Washington Times*, June 4, 1991.

7. *Washington Times*, July 5, 1990.

8. *Times of London*, April 1, 1995.

9. See, for example, *Washington Times*, June 8, 1994. The CIA's semi-annual proliferation reports to Congress also reflect this.

10. *Washington Post*, August 14, 2003.

11. *Washington Times*, April 13, 2000.

12. "Unclassified Report to Congress on the acquisition of Technology Relating to Weapons of Mass Destruction and advanced Conventional Munitions 1 January Through 30 June 2002."

13. Ibid.

14. *Washington Times*, March 9, 2001.

15. *Washington Times*, April 13, 2000.

16. *The Military Balance 2002-2003* (Oxford, 2002), 111.

17. "Ballistic Missile Development in Libya," Joseph Bermudez, Jr., *Jane's Intelligence Review*, January 2003.

18. The Rumsfeld Commission on ballistic missile threats to the United States noted a 1990 speech by Qaddafi threatening to strike the American mainland.

19. As this book goes to press, the U.S. and Libya are negotiating the end of Qadaffi's WMD and missile programs.

20. Late October 1988.

21. These travel restrictions on American diplomats were dropped during the George H. W. Bush administration. When the first Bush administration took office in 1989, the communist Chinese deduced, correctly, that the administration would take no action against their arms sales to terrorist countries no matter how outrageous their conduct. The failure of the first Bush administration to address proliferation issues and communist China [which is the same thing] is an ugly story yet to be told. To be fair, Secretary of State James Baker and some others were handicapped by total lack of support from President Bush, Sr. and his National Security Advisor, General Brent Scowcroft. The first Bush administration did apply sanctions to communist Chinese companies for missile sales to Pakistan in the summer

of 1991 but only because the chairman of the Senate East Asia Subcommittee refused to confirm the Bush administration's choice for ambassador to Beijing unless they did. The Clinton administration no doubt inherited a difficult situation but, arguably, they made it worse. See Timperlake and Triplett, *Red Dragon Rising.*

22. *Washington Post*, December 25, 1987.
23. *Jane's Defense Review*, June 25, 2003.
24. August 6, 2003.
25. This is consistent with Congressman Chris Cox's discovery that the Chinese and North Korean satellites are identical for all practical purposes. Space launch technology and ballistic missile technology are very similar which is why the American government fined the Hughes and Loral firms for transferring American space launch to China. See Edward Timperlake and William C. Triplett, II, *Year of the Rat* (Washington, D.C.: Regnery, 2000). Until the communist Chinese, Iranian, and North Korean archives are opened, we cannot determine whether American space launch technology from Hughes and Loral has provided the critical element to the Iranian-North Korean nuclear warhead program but we cannot rule it out, either.
26. *The Military Balance*, 104.
27. *The Jerusalem Post*, July 8, 2003.
28. *Chungang Ilbo*, in Korean, June 16, 2003.
29. As previously noted, the *Taepodong* missile series has a strong family resemblance to the Chinese CSS-2 and during all of this period the CIA was continually reporting to the Congress on missile and missile technology transfers to Iran. The semi-annual CIA reports on proliferation of WMDs are called "Section 721" reports and the unclassified versions can be found on the CIA website.
30. June 11, 2003.
31. Paragraph 52 of an August 2003 IAEA report on new information provided by the Iranians contains an amusing observation that "some of the information was in contrast to that previously provided by Iran," which is UN agency-speak for "They lied until we caught them at it."
32. www.IAEA.org
33. The American specialists believe the Iranians are four years away. *U.S. News and World Report*, November 3, 2003.
34. Chinese families make money selling WMDs and missiles to Pakistan but not as much as they would make if Pakistan were forced to purchase its weapons systems on the international market. Communist China supplies

WMDs and missiles to Pakistan in order to threaten India, i.e. Pakistan is China's proxy against India. Communist China's WMD sales to North Korea represent a mix of profit and political motives.

35. *Washington Times*, September 17, 2003.
36. Ibid.
37. *The Military Balance*, 118.
38. March 5, 1992.
39. Burroughs and Windrem, *Critical Mass*, 334.
40. July 24, 1996.
41. August 23, 1999.
42. Communications, 2002.
43. One defector claimed the North Koreans had transferred nuclear-tipped missiles to Cuba, an unlikely prospect given how closely both places are watched. *Gendai*, in Japanese, June 2003, 28–40.
44. See Timperlake and Triplett, *Red Dragon Rising*.
45. Yossef Bodansky, *Bin Laden: The Man who Declared War on America* (Rocklin, California: Prima Publishing Co., 1999).
46. March 30, 1994.
47. *New York Times*, November 15, 1991.
48. March 24, 1993.
49. *Washington Post*, March 30, 1994.
50. *Washington Post*, April 4, 2003.
51. "No Legal Grounds for Stopping Ships," *China Daily*, July 12, 2003.
52. "Chinese aide faults U.S. on nuclear negotiations," *the International Herald Tribune*, September 1, 2003.
53. The author is a registered Republican who has worked successfully over several decades with both Republicans and Democrats.
54. Madeleine K. Albright, *Madam Secretary* (New York: Miramax, 2003), 455.
55. "Nuclear Nightmare: Understanding North Korea" from www.discovery.com
56. James A. Baker, III, *The Politics of Diplomacy* (New York: Putnam, 1995), 598n.
57. National Security Council staff member Daniel Poneman, who had persuaded President Clinton to send a condolence message ("On behalf of the people of the United States, I extend sincere condolences to the people of North Korea on the death of President Kim Il Sung") in 1994. Don Oberdorfer, *The Two Koreas* (New York: Basic Books, 2001), 343.
58. Interview, 2003.
59. *Washington Post*, October 23, 2000.
60. Interview with a participant, July 2003, Washington, D.C.
61. October 26, 2000.

62. Japanese and South Korean television ran the Albright/Kim/Sherman applause clips repeatedly over several days. Personally observed by author in Japan.

63. At least in Tokyo by senior political figures in private discussions with author.

64. October 27, 2000.

65. October 23, 2000.

66. Interview with a knowledgeable American journalist, 2003.

67. "Inside the Ring," *Washington Times*, October 31, 2003, and "Inside the Loop," *Washington Post*, November 3, 2003.

68. State Department source, 2003.

69. AP, November 1, 2003. "Ambushed" is Gedda's interpretation of Albright's statements. George Gedda has covered foreign affairs for the Associated Press since 1968.

10: NORTH KOREA: CHINA'S KNIFE

1. Interview, Seoul, 2003, with the matriarch's grandson, now an ROK officer.

2. James A. Baker III, *The Politics of Diplomacy*, (New York: Putnam, 1995,) 593.

3. See "China's Strategic Proxies" by Justin Bernier, in the fall 2003 issue of *Orbis*, beginning at page 629.

4. Title 18, US Code, Sections 1961–1968.

5. 22 US Code 5001 et seq. Repealed in stages beginning in 1993.

6. The U.S. portion amounted to 24 percent of the total. *Yonhap*, November 20, 2003.

7. Reuters, November 20, 2003.

8. Ibid.

9. It is always possible that the administration has a secret plan to permanently resolve the North Korea problem. However, at present there are no indications of this.

INDEX